Collateral Damage

A Candid Look at the
Brock Turner Case

and Recall of
Judge Aaron Persky

Humane Justice

February 9, 2021

Contents

A Note from the Author

"Justice without mercy is justice denied." -- Anonymous

As a feminist, mother, registered nurse, and concerned citizen, I have a strong interest in ensuring that this nation's freedoms and civil liberties remain whole. And like most nurses, my empathy and compassion for others, and strong desire to lessen others' suffering – even for total strangers – does not end outside hospital doors.

I also know that facts matter. Not name-calling and not shouting down anyone with contrary views but rather a careful and clinical examination of the facts. It is not lightly, therefore, that after exhaustive research on my part, and with the input of as many as 100 other volunteers and information provided by people at Stanford and elsewhere who had firsthand knowledge of what was taking place, I believe the conclusion is inescapable. Brock Turner, the Stanford swimmer convicted in 2016 of sexual assault, was wrongfully prosecuted and convicted and the subsequent recall of the judge in the case likewise was not justified. Both vengeful actions were not supported by the facts.

You may have already come to conclusions about the highly publicized case several years ago involving Brock Turner and Chanel Miller. Turner's sensationalized trial was followed a year later by the recall of the judge in the case, Judge Aaron Persky. What is presented in this book may therefore be contrary to everything you know, or think you know. Assuming you are a fair-minded and rational person, I simply ask that you read what follows, and if you know of any facts presented here that are incorrect, let me know at the web address at the bottom of this author's note so that appropriate revisions can be made.

Why did I get involved? Upon reading local newspapers and online news sources about the Turner incident at Stanford (my alma mater), I started making inquiries about what had happened. I was shocked and saddened by what I learned in subsequent months in how Turner, a young man barely out of high school, was made the subject of an unconscionable and unprecedented nationwide and international campaign of bullying, hatred, abuse, and falsehoods that were far beyond what I had ever observed in the case of anyone accused of far more egregious crimes. Something seemed very wrong in what was happening. And then, after Turner's trial, I watched a similar massive and cruel disinformation campaign against Judge Aaron Persky, the judge in Turner's trial.

And I want to be clear. My involvement in the Turner matter was for humanitarian rather than political or financial reasons, unlike third parties who have played a significant role in causing inhumane harm to both Turner and Judge Persky, and even to Chanel Miller. Just as I would, without a second thought, help an accident victim suffering on the side of the road, it would have been impossible for me to throw aside empathy and compassion and walk away from what I observed in the Turner matter, and where the facts and truth needed to be set forth.

I decided to learn as much as possible about what actually happened at the Stanford fraternity party that night and, more than a year later, the campaign to recall Judge Persky, with the result being a vast collection of research and observations that culminated in the writing of this book.

Throughout my inquiry, I was struck by a continual lack of compassion for two young people (Brock Turner and Chanel Miller), both of whom I believe were being used for the personal motivations of others and without regard to the short- and long-term impact on them and their families. Facts were distorted, evidence was eliminated, a mob frenzy was created, and no one questioned what was happening or who was orchestrating it. As a result, a 19-year-old freshman was sacrificed for a cause and the misguided attacks against Judge Persky were used to send a warning to other judges to ignore both justice and mercy.

Even if you read just portions of this book, you will learn of the cruel and vicious exploitation of young Turner by third parties; of a campaign that raised legitimate issues about alcohol and sex on college campuses but without regard for the facts or the truth; and of a District Attorney up for re-election who used the case for his own political purposes and that of his associates. Traditional and social media likewise were skillfully used for an ongoing and untruthful propaganda campaign against Turner and Judge Persky.

Read what follows and ask yourself, why didn't you ever hear this side of the story along with these documented facts?

Learn how 19-year-old Turner was seen by his teammates as a very respectful and level- headed future Olympic swimmer. Learn how Chanel Miller, undoubtedly a talented young woman (age 22 at the time and who had already graduated from college elsewhere), went to a fraternity party already drunk even though she knew from past experience that she doesn't appear to others as drunk yet can't remember the next day what she did.

Turner and Chanel, both already drunk, continued drinking at the party and started talking. From what is known, they left the party together and then slipped and fell less than a minute from the fraternity house and in full public view – there was no attempt to hide anything. They started making out and engaged in activity that modern generations don't even consider sex – that is, manual stimulation and dry humping – and in the process, Turner believed he had Chanel's affirmative consent as modern generations also are taught. At that point, the two Swedish graduate students bicycled by and saw them. The rest is history.

Turner's DNA was not found on Chanel's clothing nor on her. Think about that for a moment. Turner never opened his pants or other clothing even though he could have, thereby disproving any intent of committing rape. Turner nevertheless was arrested by Stanford police who then oversaw the subsequent investigation under the direction of the District Attorney. Somehow critical evidence taken by Stanford police disappeared and one or more Stanford police officers seem to have intentionally misrepresented the facts.

As you will see in a single chapter in this book, the shortcomings in Turner's defense are astonishing. Especially alarming is the fact that the prosecutor had failed to present evidence of essential elements of her case against Turner, but rather than seeking a directed verdict, Turner's lawyer inexplicably put Turner on the stand and made up for the prosecutor's own shortcomings. There also were serious defects in the jury instructions and other actions involving the jury.

Stanford had long been aware of problems in prior cases involving their own students and one of their faculty members but stood by in silence, even if they knew critical facts that should have been brought forward in Turner's case, and notwithstanding the involvement of their own police and one or more of their own faculty members and staff. And although they are fully aware of Turner's being blocked from continuing his education at other colleges and universities, Stanford continues to do nothing to clear the way for him to get his undergraduate degree and possibly an advanced degree in bio-engineering or related fields.

Misinformation was carefully circulated to the media for over a year leading up to the trial and then afterwards. Such as blaming Turner for taking a photo of Chanel and then circulating it, even though the parties disseminating this information knew it was false. Such as intentionally creating the impression that Turner somehow found Chanel passed out, dragged her inert body behind a garbage dumpster, and then raped her. No such thing happened. By the time of his trial, Turner had already been convicted in traditional and social media and in the minds of the general public as a result of a massive campaign of misinformation. Yet Stanford continued to stand by in silence, even when they were fully aware of the untruths being circulated against one of their own students or former students by one of their own faculty members and others at Stanford.

Also disturbing were the breaches of professional ethics displayed by members of the District Attorney's office. A prime example is that the prosecutor in the case deliberately confused and misled the jurors in her overzealous pursuit of obtaining a conviction, often without regard for facts or the truth. Moreover, Santa Clara County District Attorney Jeff Rosen claimed he was opposed to the recall of Judge Persky but nevertheless watched in silence as Stanford law school Prof. Michele Dauber misrepresented Judge Persky's past cases to the public in her effort to convince voters to vote Judge Persky out of office. All of the cases cited in Prof. Dauber's campaign had been prosecuted under DA Rosen, and he almost certainly would have participated in key decisions about them. He therefore would have known that Prof. Dauber's renditions of the cases were false, yet he did nothing to publicly correct the misrepresentations. And again, Stanford stood by in silence even as their own law professor was widely misrepresenting important legal issues.

What is particularly troublesome is that, as a result of Turner engaging in what he thought was a consensual hookup (and not even sex in the view of current generations – and remember, Turner's DNA was not even found on Chanel), he is required to register as a sex offender for life. Not five or ten years, but for life. This has resulted in his education being blocked, and he is not allowed to live near schools, playgrounds, or other places where children are present even though his alleged crime had nothing to do with children. If he someday has children of his own, he will likely be restricted or even prohibited from attending school meetings or having his own kids' playmates at his home.

Current studies have shown that the National Sex Offender Registry program is a barbaric, oppressive, and mostly failed program. Even its originator Patty Wetterling now opposes it, especially for young offenders, and Prof. Dauber herself has publicly stated that ten years would be more than adequate in Turner's case. No modern society should continue to punish former offenders, especially redeemable young people, who have paid their debts to society. But many young former offenders are ostracized, may end up homeless, and are prevented from reaching their full potential as productive members of society as a result of misguided and archaic sex offender registry programs.

A star competitive swimmer, Turner also lost all potential opportunities to compete in the Olympics and other major U.S. and worldwide swimming competitions, something that had required grueling preparation ever since he was a young boy. Many commenters and others ignore this impact, even though it would be like telling an accomplished teenage and widely heralded concert pianist that she may not, for the rest of her life, play at concerts, or a distinguished professor that he may not for the rest of his life publish his research or attend meetings of his peers.

Read the factual analysis in this book, note the endnotes if you want to check the sources, and decide for yourself. Again, helping shine a light on the abuses of campus alcohol and sex is important, but so is truth. How did leaders at Stanford, in Silicon Valley, and nationwide deviate so far from the truth? Why didn't these people and the media question what was happening but instead stood by in silence, even when they knew the truth and in some cases were active participants? Most of all, how could the people who contributed to the harm done to Turner and Judge Persky – that continues even to this day – have so severely lost sight of basic humanity and compassion for others?

Third parties may claim what is presented in this book is nothing but a wild conspiracy theory. Ignore their blowing smoke. Ask them instead, what factually is incorrect in what is presented here. Tell them to be specific and to show evidence of the errors, and if anything stated here is incorrect, please forward that information as provided below.

There also were many frustrations in gathering the information for this book, including information to which the public was entitled under California's Public Records Act. Much of that information remains unlawfully hidden and, in some cases, seems to have been improperly erased or destroyed by Santa Clara County officials. Also, a prepublication copy of this book was sent to the leaders at Stanford with a request that they advise of any errors or of information that should be included. No one from Stanford responded. If anyone has access to information that should be included or is aware of any errors of fact in what is presented here, please send the appropriate information to *humanejustice@protonmail.com*. I also apologize that some items may appear in more than one place. This is because I felt it best that each chapter stand on its own and contain the key information even if that information appears elsewhere as well.

While the individuals mentioned in this book are regularly referred to by their surnames, to distinguish Chanel Miller's name from her sister's, both Chanel Miller and Tiffany Miller are frequently referred to by their first names.

It should be noted that what is presented here is by no means intended as victim blaming. Nor is it to condone excessive drinking by either men or women, or engaging in any sort of aggressive or inappropriate sexual activity. Rather, the purpose is to seek truth and compassionate justice for everyone involved. That said, what follows are solely personal opinions.

Chapter 1

Overview

T he night of January 17, 2015 started a cascade of heartbreaking and life-changing events that will forever haunt two young people and their families. Brock Turner, a 19-year-old freshman and recipient of a revered swimming scholarship at Stanford, was at a campus fraternity party where drinking was rampant and where apparently no one was enforcing Stanford's alcohol policies. An hour into the party, Turner met 22-year-old nonstudent Emily Doe, later disclosed as Chanel Miller, who was there with her sister Tiffany and three friends. Chanel and Turner, both drunk, left the party together, slipped on the ground all of 49 feet from the fraternity house and in full public view, and engaged in what Turner believed was consensual fingering of Chanel and his own dry humping. In the course of events, Turner never opened his pants or any of his other clothing.

Sometime during the encounter and unbeknownst to Turner, Chanel passed out from drunkenness, and it was at that point in time that Turner and Chanel were found by two Swedish graduate students bicycling past. Turner was charged with – albeit wrongly and without evidence – rape even though lab tests that very day showed no sperm present, and not long after that further lab tests showed that even his DNA was not on Chanel's body or clothing.

With the criminal charges pending, Turner was forced to leave Stanford. Upon his conviction a year later, he was banned for life from competitive swimming thereby dashing his Olympic swimming hopes, and after serving jail time he was required to register for life as a sex offender – an inappropriate and extraordinarily harsh punishment for anyone, and especially for a then 20-year-old.

This is a true story of the people and institutions including Turner, Chanel, Judge Persky, Stanford, judicial independence, honest media, and many others that were collateral damage brought about by the wrongful actions of third parties. It is also a story of the collateral damage done and still being done by people who know the truth and could correct the wrongs but instead have stood by in silence, apparently hoping someone else will correct the wrongs.

A review of the police reports, the trial transcripts, and other evidence demonstrate an extraordinary injustice throughout the case. To start, Chanel gave two contradictory accounts of her activities that day. Under the first version, as Chanel told Stanford police when she first woke up in the emergency room where she had been admitted for acute alcohol intoxication, Chanel said she, her sister Tiffany, and a friend went to the Lagunita Court dorm area at Stanford earlier in the evening and later went to the Kappa Alpha fraternity party.[1] Fifteen hours later, however, Chanel and her sister went to pick up Chanel's cell phone from Stanford police and this time Chanel gave a very different accounting. In this version, Chanel told Stanford police that after she and her sister drank a substantial amount of alcohol at home, their mother drove them and two friends to the Kappa Alpha party around 11 p.m. where they continued to drink. Under either version, Chanel ultimately drank herself into an alcoholic stupor (back-extrapolated blood alcohol concentration "BAC" of 0.242 to 0.249%). Both versions were written up by Stanford police and attached to the formal criminal complaint filed against Turner without anyone apparently trying to reconcile the discrepancies.

What ensued was a massive frenzy in both traditional and social media orchestrated by Stanford law school professor Michele Dauber, an activist in the #MeToo movement and longtime friend of the Miller family. Prof. Dauber engaged in ongoing attacks against Turner and, following Turner's trial, she similarly led a massive disinformation campaign against the judge in the case, Judge Aaron Persky. The unfounded and cruel attacks against both Turner and Judge Persky inexplicably continue to this day.

Trial and other records confirm the prosecutor's intentional misconduct of charging Turner with rape while allowing DNA and other evidence that would refute rape to sit undisclosed for months. This wrongful and longstanding charge of rape provided the court of public opinion, largely fueled by Prof. Dauber, with ample time and ammunition to falsely label Turner "the Stanford rapist" via Twitter, Facebook, and other media outlets before the trial even began. It created an atmosphere of pretrial bias in which a fair trial could not occur.

A major factor in the Turner case was the issue of consent. Turner believed Chanel gave consent. Chanel said she couldn't remember. This is because of a condition known as blackout amnesia, a condition Chanel told Stanford police she had experienced at least four to five times during previous parties while in college. Alcohol-induced blackout is medically defined as a type of anterograde amnesia where the drinker is uninhibited, conscious and functional, yet the hippocampus part of the brain is unable to form new memories. From a detailed review of events that night, Chanel likely agreed to leave the party with Turner while she was in an early alcoholic blackout state. After they slipped on the path, she engaged in limited consensual sexual activity (fingering) while conscious and alert, then subsequently slipped from consciousness to a drunken stupor. Turner would not have known when Chanel slipped into a state of stupor due to Turner's own alcohol-induced mental impairment (back-extrapolated blood alcohol concentration "BAC" of 0.171%). Additionally, there is significant medical evidence that a person suffering from blackout amnesia will often appear to third parties, including someone like Turner, to be functioning totally fine and sometimes not even appearing to be excessively drunk.

Turner's case proceeded to trial where numerous other abuses took place by the District Attorney's office and the prosecutor, and where Turner's lawyer also proved extraordinarily deficient even though he was long recognized as a capable and experienced criminal defense lawyer. After Turner was found guilty (a verdict not supported by the facts), Judge Persky accepted the sentencing recommendations of the professionals in the county probation department, as is standard practice. He had the courage to do this in the context of managing a case in which the defendant had already been deemed guilty in the court of social media-led public opinion. Because of his sentencing decision, a massive campaign of misinformation was waged against him, with the result that Judge Persky was recalled from the bench in a subsequent county election.

The campaign to recall Judge Persky, which raised approximately $1.4 million, was spearheaded by Prof. Dauber. Prof. Dauber, who did not have a license to practice law and was not employed by the DA's office, made extensive use of the DA's office resources to compile her own and wrong summaries of Judge Persky's prior cases. These were resources that would not have been available to ordinary citizens. In fact, subsequent Public Records Act disclosures showed hundreds of emails between Prof. Dauber and District Attorney office employees including District Attorney Jeff

Rosen, several of Rosen's deputies, and numerous others. Prof. Dauber proceeded to twist and distort Judge Persky's past cases in order to sway voters into believing that Judge Persky was biased in favor of wealthy, White male athletes, which a review of his cases shows is demonstrably false.

This narrative of the Brock Turner case highlights Prof. Dauber's inappropriate actions, a prosecutorial system in dire need of reform, the actions of a DA up for re-election, the unjustified and dishonest campaign against a fair-minded judge, and the deep pitfalls of a barbaric and ineffective national sex offender registration system that is counterproductive and causes irreparable harm. Throughout all of this, Turner was the subject of unprecedented and unbelievably inhumane, brutal, and untruthful global traditional news and social media attacks against him.

Among the most shocking issues uncovered and discussed in detail in the chapters that follow are:

- As already noted, Chanel told totally contradictory stories to Stanford police at different times on the very day of the incident, and she then changed various parts of her story in the subsequent months and years. The same seems to be the case with her sister Tiffany and others.
- Stanford police appear to have gotten rid of critical and likely exculpatory evidence, and then misrepresented what happened.
- Prosecutor Alaleh Kianerci engaged in prosecutorial misconduct, and with the almost certain approval of and coordination with District Attorney Jeff Rosen.
- In violation of applicable ethics rules, extrajudicial false statements were constantly being made, directly and through third parties, that heightened public condemnation of Turner and yet both Rosen and Kianerci made no apparent effort to correct what they knew were untruths.
- During their deliberations, the jurors asked a critically important question about intent, indicating that one or more had doubts, and in response they got the exact wrong answer from what their instructions had been at the start of the trial and again at the end of the trial, and with no explanation.
- Turner's own lawyer, Mike Armstrong, had reportedly represented Prof. Dauber or her family on at least two prior occasions and never

4

told the Turners. He likewise was speaking at her classes while preparing for the trial and then again after the trial, and again never told the Turners. As already noted, there were very serious deficiencies in how Armstrong prepared for and then defended Turner.

- Not surprising is the role alcohol plays in relation to college and university sexual assaults and other injuries, but where little effort is made to effectively mitigate this problem by all involved.

It is important for society to reflect on how quickly and effectively one person can destroy the lives and careers of others by continually feeding untrue and hurtful content to traditional and social media, as was done to both Turner and Judge Persky. Unfortunately, and as Dr. Jim Taylor's article, "How Social Media Can Ruin Lives" so rightly states:

"Research has shown that information that makes it to the Web continues to be believed even when later information is posted that demonstrates it to be false."[2]

Hopefully, those reading this book will look at the facts presented here and come to realize and believe the extraordinary injustices that were done to both Turner and Judge Persky and the need for fundamental reforms so that what happened here doesn't happen again.

The many wrongs in this case ended in society's loss of a bright young man's future and the unseating of a fair judge who simply followed the rule of law. As documented in the chapters that follow, the damage was wrongly but intentionally created, was widespread, and continues to the present.

Chapter 2

Before, During, and After the Party

On January 17, 2015, Emily Doe, later revealed to be Chanel Miller, was a 22-year-old who six months earlier had graduated from the University of California at Santa Barbara where she had majored in literature. Chanel had not attended and was never otherwise affiliated with Stanford. Chanel lived at home with her family, including her 20-year-old sister Tiffany, at the time a Cal Poly student who had recently returned from abroad. Chanel held a job as a content creator at a company that developed educational apps for kids. Chanel had a boyfriend, 25-year-old Lucas Motro, with whom she said she was in an exclusive relationship and whom she said she had started dating in November of 2014. Motro, who hailed from Los Gatos, California, was attending Wharton School of the University of Pennsylvania, and intended to seek employment in California.

Brock Turner was a 19-year-old freshman, barely out of high school, attending Stanford on a swimming scholarship. He was an outstanding student and an NCAA Division 1 swimmer with promising prospects as an Olympic swimmer. Before arriving at Stanford, Turner lived with his parents and siblings in Ohio.

Chanel and Turner, both of whom were drunk and who hadn't previously known each other, became involved in an apparent sexual hookup at Stanford that both would forever regret. Judge Aaron Persky, from all prior accounts a fair-minded Santa Clara County Superior Court judge and who presided at Turner's trial, got caught in the crossfire of a vengeful #MeToo movement that was seeking money and publicity and that succeeded through misrepresentations and a carefully orchestrated media campaign in unseating Judge Persky from the bench.

Before the Kappa Alpha Party

There are at least two very conflicting accounts of what Chanel told police took place prior to her attending the party at the Kappa Alpha fraternity house at Stanford. Both accounts were attached to the criminal complaint later filed in Santa Clara County Superior Court but apparently no one pursued the discrepancies, including the Stanford police who were charged with that task.

Pursuant to Chanel's account to Stanford police deputy Jeffrey Taylor when she first woke up at a hospital emergency room, Chanel and her sister Tiffany went to the Stanford campus in the early evening and met up at the Lagunita Court dormitory area with Tiffany's friend Julia [last name deleted]. After spending time there, they either walked or drove to the party at the Kappa Alpha fraternity house; Dep. Taylor's written report doesn't indicate their mode of transportation to campus and later to the Kappa Alpha fraternity house.

Under an alternative account Chanel gave 15 hours later to Stanford police deputy Carrie DeVlugt, Chanel was at home when her sister Tiffany received a phone call at around 8 p.m. from Julia inviting her and her sister to a fraternity party at Stanford. In this accounting, Tiffany then invited her friend Colleen [last name deleted] and Colleen's friend Trea [last name deleted] to the party, who arrived at the Miller house after attending a dinner party, and then Chanel's and Tiffany's mother drove them at around 11 p.m. to the Stanford campus. Chanel told Dep. DeVlugt they were dropped off at the Tresidder Memorial Student Union parking lot,[3] Colleen said they were dropped off "right in front of Kappa Alpha,"[4] and Tiffany said she did not remember where they had been dropped off.

Under still another accounting of that day, as given on later occasions, at approximately 6:00 p.m., Chanel, her sister Tiffany, and their friend Julia went for a walk at the Arastradero Preserve, a nature preserve in Palo Alto where the women walked on trails and took photographs. After their visit to the Arastradero Preserve, they ate at a nearby taqueria, where Tiffany and Julia discussed attending a fraternity party at Kappa Alpha on the Stanford campus.

Julia, a student at Stanford, had attended middle school with Tiffany and Gunn High School in Palo Alto with Chanel and Tiffany. Julia had been on the Gunn High School varsity volleyball team with Chanel. Julia and Tiffany decided they would go to the Kappa Alpha fraternity party, while Chanel said she would decide whether to attend the party after she and Tiffany arrived home. Chanel later said she had been hesitant to attend the party with her sister because she felt like a mother to Tiffany. In any event, under this

7

accounting, Chanel and Tiffany returned home at approximately 8:00 p.m., where their father later prepared for them a meal of broccoli stir fry.

Pre-Party Drinking

Tiffany's friend Colleen, who Tiffany had met while both were students at Cal Poly, and Colleen's friend Trea, who was home from school in New York, had planned to meet at the Miller home before attending the Kappa Alpha party. Chanel had already met Colleen in the past when Colleen and Tiffany had to pick up Chanel, who Colleen had described as "pretty drunk,"[5] from a party when Chanel was a senior at UC Santa Barbara.

Under some of the accounts, Colleen and Trea arrived at the Miller home between 10:00 p.m. and 10:30 p.m. Trea had consumed a few drinks at a bar before going there. Under this accounting, all four women, including Chanel, then decided to go to the fraternity party at Stanford's Kappa Alpha fraternity house where they would meet up with Julia. Chanel said she had decided to go to the Kappa Alpha party after all but also said she might afterwards possibly go to some bars in downtown Palo Alto. Between 10:00 p.m. and 10:45 p.m., under this accounting, Tiffany drank approximately four shots of rum or whiskey, and Chanel drank four shots of whisky and a glass of champagne. Colleen and Trea brought their own champagne to drink. Under this accounting, sometime between 11:00 p.m. and 11:15 p.m., Chanel's mother drove the four women to the Stanford campus, although as already noted, with conflicting testimony as to where they were dropped off. Chanel and Tiffany brought with them an empty water bottle containing alcohol.

The Kappa Alpha Fraternity Party – an Alcohol Fest

Pursuant to testimony later given at the preliminary hearing and then at the trial, notwithstanding the prior conflicting stories, Chanel, Tiffany, Colleen, and Trea entered the Kappa Alpha fraternity house, where they met Julia. They first appointed themselves as what they described as a "welcoming committee," and then the women danced and continued to drink more alcohol. Prior to the other women's arrival, Julia had engaged in a drinking game called Red Cage, at which time she drank three solo cups of beer. Shortly after, Julia found a large Costco-size vodka bottle, which she

8

shared with Chanel and the other women by free-pouring shots into red Solo cups.

Chanel danced on a chair or table, sang songs, and embarrassed her sister Tiffany by "acting silly." Other party-goers were dancing on tables and drinking alcohol, and participated in drinking games. While Chanel was in the Kappa Alpha kitchen, she "slapped" the juice dispensers and made what she described as "silly concoctions." Chanel was also throwing cereal in the kitchen, saying, "F___ yeah. College. I love this." According to Tiffany, someone who appeared to be "mad" about the women's activities in the kitchen told them to stop. A short time later, Julia, Chanel, and Tiffany walked to an area away from the fraternity house near some bushes where Julia and Chanel proceeded to urinate. Chanel was laughing and "running around in circles rapping." They took photos and/or videos of their doing this; for some reason, the phones with those photos and/or videos were either not obtained, or as with Chanel's phone, was immediately returned to her by Stanford police with the request that she simply send back to them whatever she thought might be of use. And at least according to the District Attorney's office, without keeping information that could have been important evidence of what took place and when.

After urinating near the bushes, the women went to the Kappa Alpha patio area where they talked with several men attending the party. One of the men was Tommy, who said his sister attended Cal Poly. Turner was also in the group. The men were shotgunning beer and offered some to the women. Tiffany and Chanel both drank the beer. At one point, while Tiffany was standing with Colleen, Turner tried to kiss Tiffany, which made her laugh, and she moved away from him. It should be noted, Chanel's group had already started calling Turner by another name – the name of someone Tiffany knew at Cal Poly and who they thought looked like Turner. Turner later came back and held Tiffany's waist and kissed her, at which time Tiffany again walked away.

As the party wore on into the early morning, Trea had become excessively drunk and didn't look well. Tiffany and Colleen texted Uber for a car to take them and Trea to Julia's dorm so that Trea could rest on a bed in Julia's room. According to the Uber receipt, the Uber car arrived to pick them up at 12:17 a.m. Chanel remained at the party, and according to Tiffany, when she saw Chanel at about 12:00 a.m. - 12:10 a.m., Chanel appeared to be "fine" and told Chanel she would be right back. Tiffany later testified that she was not worried about leaving Chanel at the party (police report "PR" 048). At 12:29 a.m., Chanel attempted to call Tiffany, but Tiffany was unable to hear or understand her. At the preliminary hearing Tiffany said, "I could not understand anything that was on the other end. I remember just saying, 'Hang up and call me again. I can't hear you.'"

When Tiffany and Colleen returned from Julia's residence, they looked for Chanel inside the Kappa Alpha fraternity house and outside the building, but were unable to find her. Tiffany also called Chanel multiple times but received no response. After failing to locate Chanel, Tiffany, Colleen, and Trea went home by Uber at 1:46 a.m. (per an Uber receipt). Before they left, they noticed there were police nearby, but they believed the police were there due to noise violations or to "shut down" the party. They did not report that Chanel was missing but instead thought she may have gone to downtown Palo Alto, as she previously had said she might do.

Communication with Lucas Motro (Chanel's boyfriend)

At 11:30 p.m. PST (2:30 a.m. EST), Chanel sent Lucas Motro (whom she had started exclusively dating two months prior), who was asleep, a text in which she said "Too turnt, at baseball house." According to Lucas, "turnt" meant drunk, and the "baseball house" referenced the Kappa Alpha fraternity – which would imply that both Chanel and Lucas were previously familiar with that particular fraternity. In any event, at 11:54 p.m., Chanel called Lucas, during which she was slurring some words and some words were incomprehensible. The call lasted two minutes. At 12:14 a.m., Lucas sent a text saying, "You're done [drunk]. Tell Neegus [Tiffany] to take care of you, please." At 12:16 a.m., Chanel left a voicemail for Lucas in which he could "hear—understand some parts." According to Lucas, "she [Chanel] said she missed me and she said that males were presenting themselves to her but that she liked me." In that same voicemail, Chanel said, "Even though you are so far, I'll reward you . . . I'll reward you by you know what."[6] At 12:18 a.m., Lucas called back at which point he was unable to understand Chanel and left his phone on his pillow until she "either hung up or fell asleep." The call lasted 10 minutes. A final text from Lucas at 12:40 a.m. PST was "I'm worried about you, Boo." Chanel later said she did not recall receiving or sending texts or phone calls between her and Lucas, which if true might confirm that she had already been in a state of alcohol-induced blackout amnesia.

It should be noted that according to nationally recognized researcher and expert on alcohol-induced blackout Dr. Kim Fromme, "about the only thing that is impaired during an alcohol-induced blackout is memory."[7] Dr. Fromme goes on to say, "you can't infer from slurred speech that cognition, behavior, decision-making, are necessarily impaired beyond the level in which you could engage in voluntary actions."[8]

The Alleged Assault

Sometime between the hours of 12:30 a.m. and 12:55 a.m., Chanel was apparently in the company of Turner. Turner said he had left the Kappa Alpha house with Chanel and as they were heading to his dorm, Chanel slipped, and because they were holding hands, Turner fell down as well. The two apparently started making out on the ground and with another couple making out within a short distance from them and likewise in full view of all passersby. Turner said Chanel consented to his fingering her, a form for this generation of safe sex or not even sex, after which Turner engaged in "dry humping" which also is considered by this generation as safe sex or not even sex.

Chanel had a history of alcoholic blackout amnesia. In alcoholic blackout amnesia, the drinker is alert, uninhibited, more likely to engage in sexual risk-taking than when sober, and can engage in activities such as driving a car (illegally) and decision-making, but the hippocampus portion of the brain is unable to form memories. It is believed that Chanel consented to sexual activity including being fingered while she was in a state of alcoholic blackout amnesia, and then gradually slipped into a state of alcoholic stupor. Turner would not have known Chanel was in alcoholic blackout, as alcoholic blackout is not detectable by an observer, even a sober one. Turner was also apparently unaware when Chanel's mental status had changed from functionally blackout drunk to drunken stupor, and Turner himself was drunk. Chanel would later say she remembers nothing.

The Two Witness' Accounts

Carl-Fredrik Arndt and Lars Peter Jonsson were two Stanford graduate students from Sweden. Carl-Fredrik was a Ph.D. student in computational mathematics, and Lars Peter was a Master's student in management, science, and engineering.

On January 17, 2015, Carl-Fredrik had been at a birthday party held at the Terun Italian restaurant in Palo Alto at approximately 6:00 p.m., where he consumed one beer. He remained at the restaurant for about two hours. At around 8:00 p.m., Carl-Fredrik left the restaurant and played video games with his friend Lewis, at which time Carl-Fredrik drank two beers. Lars Peter, who had been in San Francisco to visit a friend, arrived at Carl-Fredrik's residence around 8:00 p.m. – 8:30 p.m. to play video games. Around 10:30 – 11:00 p.m., Carl-Fredrik and Lars Peter went to a birthday party in Escondido Village on the Stanford campus. Carl-Fredrik and Lars Peter each drank one beer, and they left the party around one to two hours later. Carl-Fredrik later went with Lars Peter to his residence where Lars Peter picked up his bike, from where they planned to head to the Kappa Alpha fraternity party. Lars Peter had consumed a total of four beers between approximately 8:30 p.m. and 11:00 p.m. Carl-Fredrik had also consumed about four beers.

Around 12:15 a.m. – 12:45 a.m., Carl-Fredrik and Lars Peter were riding their bikes in the direction of the Kappa Alpha fraternity house when they saw what they believed were two people making out. Initially they bicycled past and noted the couple were having "their personal moment." But then the two graduate students said they felt something wasn't right, as they saw the male, who was later identified as Brock Turner, thrusting (dry humping) on top of a female, who was later identified as Chanel Miller. Turner was fully clothed. Chanel was in a supine position with her arms out. The graduate students sensed Chanel wasn't moving, thus Lars Peter shouted at Turner asking, "Hey, what's going on . . . What the f----- are you doing . . . She's f---ng unconscious." Lars Peter said that after yelling at Turner, he (Turner) got up and started taking steps in a backward direction, and then started running. Turner, on the other hand, in his first words at the police station said he didn't recall running but that he was feeling sick and got up to move away. Lars Peter said he chased Turner, and Carl-Fredrik said he checked to ensure Chanel was breathing and then went to help Lars Peter. Lars Peter had caught up with Turner and tripped him, holding Turner down. Two other men saw Lars Peter holding down Turner and asked, "What are you doing? . . . let him go." To prove Lars Peter wasn't fighting Turner, Carl-Fredrik directed the two men to Chanel's location, where another male was sitting next to her, who apparently called 911. Lars Peter held Turner down until first responders arrived at approximately 1:05 a.m.

Fig. 1. The view the two Swedish graduate students had of Chanel Miller and Brock Turner in full view of all passersby, IN FRONT of the wooden shed and a 15- to 30-second walk from the fraternity outdoor patio.

Fig. 2. Kappa Alpha fraternity house on right, Jerry House on left.

1. Kappa Alpha patio.
2. Path where Turner and Chanel walked from the Kappa Alpha patio.
3. Where Turner and Chanel were making out.
4. Where graduate students tackled Turner.
5. Path the graduate students came in on bikes.
6. Area in bushes where Chanel, Chanel's sister, and their friend went to urinate an hour earlier.

Before first responders arrived and when Carl-Fredrik had returned to Chanel's location, he noticed that Chanel was in a different position from when he had last seen her. It was unknown if someone had helped Chanel change her position or if she had changed her position on her own. Reportedly there also was a flash of light around this time, and it wasn't clear if someone had taken a photo or was using their mobile phone to illuminate the area. It is very strange, however, that someone would flash a light over Chanel, as reported, but then flee the scene rather than remain to help.

Carl-Fredrik and Lars Peter did not witness the fingering or anything that had led up to it. Assuming Chanel really had no memory of the events, the only person who could testify as to what happened would be Turner himself.

Police Arrived at the Scene

Stanford Deputy Jeffrey Taylor arrived at the scene at approximately 1:01 a.m. He had been dispatched in response to a call regarding an unconscious person with possible alcohol poisoning. Dep. Taylor was led to Chanel's location by two men. There were other bystanders about 10-15 feet away from Chanel's location. Chanel was no longer in the supine position in which Carl-Fredrik and Lars Peter had originally found her. Dep. Taylor described Chanel's location as "directly center behind a shed" although technically they all were in front of the wooden shed from the perspective of the basketball court, bike path, and surrounding area. (The police initially said "behind" the wooden shed because they had to walk around it when walking downhill from the fraternity driveway.)

Chanel made snoring noises when Dep. Taylor moved Chanel's head to check for breathing and a pulse. Medical experts note that someone who is snoring, who is able to change positions, and who is able to clear her airway as Chanel did is not what is medically defined as being unconscious, although at the trial it was repeatedly stated by the prosecutor that Chanel was "unconscious" but without supporting evidence of that medical fact and apparently without Turner's lawyer objecting to the intentional mischaracterization. Chanel was wearing a skin-tight dark gray dress that was pulled up to her waist, her underwear was off, and some of her top clothing was pulled down partially exposing one breast.

Paramedics Arrived

Paramedics arrived at the scene at approximately 1:12 a.m. They reported Chanel was breathing and in no respiratory distress, her vital signs were within normal limits, and there were no signs of trauma. Later, however, there were areas on Chanel's arm where the paramedics had twice attempted to start an intravenous line. An intravenous line was successfully started on the third attempt. According to paramedics, Chanel was difficult to rouse, but she vomited one time at the scene at which time she was able to move her head and clear her own airway. Chanel responded to painful stimuli by briefly opening her eyes. Using the Glasgow Coma Scale, an assessment tool initially designed to quantify responsiveness in neurological injury due to head trauma, paramedics calculated Chanel's Glasgow score to be 11.

The Glasgow scale is numbered from 3 – 15, with a score of 15 indicating the highest degree of responsiveness, and a score of 3 indicating deep coma or brain death. Because the Glasgow Coma Scale is designed to assess brain trauma, in cases such as acute alcohol intoxication, the Glasgow Coma Scale is more or less suited to detect trends in the patient's condition with respect to changes in levels of consciousness. Chanel's Glasgow score was still 11 upon arrival at the hospital.

At the Hospital

Chanel was transported to Santa Clara Valley Medical Center where she received treatment for alcohol intoxication. Upon waking up in the emergency room at approximately 4:15 a.m., Chanel found herself in the company of Dep. Jeffrey Taylor and Stanford's Dean of Students. Chanel believed she was in trouble for becoming too drunk and that she was "in an administration office at Stanford." (She had later told Dep. DeVlugt that she thought she was "at a campus drunk tank."[9]) Dep. Taylor told Chanel that she may have been sexually assaulted and asked her if she would be willing to undergo a sexual assault assessment procedure. Chanel was medically cleared at 4:30 a.m. Upon medical clearance, Chanel was moved to the hospital's Family Room, where she awaited examination and testing by the Sexual Assault Response Team (SART). Chanel's blood was drawn at 7:45 a.m., which included testing for blood alcohol concentration (BAC). Chanel's BAC, which was later back-extrapolated to 1:00 a.m., was determined to be 0.24 - 0.249%.

At 8:30 a.m., Dep. Taylor was relieved of his duty by Stanford Detective Mike Kim who had been one of the first people at the scene as well. Det. Kim was also designated as the District Attorney's Official Investigating Officer, which gave him considerable leeway in his activities, but where a key obligation was to ascertain all of the evidence, including evidence that might be exculpatory on Turner's behalf. As is shown elsewhere, it appears Det.

Kim and many/most of the rest of the Stanford police – unless there is an explanation that has never been provided – even got rid of what could have been exculpatory evidence such as the license plate numbers police took as indicated in the police report. Stanford police devoted their time and resources to proving Turner guilty of a crime, they apparently coached witnesses to change their testimony (e.g., Det. Kim took the two Swedish witnesses *together* to the alleged crime scene four days before the preliminary hearing), and fabricated other items in their reports. They also filed with the criminal complaint summaries of interviews with Chanel that were wholly contradictory but with no indication that any of the police, including Official Investigating Officer Kim, tried to determine which reports were true and which were false.

At around 6:00 a.m. – 7:00 a.m. that same day (January 18), Chanel's sister Tiffany received a call from Stanford notifying her to pick up Chanel from Santa Clara Valley Medical Center in San Jose. Later in the evening, Tiffany and Chanel went to the Stanford police station to pick up Chanel's cell phone and for Chanel to again talk with police. Chanel gave a different accounting, as mentioned in Chapter 1, of when they went to campus. It was also in the earlier interview that Chanel said she only drank Keystone Light beers (omitting her intake of vodka) at the party, so when she first woke up, she apparently was already developing her own version of what had happened, whereas she and others would later testify as to her much heavier drinking at the party. That day and evening, neither Chanel nor Tiffany told their parents what had happened.

Brock Turner's Account of What Happened

According to Turner, prior to the Kappa Alpha fraternity party, he attended Peter Arnett's dorm room party at the Roble student residence at around 8:00 p.m. or 8:30 p.m. At the Roble party, Turner consumed approximately five Rolling Rock beers and took some sips of Fireball whiskey. Sometime around 10:30 p.m., Turner and about eight other males from the Roble party headed to the Kappa Alpha party, where Turner danced and drank beer. Turner engaged in a type of dancing called grinding with several different females. According to Turner, at one point he was talking with Tiffany who had said Turner looked like somebody she knew at Cal

17

Poly. Turner then leaned in to kiss Tiffany's lips, during which Tiffany's and Turner's teeth touched, which he found "weird." Both Tiffany and Turner laughed, and Tiffany left.

At approximately 12:30 a.m., Turner saw Chanel dancing by herself near the patio door, at which time he walked up to her and told her he liked the way she danced. Turner said that when he asked Chanel if she wanted to dance with him, she said yes. Turner allegedly kissed Chanel while they danced. According to Turner, he asked Chanel if she wanted to go to his dorm room—she said sure. As the two were walking outside towards Turner's dorm, Chanel fell; in her attempt to break her fall, Chanel caused Turner to fall as well. They started kissing, at which point Turner asked if Chanel wanted him to finger her, and she agreed. With Chanel's assistance, Turner said he removed Chanel's underwear (although his DNA later was not found to be on her underwear) and adjusted Chanel's clothing in order to touch her breasts. According to Turner, after the consensual fingering episode, Turner and Chanel started dry humping.

Turner said that at one point while dry humping he started feeling ill, and began getting up because he felt the need to vomit. As he was walking away to avoid vomiting on Chanel, he was confronted in a threatening manner by two adult males, whom Turner was at times unable to understand when they spoke Swedish. Out of fear, Turner believes he may have started running. Turner was unclear of the facts surrounding running, as he was drunk and may have even been in a state of partial (fragmentary) alcoholic blackout amnesia, where he would be alert and functional but unable to recall some events during his own period of alcoholic amnesia.

Turner's Transport to the Stanford Police Station

Turner was handcuffed and taken to the Stanford police station. At the Stanford police station, body samples were taken, reportedly before Turner was even read his Miranda rights. Initially Turner thought he was being protected from an attack by the two Swedish graduate students. When he was finally read his Miranda rights by Stanford police, Turner was both underage for drinking and was legally drunk and incapable of giving informed consent, even if the law in many jurisdictions currently (and wrongly) ignores that fact.

18

Worse, this was a Stanford student in the custody of Stanford police, so at very least one would hope that campus police would first assure a student in trouble is capable of understanding a Miranda warning including the right to obtain counsel before proceeding with anything more, including getting a drunken statement from the student. That didn't happen, and Stanford police recorded a statement from a very drunk Turner who believed he was innocent and admitted without hesitation that he had fingered Chanel. That recorded statement was used against him at the trial, although curiously it was not introduced by the prosecutor as part of her case against Turner. Rather, she had been told ahead of time that Turner's lawyer planned to put Turner on the stand (another wrongful trial action) and thus she planned to use it and did use it to challenge Turner's testimony in front of the jury.

Medical experts who have reviewed the transcripts and related materials also suggest that Turner may have been in an early stage or partial (fragmentary) alcohol-induced blackout which, if true, would have affected what he remembered and didn't remember and what he told police and others afterward.

What Happened at Stanford

Turner subsequently posted bail and was released from jail. He was removed that same day from his dorm by Stanford and left without any ID, money, or his cell phone. He was allowed to go to one or two classes accompanied by Stanford police and then was ordered by Stanford to no longer go to classes.

Stanford had wanted to immediately undertake what is known as a Title IX investigation even though Chanel was not a student, and it's also not clear from the public record who was the official reporting party that would trigger a Title IX investigation. Turner's lawyer was worried that any information obtained in such an investigation would not be subject to the rules of evidence or other protections required in a criminal action and might even be turned over to the prosecutor and used at the trial whereas it would otherwise be tainted or inadmissible. More recently, there were reports that Stanford did in fact turn over materials about students to the District Attorney.

In any event, instead of seeking a restraining order, Turner's lawyer had Turner voluntarily withdraw from Stanford on January 20, 2015, two days after the alleged sexual assault. In response, and before there even was a trial, Stanford banned Turner from the Stanford campus and later specified that Turner was not to step foot on the Stanford campus for life.

False Rape Charges

On the very day of the alleged assault, what is called a "wet mount evaluation" was done of Chanel's lab specimens for the presence of sperm and sperm motility. That test showed no presence of sperm, indicating that the Stanford police and the DA's office would have known within hours of the alleged assault that there was no evidence of rape.

Other lab tests not long after showed Turner's DNA was not on Chanel's body or her clothing although another person's DNA was found on her clothing, indicating any DNA residue would likely be retained. Nevertheless, the District Attorney filed rape charges and then took approximately nine months before releasing the test results which disproved rape. That delay allowed a constant nationwide and worldwide media frenzy, including labeling Turner as "the Stanford rapist" as continually promoted by Prof. Dauber and others.

The Photo That Turner Didn't Take

Police found a GroupMe text message dated January 18, 2015 (meaning the same time that Turner and Chanel were together) on Turner's cell phone and that referenced a photo of an unknown female's breast that had been circulated by one of the swim team members, reportedly the one who later wrongly accused Turner of circulating the photo. While prosecutors attempted to blame Turner for having taken and circulated the photo, it would have been impossible for Turner to have done so because he was being held down by the two Swedes at the time the photo was circulated and police had then taken his cell phone as evidence. Moreover, the name of the swim team member who had circulated the photo was known (there are references even in the GroupMe message); he should have been pursued by both the Stanford police and the Santa Clara County prosecutor, but apparently, he wasn't.

Stanford police and the DA either did not try to determine who actually circulated the photo let alone who was depicted in the photo, or they concealed these facts – all major <u>Brady</u> violations (a 1963 Supreme Court decision that requires prosecutors to promptly disclose to defense counsel evidence that would support the defense or undercut the prosecutor's own case, both at the trial and at sentencing; see Ch. 7).

Worse, a year later prosecutor Kianerci intentionally and falsely accused Turner of having taken and circulated the photo in her sentencing memorandum to Judge Persky, notwithstanding it being known from the outset that Turner had not done so. Kianerci's wrongful action resulted in still another media frenzy that continued for years afterward and with no one in the DA's office or the media offering a correction (see p. 67).

The question also arises, how much did Stanford know about swim team members circulating photos like this, that night and possibly as a regular activity? Did Stanford or their police know who circulated the photo and who was depicted in the photo, and if so, how could they justify remaining silent? Did Stanford meet with the swim team members the following days and admonish them to remain silent about the photo activity generally as well as what happened at the Kappa Alpha fraternity party that night specifically? It's highly likely that Stanford would do so, in which case, their silence is even more inexcusable.

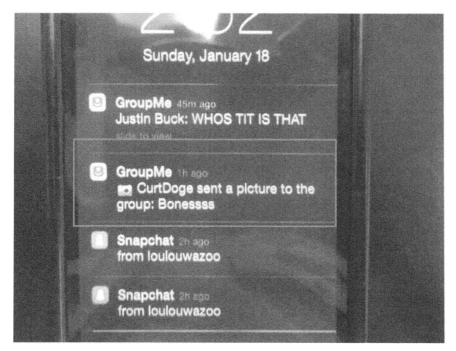

Fig. 3. Screenshot of GroupMe text regarding photo circulated by CurtDoge (not Turner).

Media Frenzy

With the ongoing involvement and encouragement of Stanford law school Professor Michele Dauber, the alleged assault was continually sensationalized and falsely depicted in traditional news and social media nationally and internationally, including falsely branding Turner as a rapist. The facts did not matter to the media. Turner had not been prosecuted for, let alone convicted of, rape.

And as already mentioned, the various lab test results showed there was no evidence whatsoever of rape but those lab results were not released for almost nine months, all of which helped fuel the traditional news and social media circus, and gave Prof. Dauber and others the opportunity to continue branding Turner a rapist and viciously maligning him with no regard to the actual evidence.

USA Swimming Banned Turner for Life

Under their zero-tolerance policy regarding sexual misconduct, upon his conviction, USA Swimming banned Turner for life, quashing all hope Turner may have had for competing in the Olympics, an aspiration he had since childhood.

Judge Persky Recalled from the Bench

Notwithstanding all of this, after Turner was found guilty and sentenced (see Chs. 4 and 5), Stanford Prof. Michele Dauber was unhappy with the fact that Judge Persky followed the probation department recommendations, as virtually all judges would do, and she immediately launched a campaign to recall him, something that hadn't happened to California judges for at least 86 prior years.

In the recall campaign that went for two years, Prof. Dauber used social and traditional media to spread continual untruths about Turner, Judge Persky, and Judge Persky's record as a judge.

A carefully orchestrated campaign portrayed Turner as a rich White privileged athlete who somehow dragged an unconscious woman behind a dumpster where he raped her—all of which was patently false. The recall campaign also attempted to portray Judge Persky as a racist and biased White judge who continually favored rich White male athletes – all of which also was patently false, especially since Judge Persky's wife is a woman of color and his kids are bi-racial. A detailed review of the cases Prof. Dauber cited also shows no bias whatsoever in Judge Persky's actions (see Ch. 15). Judge Persky was ultimately recalled in the June 5, 2018 Santa Clara County election. The details of the intentional and extreme distortions about Judge Persky's past actions as well as his actions in the Turner case are discussed in greater detail in Chapters 14 and 15.

Chapter 3

The Police Investigation

Brock Turner and Chanel Miller left the party consensually and in full view of others, but it appears no one bothered to interview others at the party who may have seen them leave. In reality, there is no way Turner could have carried or dragged an unconscious Chanel outside nor done anything else without other attendees seeing whatever was happening.

And since the only person who could tell what actually had happened was Turner (Chanel said she couldn't remember and the two Swedish graduate students came upon them only after Turner and Chanel had been making out), having other witnesses from the party confirm what Turner testified at the trial (he and alcohol expert Dr. Fromme were the only witnesses for the defense) would have been essential.

A careful review of the records shows that a thorough and fair investigation was never conducted in the Turner case. As discussed in greater detail, it is extraordinary that Stanford police were allowed to do this sort of deficient investigation. Here are some of the major defects:

1. Other than the tainted DNA lab tests (discussed in Chapter 2), the major part of the investigation by Stanford police consisted of interviewing the two Swedish graduate students.
2. Stanford police never tried to find and interview others at the fraternity party who might have seen Turner and Chanel leaving together consensually. Nor did they try to find the couple who were making out a few yards from Turner and Chanel and likewise in full view of passersby. Nor did they try to find any of the other potential witnesses, discussed in greater detail below.
3. Officers working with Det. Kim took down the license plate numbers of all the attendees at the fraternity party and made specific references to their doing so in their initial police reports and later in the attachment to the criminal complaint. Yet when Turner's lawyer asked

for the license plate numbers, as discussed in greater detail below, the DA's office responded in writing that Det. Kim is "not aware of any license check done."

4. Stanford police returned Chanel's cell phone to her the very day of the incident. They simply asked that she send back to them anything on her phone she thought might be relevant, which according to her book she did within a day or two later. In all of this, it is not clear if Stanford police didn't, in fact, keep any records from Chanel's or others' phones. Nevertheless, when Turner's lawyer asked for any and all phone records, he was informed in writing by the DA's office on February 25, 2015 that "Per Det. Kim, there was no analysis done on the victim's phone," and that "Per Det. Kim, there are no phone records for the victim, the victim's sister, or Julia." And this was several weeks after Chanel in fact had returned at least some of what was on her phone.

5. When Turner's lawyer similarly asked for the results of any investigations done at Stanford, the DA's office responded, again in writing, that Det. Kim didn't "have access" to anything at Stanford – even though Det. Kim is employed by Stanford, he and other Stanford police were the ones doing the investigations, and even though his boss, Stanford's police chief, reports directly to senior Stanford administrators as well as the Santa Clara County sheriff.

6. This is on top of the contradictory statements Chanel gave that very same day to Stanford police as to when she and others came to Stanford, where they were dropped off, and what they had been drinking but where Stanford police never tried to reconcile the blatant inconsistencies. See Chapter 2.

Detective Mike Kim's Role in the Investigation

Stanford Detective Mike Kim was the official investigating officer from the outset. He was then and presumably remains employed by Stanford's police department and not the Santa Clara County sheriff's department. As with the other Stanford police, however, Det. Kim is a sworn Santa Clara County deputy as well.

Because of his special role in the case as the official investigating officer, not only was Det. Kim in charge of the entire investigation, but he also was allowed to sit with the prosecutor Alaleh Kianerci throughout the trial, and she even referred to him in her opening statement to the jurors as *"my investigating officer seated to my right."* On top of that, Chanel and Chanel's sister Tiffany referred to Det. Kim throughout the trial and in front of the jury as "Detective Mike," as if he were a longstanding and trusted family friend.

Det. Kim along with prosecutor Kianerci had what are known as <u>Brady</u> and other obligations to turn over to Turner's lawyer any evidence that might have supported Turner's innocence or might have undercut the veracity of the prosecutor's own witnesses and case, including Det. Kim's own case files. There are many indications these obligations weren't met. These obligations continue even now, especially for members of the bar, police, the DA, the prosecutor, and other government officials as well as attorneys and other officers at Stanford, especially those who currently supervise or previously supervised Stanford's police.

Stanford's role and obligations were further complicated by the fact that one of its tenured law school faculty members, Prof. Michele Dauber, was leading a campaign aggressively attacking Turner, making it very difficult if not impossible for any investigations and hearings to proceed fairly.

As a Stanford police officer, and especially as the District Attorney's official investigating officer for the case, Det. Kim had obligations to be factual and to be open to all possibilities. Rather, it appears Det. Kim prejudged the case from the outset, or was told to do so by the District Attorney and the prosecutor. For example, the very first paragraph of Det. Kim's nine-page official report, as attached to the criminal complaint filed in Santa Clara County Superior Court, states:

"On 1/18/15, at about 0143 hours, **Lt. Havig called to inform me of a rape that occurred** on the Stanford University campus at the Kappa Alpha fraternity house. He also stated that they have a suspect in custody **for the crime**. I arrived at the [Stanford police] station at about 0310 hours and checked in with Lt. Havig to receive some more information regarding the case." [Boldface added]

The initial 911 call actually was for alcohol poisoning, yet even before an investigation had begun, Det. Kim seems to have decided this was a rape case and wrote up his report calling it that. There was no evidence of rape in the first hours that Det. Kim is discussing, and in fact, there never was any such evidence. Nor were there ever claims of rape by the parties involved including by Chanel herself.

On January 27, 2015, nine days after the alleged assault, Det. Kim signed a felony complaint with five charges against Turner that included the following:

"The undersigned [Det. Kim] is informed and believes that . . . BROCK TURNER who did accomplish **an act of sexual intercourse** with Jane Doe . . . where the person was prevented from resisting by an intoxicating and anesthetic substance ..." [Boldface added]

Det. Kim was obviously not "informed," and he had no evidence whatsoever that sexual intercourse had occurred. Det. Kim didn't wait for DNA test results, and he evidently didn't bother to contact the SART team about preliminary findings such as wet mount evaluation for sperm, which showed that *no sperm were found*, and which would have been available almost immediately after the alleged assault occurred. In fact, findings from Chanel's SART exam weren't even ordered until February 4, 2015, and apparently nobody bothered to make a timely or earnest effort to examine the results. In other words, Det. Kim had no justification for filing rape charges, yet rape charges, which were later found to be false, were allowed to stand for nearly nine months.

The Missing License Plate Records

Stanford police said in their written reports that they took down the license plate numbers of the vehicles in the Kappa Alpha parking lot, presumably to do follow-up investigations. In fact, Dep. Shaw wrote in his police report:

"Sgt. Barries and Dep. Edwards logged vehicle license plates that were found in the parking lot of 664 Lomita Ct. (Kappa Alpha.)."[10]

The implication is that the Stanford police, headed by Det. Kim, intended to locate and interview witnesses based on the license plates of the cars in the parking lot, and it appears that Det. Kim was on site and supervising the case when the license plates were being recorded by his fellow Stanford police officers.

On February 5, 2015, which was two weeks after the incident, Turner's lawyer requested in writing these license plates and the results of any investigations, but three weeks after that (that is, on February 25), the Santa Clara County DA's office responded in writing: *"Per Det. Kim, he is not aware of any license plate check done."* [Italics added]

In other words, and despite official documentation that two officers had recorded vehicle license plates, the Stanford police department, the Sheriff's office, the DA's office, and the prosecutor either hid the information or forgot that they had previously documented, in writing, what they had done, including in the statements attached to the criminal complaint itself. Note also that the answer from the DA's office carefully refers only to Det. Kim and not whether others at the Stanford police department, the Sheriff's office, the DA's office, or others had the information being requested by Turner's lawyer. They all had obligations under the law to bring this and all other similar evidence to Turner's lawyer, but they apparently didn't. Many questions remain, including:

1. Did Det. Kim or others do an investigation as a result of their having written down the license plate numbers, and then kept the results hidden?
2. Or for some reason did they decide not to do the investigation, in which case, who decided not to investigate, and why?
3. What role, if any, did the Santa Clara County District Attorney Jeff Rosen, the prosecutor Alaleh Kianerci, Stanford Detective Mike Kim, and others play in these decisions and actions?

The Missing Witnesses

Regrettably, and almost certainly to the detriment of Turner's trial outcome, there was minimal and even non-existent effort by Stanford police, the DA's office, and even Turner's own lawyer Mike Armstrong to interview and subpoena key witnesses, including Kappa Alpha residents and visitors, attendees at the Kappa Alpha party, members of the Stanford swim team, and the couple making out nearby, all of whom may have seen the interactions between Chanel and Turner at the Kappa Alpha party, who may have seen Chanel and Turner leave the party together, and/or saw the subsequent interactions of Chanel and Turner.

The initial police report said there were five witnesses. Other than the two Swedish graduate students, there appears to have been little if any follow-up with the other three witnesses.

One of the most surprising defects concerns the people who were standing over Chanel, including the unidentified person who flashed a light over her and then fled. Who was that person? Was the flash of light the result of his also taking a photo? Was he one of the people named in the GroupMe text message and photo that was circulated within minutes of Turner's being tackled by the Swedish graduate students and then taken into custody by the police?

During the trial, Turner's lawyer asked Det. Kim the following questions, which indicates a sloppy investigation and possibly intentional framing of Turner, and also highlighted Kianerci's attempts to block potential factual evidence:

Armstrong: "So, Detective Kim, more specifically, let me ask a more directed question. You don't have any evidence that has been turned up in the entire investigation from a witness who saw [Chanel] between 12:29 and 1:10?"
Kianerci: "Objection. Misstates the evidence."
Armstrong: "Well, he can answer the question."
The Court: "All right. Well, I'll allow the answer. You can answer."
Armstrong: "Do you have evidence as to what she was doing or where she was between 12:29 and 1:01?"
Det. Kim: "No."[11]

Then Armstrong queried Det. Kim regarding more lack of follow-up, asking:

Armstrong: "Now, one of the things you told Brock Turner on the audio tape that we just listened to was, the more people we can talk to at KA the better. You said that, didn't you?"
Det. Kim: "Correct."
Armstrong: "Okay. So since January 18th of 2015 until today, have you personally interviewed any member of the Kappa Alpha Fraternity related to this evening?"
Det. Kim: "No."
Armstrong: "All right. So at this point, you're not aware of any identifiable witness that was ever interviewed by you or anyone at your direction in your department that was a member of Kappa Alpha Fraternity as it relates to this incident; right?"
Det. Kim: "Correct."[12]

Later during the same testimony, Armstrong asked Det. Kim:

Armstrong: "Other than the people who have testified here at trial, did you personally interview anyone else who was at the party?"
Kianerci: "Objection. Vague as to party."
Armstrong: "I'm talking about the party on January 17/January 18th of 2015 at the Kappa Alpha house."
Court: "All right."
Det. Kim: "You mean for me personally or our department?"
Armstrong: "Yes. I'll start with you first."
Det. Kim: "I don't believe so."
Armstrong: "Of the women who have testified in this trial, the only one that was actually a student at Stanford University on that occasion was Julia; correct?"
Det. Kim: "Correct."
Armstrong: "Did you ever ask Julia for names of other people who were at the party that could be potential witnesses?"
Det. Kim: "I'm not sure if I asked her that question."
Armstrong: "Did you ever go to the Kappa Alpha house yourself to try and find witnesses to this incident?"

Det. Kim: "No."
Armstrong: "That's all the questions I have."

In summary, Det. Kim and the rest of Stanford police failed to locate any witnesses from 12:29 a.m. until the arrival of the two Swedes, they did not attempt to locate and interview other essential witnesses, that night or at any time, they did not interview anyone who attended the party other than Chanel, three members of her group, and Turner, and they did not ask Julia, the only Stanford student in Chanel's group, for the names of other people who were at the party. And from what is known, Det. Kim and the rest of Stanford police likewise did not bother to interview members of the Stanford swim team other than Tom Kremer (who was actually interviewed by Dep. Dotsy), who nevertheless was not brought in to testify at the trial.

What's also interesting is that Det. Kim was careful to limit his answers to what he did personally ("you mean for me personally or our department") and yet Armstrong did not ask the obvious follow-up question: "Did anyone else conduct such inquiries?" A related and obvious question is, how come Armstrong never bothered doing any of this?

It was particularly odd that during questioning, Det. Kim seemed to have difficulty identifying areas of the scene of the alleged assault. It would seem that because he was the lead detective and was overseeing the investigation, Det. Kim would have a very detailed knowledge of the scene, but inexplicitly, he didn't.

Another example of the missing witnesses is the fact that prosecutor Kianerci had listed a number of people as possible witnesses she might call as part of the prosecution's case but who she then didn't call. Which leads to the question, why not? Did one or more of these potential witnesses have exculpatory information that Kianerci, District Attorney Rosen, and even Stanford police had obligations to disclosure to Turner's lawyer?

It's also noteworthy that one of the Stanford swim team members said in a pre-sentencing character reference letter to Judge Persky that:

"We were all shocked by the verdict in Brock's case. **I personally struggle with it given the events I witnessed on the dance floor shortly before the events took place.**" [Boldface added]

31

What did this swim team member witness that led him to struggle with the verdict based on what he saw on the dance floor? What else did he see? And why was this witness, along with other swim team members and partygoers, not interviewed and asked to testify at the trial? How could Armstrong have known about this person's eyewitness account and not have called him at the trial?

Separate from these important eyewitness accounts, a critical element in the trial was Turner's credibility since, even though the prosecutor had failed to show essential elements of the alleged crimes, Armstrong inexplicably put Turner on the stand (see Ch. 4). Turner's reputation for honesty therefore was very important, but the testimony of this swim team member and others wasn't even presented to the jury.

In summary, the half-baked efforts by Stanford police and the DA's office to identify and interview witnesses, including witnesses whose testimony might have been exculpatory to Turner's case or undercut the prosecution, as is required by law to be disclosed, were shoddy at best or an intentional framing of Turner at worst

The Missing Phone Records

It is unclear from the record whether Stanford's police searched Chanel's cell phone when they first took possession of it even though they carefully searched Turner's phone. The information on Chanel's phone contained photos, videos, text and voice mail messages, calling details, GPS location history, and timelines of what was happening and when. That information obviously could have led to important exculpatory evidence on Turner's behalf.

Remarkably, when Chanel went to the Stanford police station to pick up her phone on the very same day as the incident, Stanford Det. DeVlugt, according to Chanel's book, *Know My Name,* gave the phone back to Chanel and simply asked that Chanel send back to Stanford police any relevant information on the phone. It appears that Chanel, a day or two later, then selectively decided what to send back. Even then, when Turner's lawyer sent a written discovery request to the DA's office on February 5, 2015 for all of the phone records including Chanel's, he was told in writing on February 25, 2015 by the DA's office that "Per Det. Kim, there was no analysis done on the victim's phone." And, "Per Det. Kim, there are no phone records for the victim, the victim's sister, or Julia [last name deleted]."

Here's what then was revealed at the trial itself:

Kianerci: "And did you show all of these [screenshots] to the lady detective that was giving you your phone?"

Chanel: "No. I showed—I—I thought that the important—not transaction—the important screenshots would be between me, [Tiffany], and Julia and Colleen, because I knew they were part of the evening, but I was not aware that I had called Lucas or that he was involved in any way."

Kianerci: "Okay. At some point, when you became aware that you had called Lucas, did you provide all that information to Detective Kim?"

Chanel: "Yes."[13]

But apparently no questions were asked by Armstrong or Kianerci: What didn't you send back that was on your phone? Did anyone advise you what to send back and what not to send back? If so, who? And did anyone advise you to delete items on your phone? If so, who?

The Questionable DNA Testing

Turner's DNA was NOT on Chanel's underwear nor was it found anywhere on her body. Chanel's DNA was found on Turner's hands and under his fingernails, but at least some of that may well have come from their holding hands. Turner also admitted to "fingering" Chanel but it's not clear he fully understood at the time what that meant.

The lab technician's DNA, on the other hand, was found on body samples taken from Turner, indicating improper procedures. Still another person's DNA was found on Chanel's underwear, and it was specifically determined NOT to be Turner's. [14] This fact is important not only because of the discrepancies, but also because it shows that if someone had touched Chanel's underwear, including Turner, there is a very high likelihood their DNA would have remained on the underwear. The question also arises whether the SART examination kit showed other evidence that might not have been provided to Turner's lawyer, as required under the law. Presumably that kit and any related evidence have been preserved.

Of note is that the vaginal and cervical swabs taken from Chanel were positive for presumptive blood, but the rectal swab was also positive for presumptive blood. This makes no sense, as a rectal swab positive for presumptive blood in this case would have been nearly impossible, leading to the suspicion that perhaps all three specimens – the vaginal, cervical, and rectal specimens – were incorrectly obtained, processed, or were somehow contaminated. A presumptive test for blood can only indicate the possible presence of blood, while a confirmatory test for blood can accurately identify the presence of blood. No confirmatory tests for blood were conducted, and no follow-up as to the questionable test results had taken place.

The Santa Clara County District Attorney's Crime Laboratory that conducted the DNA testing was one of only two labs in the U.S. that the FBI had threatened at the time to deny access to the national DNA data base. This was because of the lab's repeated misconduct while handling and testing DNA evidence. Despite these serious problems, the Santa Clara County DA's office, in Turner's case and others, continued to present this lab's work as trustworthy. (See book by Erin E. Murphy, *Inside the Cell.*) It also is reported that the Santa Clara County Crime Lab is one of few anywhere that isn't independent but instead reports to the Santa Clara County District Attorney.

Notwithstanding these serious defects, Turner's lawyer reportedly agreed with the prosecutor in advance of the trial not to challenge any of the DNA evidence.

Other Missing Evidence

Photos reportedly showed a beer can lying near Chanel's hand. In fact, Stanford Dep. Campos had collected an empty Coors Light beer can found at the scene for evidence.[15] That beer can seems to have been carefully cropped out of photos used at the trial. As far as is known, no one even checked whose DNA was on the beer can, and what were the implications, if true, of Chanel walking with Turner, a beer can in one hand and her other hand in his hand? Why was this important part of the photo cropped out and its implication (that Chanel was voluntarily walking with Turner to his dorm) not shown to the jury? And again, where was Armstrong in all of this?

The original 911 caller reported only a case of alcohol poisoning and apparently made no mention of any alleged assault or other questionable activity. Presumably Chanel, Turner, and the two Swedish graduate students were in front of whoever made the call but it seems that no one bothered to track down the phone number and interview the caller.

As discussed in Chapter 2, there were reports of a bright flash over Chanel while she was on the ground. The person who was standing over her and caused the flash reportedly then fled the scene. Shortly after that, a photo of a female's breast was circulated among members of Stanford's swim team, although as far as is known, it isn't clear who the photo was of. Incredibly, both prosecutor Kianerci and Prof. Dauber accused Turner of taking and circulating the photo and used this untruth in a national (even worldwide) media campaign against Turner that was already underway, and the falsehood about the photo was repeated by Kianerci at Turner's sentencing a year later. This is another element of prosecutor misconduct, by the way, since both Kianerci and Prof. Dauber surely knew early on that the photo was circulated while Turner was being held down by the two Swedes, was later distributed to others while Turner was in custody and the police had confiscated his phone, and that the name of the swim team member who circulated the photo (not Turner) was already known by the swim team and others and even appears to be referred to in the message that accompanied the photo. Yet Det. Kim, the rest of the Stanford police, and the DA's office apparently did nothing to investigate why there was a bright flash over Chanel, whether that flash included someone taking a photo that was subsequently circulated, why the person who caused that flash then fled the scene, and the identity of that person.

There Was Never Probable Cause to Charge Turner with Rape, and It's Even Questionable Why He Was Prosecuted

In a 2019 *Palo Alto Daily Post* article, **"0-for-16: No Sex Cases Stanford Police Submitted to the DA Were Prosecuted"** by reporter Allison Levitsky, Assistant DA Terry Harman, who now heads the Santa Clara County Sexual Assault Unit, admitted that:

"We received criticism from a lot of defense attorneys that we were wrong to pursue the Brock Turner case, that there was insufficient evidence there and we should have declined to file."[16]

As shown throughout this book, this assessment seems quite accurate. And in fact, several years after the incident, Stanford's police chief told one of the volunteer alumni who has been reviewing the case that she (the police chief) was surprised Turner was prosecuted. She thought both Turner and Chanel deserved counseling, and that Turner might have been subject to campus disciplinary procedures.

Another senior Stanford official similarly has said that Santa Clara County District Attorney Jeff Rosen routinely refused to prosecute cases like this, so senior officers at Stanford were very surprised at how Rosen and his office acted in the Turner matter, and from the very outset. Which again leads to questions about what role Stanford's law school professor Michele Dauber had in the case, and possibly from the very beginning. And since the Stanford administration had long been aware of complications created in other cases, on what basis did they simply stand back here?

Wet Mount Testing the Day of the Alleged Assault Showed No Evidence of Rape

What's also particularly disturbing is that the Stanford police, Kianerci, and the DA's office would have known almost immediately after Chanel's SART exam, which took place the day of the alleged assault, that rape did not occur. This is because the SART team conducted an on-site wet mount evaluation during Chanel's SART exam using a microscope to examine specimens for motile and nonmotile sperm, which showed no sperm. Wet mount evaluations are conducted during SART exams since sperm motility can decline rapidly after specimen collection. Specifically, the SART team's finding was that "we did not see anything on that slide,"[17] meaning there were no sperm found. It's outrageous that the wet mount findings were available the day of the alleged assault, yet police and the prosecution chose to ignore this crucial information and instead charged Turner with rape when there was never probable cause to do so. Worse, months later the DA office's own crime lab reported that they had not found Turner's DNA on either Chanel or her clothing.

Chapter 4

The Preliminary Hearing and Trial

Turner's Initial Charges

Turner was arraigned on February 2, 2015. He was charged with five felony counts: two rape charges, one count of intent to commit rape, and two counts of sexual assault. Turner pleaded "not guilty" to all five counts. A bail hearing was set for March 7, 2015.

It should be emphasized that Turner's trial was tainted before he even stepped into the courthouse. Traditional news and social media had spread disinformation, reported intentional falsehoods, and engaged in cyber-shaming and bullying for over a year before the trial. With the enormous amounts of cruel and false publicity against him prior to the trial, Turner could not possibly have received a fair trial.

Among other things, prosecutor Kianerci waited nearly nine months before releasing DNA test results disproving rape. The DNA test results were known months earlier but not disclosed until the pretrial hearing, at which time Kianerci left the task of removing the two rape counts for the court to handle. The totally unnecessary wait to disclose these important DNA results allowed the false rape charges to stand for almost nine months and gave Prof. Dauber, the District Attorney's office, traditional news sources, and social media the benefit of close to nine months to malign Turner and falsely publicize him as a rapist.

What's especially shocking is that Kianerci claimed:

"the [nine-month] delay in dismissing the rape counts was really to accommodate the defendant who was on a 977 waiver, in Ohio, to avoid having him to come back to court for an arraignment on a new Complaint."[18]

In reality, the fraudulent nine-month delay in disclosing the DNA results and dismissing the rape charges served only to promote the relentless false publicity against Turner. Contrary to Kianerci's above statement, it would not have been necessary for Turner to be present in California in order for the DA's office to inform the public that DNA test results showed no evidence of rape. Here, the DA's office and Kianerci selectively chose when and what they wanted the public to hear in an obvious ploy to sway public opinion against Turner.

Kianerci's actions were contrary to the American Bar Association's Model Rule 3.8: Special Responsibilities of a Prosecutor, including:

- Section (a) whereby a **prosecutor must "refrain from prosecuting a charge that the prosecutor knows is not supported by probable cause,"**
- Section (d) that requires a prosecutor to **"make timely disclosure to the defense** of all evidence or information known to the prosecutor that tends to negate the guilt of the accused or mitigates the offense," (see the discussion elsewhere about the license plate records and other evidence that went missing or was destroyed), and
- Section (f) that provides a prosecutor must "refrain from making extrajudicial comments that have a substantial likelihood of heightening public condemnation of the accused and **exercise reasonable care to prevent** investigators, law enforcement personnel, employees or **other persons assisting or associated with the prosecutor in a criminal case** from making an extrajudicial statement that the prosecutor would be prohibited from making under Rule 3.6 or this Rule." [Boldface]

California's rules of ethics impose similar duties. It's surprising that prosecutor Kianerci got away with breaking the above rules.

The Preliminary Hearing and Conflicting Testimony

The preliminary hearing occurred on October 5, 2015, during which time preliminary motions were discussed and Chanel, Chanel's sister Tiffany, and one of the two Swedish graduate students, Lars Peter Jonsson, were queried. A useful way to see some of the more obvious conflicts in testimony is to take each witness separately, as follows.

38

Chanel Miller's testimony at the preliminary hearing versus the trial:
Chanel made statements that were contradictive to statements she had made earlier to the police, statements that didn't concur with other witness accounts, and statements that were contradictive to what she later said at the trial. For example, Chanel said she brought no I.D. or money to the fraternity party because the women were not going to a bar, but Chanel's sister Tiffany said Chanel had told her that Chanel would go to the fraternity party and then possibly "go downtown to meet her friends." Tiffany said when she had returned to the fraternity party after bringing one of their friends to another friend's dorm to sleep off her drunkenness, she thought Chanel wasn't at the fraternity because she believed Chanel had gone to downtown Palo Alto to meet her friends "as she was planning to do since I was gone."[19]

At the pretrial hearing, Chanel also said she, her sister, and two friends had gone only to the Kappa Alpha party. However, when she first woke up in the emergency room, Chanel had told Stanford police that the group had first gone to a party at the Lagunita Court dormitory area and then proceeded to go to the Kappa Alpha party.[20]

Prosecutor Kianerci asked Chanel at the trial, "Do you remember if anyone in your group had any alcohol with them?" Chanel responded, under oath, "I'm not sure." Kianerci: "Okay. Do you recall if anyone had a bottle of water with vodka in it?" Chanel: "I don't remember."

On the other hand, one of Chanel's and Tiffany's friends was asked at the trial about anyone bringing alcohol to the party:

Friend: "Yes. But I also know that [Chanel] and [her sister Tiffany] brought a plastic bottle of alcohol with them."
Kianerci: "How do you know that?"
Friend: "I saw it."
Kianerci: "And how do you know what was in it?"
Friend: "They told me."
Kianerci: "And you remember them telling you that?"
Friend: "Yes."

It should also be remembered, when Chanel first woke up in the hospital emergency room, she explicitly told Stanford police that the only things she drank at the party were Keystone Light beers. Among other things, it's curious that she would have gone out of her way to make such an explicit statement when supposedly she was having trouble remembering what happened. And yet she testified at the trial that she had also been drinking vodka. No doubt she, her sister, and others had to be careful what they now were saying under oath.

Tiffany Miller's testimony at the preliminary hearing versus the trial: Tiffany denied under oath having brought alcohol to the party. On the other hand, her friend Colleen testified at the trial that Chanel and Tiffany had brought to the party an empty water bottle containing alcohol.

At the preliminary hearing, Tiffany described Chanel as functioning fine:

> "Chanel seemed drunk but not out of control at all. She was still like speaking totally fine. And she was just making up silly rap things and like running around in circles. And then Julia definitely seemed more drunk than Chanel."[21]

Tiffany also said that when she had left the party to take Trea to Julia's room, Chanel "seemed drunk, but I was not concerned at all about her."[22]

What stands out in Tiffany's testimony is that shortly after the above testimony and after a brief court recess requested by Kianerci, Tiffany's testimony took an about-face, as if she had been coached during the recess. After the recess Kianerci asked Tiffany, "You indicated when you spoke to your sister she seemed really drunk but fine?" This time Tiffany's response differed significantly from her testimony before the recess:

> "I wasn't really paying attention to how she was doing. I meant more that — so everyone seemed really drunk. I was pretty drunk . . . And I remember I wasn't paying attention to anyone specifically in how drunk they were, but I felt like I was more concerned about Trea and not just passing out there because she was like stay [sic] on the bench like falling asleep, and I was way more focused on her [Trea]. I definitely wasn't paying attention to Chanel or my other friends for that matter. I just remember feeling okay with leaving her. I didn't feel like I was putting her in any danger. And I don't remember specifically like how she was doing when I said I was leaving. Like how she was doing when I said I

was leaving. I just remember that I didn't feel like if I left she would, you know, I didn't feel she was – I don't know."[23]

Kianerci then asked, "When you previously said she felt fine, what did you mean by that?" Tiffany answered:

"She [Chanel] was very, very drunk. But she was being really silly. And I was more so with Colleen at that time and think Julia and Chanel were kind of mainly hanging around and it was also the time where everyone was shot gunning beers and stuff. So I hadn't had like a direct conversation with Chanel in a while. I just – felt like she was fine in that sense, that like she wasn't – when I saw her I didn't think like she was going to throw up. I didn't think that if I left for 20 minutes like that any of my friends would – I don't know. I just – I really regret not --."[24]

Tiffany was clearly confused or coached or both.

The Swedish graduate students' testimony at the preliminary hearing versus the trial: It came out at the preliminary hearing that the two Swedish graduate students may have been improperly coached about their testimony, including being taken together to the Kappa Alpha fraternity house by Det. Kim four days prior to the preliminary hearing likely to get their testimony more in line with one another. As a matter of proper investigation protocol, it was inappropriate to take the two of them together, and even more inappropriate to try to get them to change what they would say. Even then, they kept getting it wrong.

At the preliminary hearing, Turner's lawyer, Mike Armstrong, asked Lars Peter if he recalled that Chanel was unconscious:

Lars Peter: "Yes"
Armstrong: "Because you've spoken to the police twice before, right?"
Lars Peter: "Yeah."
Armstrong: "You never mentioned that fact before, did you?"
Lars Peter: "I don't remember."
Armstrong: "You spoke to the police shortly after this happened on that night, right?"

41

Lars Peter: "Yes."

Armstrong: "Almost at the very same place that this occurred?"

Lars Peter: "Yeah."

Armstrong: "And then approximately five days later you got a telephone call from Detective Kim; right?"

Lars Peter: "Yes."

Armstrong: "And you spoke to him on the phone?"

Lars Peter: "Yeah."

Armstrong: "And you talked to him again last Thursday when you went out to the scene?"

Lars Peter: "Yes."

Armstrong: "And on neither of those occasions did you tell him that, did you [that Chanel was unconscious]?"

Lars Peter: "I'm not sure."

Regarding how the two Swedish graduate students tackled Turner:

Lars Peter at the trial: "I was **sitting on his chest**."

Kianerci: "Did your positions change at all?"

Lars Peter: "No."

Kianerci: "And when you tackled Turner, you tackled him in such a way that he ended up being **on his back**, correct?"

Lars Peter: "Yes."

Carl-Fredrik at the trial: "The defendant was **face down**."

Kianerci: "Face-down?"

Carl-Fredrik: "Yes." [Boldface added]

Since Lars Peter and Carl-Fredrick had both held Turner down and were important eyewitnesses, it's odd that Lars Peter testified that Turner was lying face up, while Carl-Fredrick testified that Turner was lying face down. That's quite an obvious difference.

Lars Peter also kept getting it wrong about Chanel's clothing. For example, when he was asked by prosecutor Kianerci about Chanel's clothing and whether any of Chanel's body parts were exposed, Lars Peter responded: "I didn't take notice of that."

- **Lars Peter at the preliminary hearing,** after Kianerci reminded him that he had talked in recent days to Det. Kim and after the

42

prosecutor then read to Lars Peter what Det. Kim had written, said "I can't say for sure that I said exactly that."

- **Kianerci** again reminded Lars Peter that he talked to police, to which **Lars Peter** then responded: "I remember describing it, yeah, but I don't remember saying exactly that."
- At this point, **Kianerci** asked: "Do you remember describing that her dress was pulled up?" to which
- **Lars Peter** responded "Yeah."
- **Kianerci**: "Do you remember seeing her dress pulled up?" **Lars Peter**: "No."
- **Lars Peter at the trial**, when asked if he could describe Chanel's state of dress: "Uh, no. Not really."
- **Lars Peter at the trial**, when being pressed still further by Kianerci: "I could but I didn't look straight there. So I just saw briefly that she looked – she had her dress pulled up."

The Trial: Background; Prosecutor Misconduct

On March 14, 2016, the <u>People v. Brock Allen Turner</u> trial commenced at the Santa Clara County courthouse in Palo Alto, California with Judge Aaron Persky presiding. Deputy District Attorney Alaleh Kianerci presented the prosecution's case against Turner, and Mike Armstrong served as Turner's criminal defense lawyer. Armstrong had long been a named partner at a Palo Alto law firm but for unknown reasons he left the firm shortly after undertaking the Turner case and was now functioning as a solo practitioner.

The witnesses for the prosecution were multiple fire and police personnel who were involved in the case (although without Turner's lawyer quizzing them on their completely contradictory official statements, as discussed elsewhere), the two Swedish Stanford graduate students who had found Turner and Chanel outdoors on the ground (but had not witnessed what actually had taken place), Santa Clara County Valley Medical Center personnel, Chanel, her sister Tiffany, Tiffany's friend Colleen who had attended the Kappa Alpha party with Chanel and Tiffany as well as another friend, Julia, who lived on campus, and Chanel's boyfriend.

Besides several character witnesses, the only other sworn witnesses at the trial for Turner's defense were alcohol expert Dr. Kim Fromme and Turner himself.

While walking into the courtroom the first day of the trial, prosecutor Kianerci handed Turner's lawyer important evidence (the EMT written report made 14 months earlier) not previously disclosed to him and thus another violation of the DA's obligations to make timely disclosures of evidence of this nature. Also, although it was agreed in advance that Chanel would be referred to as "Jane 1" and her sister Tiffany as "Jane 2," Kianerci continually and aggressively referred to Chanel as "the victim" throughout the trial. In fact, Kianerci used the term "victim" at least 71 times in front of the jury, and likewise marked all evidence with "Victim" or "V" even though the entire point of the trial was whether Chanel had in fact been the victim of a crime. Armstrong never objected.

On numerous occasions when referring to Turner's sworn testimony, Kianerci described Turner's oath as "magical." For example, Kianerci said, "But you heard him when he testified after taking that magical oath."[25] This statement was improper and contradicted the court instruction that a jury is not to disregard any witness' testimony without a reason to do so. It is improper for a prosecutor to imply to the jury that the oath does not apply equally to all testimony and witnesses.

Somehow Chanel, her sister Tiffany, and various other witnesses were on a first name basis with the prosecutor ("Alaleh") and the official investigating officer ("Detective Mike") and regularly used those first names in front of the jury.

The Trial: Lack of Evidence; More Prosecutor Misconduct

A critical element of the prosecutor's case was whether Turner had fingered Chanel, including with Chanel's consent. By the time the prosecutor rested her case, no such evidence was presented for the following reasons:

1. Turner's DNA was not on Chanel nor on Chanel's underwear.
2. Chanel said she didn't remember what had happened.

3. The Swedish graduate students did not see digital penetration, and there were no other witnesses before the Swedish graduate students arrived, which was after the fact.
4. The only possible witness therefore was Turner himself.
5. The prosecutor also didn't introduce any statements Turner may have made, with or without proper legal warnings, to the police when the prosecutor concluded presenting her case. In fact, Turner, while very drunk, told police that he had fingered Chanel but had done so with Chanel's consent, and his pants and other clothing were always closed. Turner's statement to police also may have been invalid as evidence for the prosecutor to introduce because:
   - Turner was too drunk to know what was going on, including waiving his Miranda rights while in a likely fragmentary alcoholic blackout condition.
   - The evidence from his body required separate, knowing disclosures and consent, which hadn't happened.
   - Turner actually didn't understand what fingering versus penetration meant. Incredibly, Armstrong not only put Turner on the stand to testify about essential elements the prosecution had failed to demonstrate, but he didn't ask Turner if he had "fingered" Chanel (which is all Turner had said in his drunken statement at the Stanford police station). Rather, Armstrong phrased his question, "When you say "fingered her, did you put a finger from your hand into her vagina?" – meaning, "penetrate" her, the very point that would result in the extraordinary requirement for Turner to register for life as a sex offender. Apparently unprepared for how to answer the question, Turner answered 'Yes I did." (Trial transcript Vol. 9, p. 852, Lines 8-10.)
   - Turner had no criminal intent under the statutes he was being prosecuted for, since he had every opportunity to open his pants but never did so, and he had no familiarity with the criminal process.
   - The question is, then, what caused the prosecutor to **not** introduce Turner's statements during her presentation of the case?

Even though the prosecutor's case was missing critical elements, at the end of the prosecutor's presentation, Turner's lawyer did not seek a directed verdict. Rather, Turner's lawyer put Turner on the stand and had Turner testify about the critical elements that were missing from the prosecutor's own case, which then gave the opening for the prosecutor to try to discredit Turner's testimony by subsequently playing a tape of Turner's drunken statement to Stanford police.

More Conflicting Testimony at the Trial

Sworn testimony throughout the trial conflicted with what various parties said in sworn testimony at the preliminary hearing or with known facts. Many of those conflicts are discussed in other chapters, but here are some. At the trial, for example, Chanel was asked by prosecutor Kianerci whether Chanel remembered shotgunning beers.

Chanel (under oath): "No I don't."
Kianerci: "Have you ever shotgunned a beer?"
Chanel: "I can't."
Kianerci: "Why can't you?"
Chanel: "Because it's hard."

But at the preliminary hearing, when Chanel's sister Tiffany was asked by Kianerci if Tiffany had observed Chanel shotgunning beers, Tiffany answered, also under oath:

Tiffany: "Yes, because she was making jokes about it [shotgunning beers]."
Tiffany also acknowledged that Chanel had said: "Yeah. Shotgunning. F___. Yeah."[26]

Surely, Kianerci knew about this prior testimony at the preliminary hearing and needed to somehow rectify it – falsely.

Kianerci also asked at the trial: "Do you remember if anyone in your group had any alcohol with them?"
Chanel (under oath): "I'm not sure."
Kianerci: "Okay. Do you recall if anyone had a bottle of water with vodka in it?"

Chanel: "I don't remember."
Separately at the trial, Kianerci asked: "Okay. So fair to say you guys shared the vodka around with the group?"
Chanel's friend: "Yes. But I also know that [Chanel] and [her sister Tiffany] brought a plastic bottle of alcohol with them."
Kianerci: "How do you know that?"
Friend: "I saw it."
Kianerci: "And how do you know what was in it?"
Friend: "They told me."
Kianerci: "And you remember them telling you that?"
Friend: "Yes."

When Kianerci asked Carl-Fredrik what Turner had been wearing, he said "jeans and a T-shirt." But based on photograph evidence, Turner was wearing pants other than jeans, and he was not wearing a T-shirt but rather a long shirt. Lars Peter said he believed Turner was wearing khaki pants.

Another example of conflicting testimony is the SART nurse's testimony that Chanel had not vomited, whereas the paramedics reported observing Chanel vomit with the ability to clear her own airway. The SART nurse indicated she had not read the ER documents, which would include pre-hospital reports, before Chanel was discharged from the ER and arrived at the SART office for examination. Also, in describing female anatomy, the SART nurse twice incorrectly named the female perineum as the "peritoneum," saying, "the outer surface of her vaginal area, the peritoneum,"[27] and then again saying the colposcope was at the "same level as her peritoneum area, her genitalia."[28] The peritoneum is actually a two-layered membrane that lines the abdominal and pelvic cavities, and covers mostly the abdominal viscera,[29] which has nothing to do with the female perineum. The SART nurse then later described erythema (redness) and abrasions on the labia minora (which is not part of the vagina) as "significant trauma," which it was not, as significant trauma is generally medically defined as "sudden, severe injury."[30] Furthermore, the word "trauma" can be easily misconstrued by jurors, as many people associate trauma, especially "significant trauma," with emergency trauma centers, mangled bodies due to motor vehicle accidents, and the like.

Prosecutor Kianerci Presented False Information to the Jury

Dozens of social and professional character witnesses had written letters to the court to attest to Turner's character as a responsible young man with strong moral values. Yet Kianerci told the jury:

> "Those character witnesses don't really add anything of value as to what the facts of this case are. They all say he's a good guy and they can't imagine him doing this. **None of them were there. None of them have seen him intoxicated.**"[31] [Boldface added]

But Kianerci's statement was false. In truth, one of the above referenced character witnesses was Tom Kremer, a friend of Turner's and member of the Stanford swim team who was at the Kappa Alpha party and had attended other Stanford parties with Turner when Turner was intoxicated. Moreover, when interviewed by Stanford Police Deputy Terrance Dotsy, Kremer told the officer, "Turner is a mellow, calm person when under the influence of alcohol."[32] This important testimony was not heard by the jury but was known to Kianerci.

As noted previously, another Stanford swim team member (see Ch. 3) who was at the Kappa Alpha party and who had written a letter to Judge Persky as a character witness for Turner, said:

> "We were all shocked by the verdict in Brock's case. **I personally struggle with it given the events I witnessed on the dance floor shortly before the events took place.**" [Boldface added]

Why wasn't this swim team member, along with other members of the Stanford swim team, interviewed?

Kianerci told the jury:

> "they [Swedish witnesses Lars Peter and Carl-Fredrik] also saw a girl who was lifeless, unconscious, not breathing."[33]

This was shear sensationalism, and obviously it was not true. The Oxford Dictionary defines the word "lifeless" as "Dead or apparently dead."[34] None of this applied to Chanel. In addition to having documented that Chanel was breathing at a normal rate, paramedics noted Chanel had moved her head, had cleared her own airway while vomiting, and had seemingly shifted her position on her own even while passed out. Kianerci described Chanel as "lifeless" five times in her closing argument alone.

Kianerci also told the jury that Turner had to be "effectively pulled off" Chanel, but that wasn't true either. In fact, earlier in the trial when Kianerci asked Lars Peter how Turner "got off the woman," Lars Peter said, "He just stood up."[35] Carl-Frederik said that he and Lars Peter were approximately 15 feet away from Turner when Turner started to stand up.[36] Nevertheless, in a June 14, 2016 interview with *Mother Jones*, Prof. Dauber said there were two witnesses "who literally pulled the attacker off . . . ."[37] Again, according to the two witnesses Lars Peter and Carl-Fredrik, they did not pull Turner off Chanel.

In Front of a Wooden Shed, NOT Behind a Dumpster

Throughout the preliminary hearing and trial, prosecutor Kianerci made repeated claims that Turner and Chanel were hidden "behind a dumpster." In fact, Kianerci mentioned the word "dumpster," and the phrases "behind a dumpster" and "behind the dumpster" 63 times throughout the preliminary hearing and the trial, eight of which were in her closing argument alone. Traditional news and social media repeatedly used the "behind a dumpster" slogan as well. However, according to witnesses Lars Peter and Carl-Fredrik, who were the first to find Turner and Chanel at the scene, Turner and Chanel were in full view of passersby, even from a distance, and they were not far from another couple making out. Lars Peter and Carl-Fredrik described the structure near the scene as a shed or "a wooden shed," not a dumpster, and there was nothing blocking their view of Turner and Chanel from the path on which the two Swedes were riding their bikes. Even Prof. Dauber said in her sentencing recommendations letter to Judge Persky that Chanel and Turner were in public view and, later in the same letter, it "happened in public where there were eyewitnesses."

In describing the location at which Chanel and Turner were found, Lars Peter said:

49

"They were lying between the wooden shed and the basketball court."

Deputy Shaw, who was one of the first officers at the scene said:

"The area in which we found [Chanel] is a student residential area, specifically fraternity houses with **walkways that have ambient lighting and high traffic** near a basketball court."[38] [Boldface added]

Dep. Taylor, who was also at the scene, described Chanel's location as lying "directly center behind the shed."[39] He used the word "behind" because, when coming upon the scene, he would have had to park in front of the fraternity house and walk down an embankment and to the other side of the wooden shed and where Turner, Chanel and others were always in full view of passersby and, as also specifically stated by police and others, in a high traffic area.

At the preliminary hearing, when Kianerci asked Lars Peter to describe the structure near where Turner and Chanel were located, he said it was a "small wooden shed." This apparently didn't meet the narrative Kianerci had wanted, which was to specifically use the word "dumpster" or something similar. So, in order to fit her narrative, Kianerci then asked Lars Peter, "Do you know what that shed houses?" and "Do you know what is on the other side of the shed?" Lars Peter answered, without apparently understanding what Kianerci was trying to do, "It's the Kappa Alpha house." Kianerci ended her questioning, having failed to get the graphic "dumpster" word into the testimony.

Notably, despite Kianerci calling the wooden shed a "dumpster" 63 times during the trial, there are 13 photo exhibits of the shed, all of which are labelled in the trial transcript exhibit indexes as either "shed" or "wooden shed." There is one photo of a dumpster that is labeled "dumpster," which is described as being "beyond the taped off area" and thus presumably not part of the scene of the alleged assault.[40]

The question arises as to why Kianerci, and then Prof. Dauber in her tweets and news interviews, focused so heavily and emphatically on the term "behind a dumpster"? The reasons appear to be (1) to add an element of sordidness in order to elicit sensationalism and to direct disgust at Turner, and (2) to plant in the minds of the jury and public the notion that Turner specifically and intentionally sought a hidden location away from public view to engage in sexual activity with Chanel, which of course, was not true. And again, where was Turner's lawyer, Mike Armstrong, in all of this?

Most importantly, whether Turner and Chanel were found in front of the shed or behind it, the heart of the matter is that Turner and Chanel were not hidden or out of sight — they were in a public area and in full view of passersby.

More Misrepresentations

Kianerci claimed Turner had "lured" Chanel to the shed area, but there was no evidence to indicate Chanel was "lured" anywhere.[41] Rather, the evidence indicates Turner and Chanel left the party together to evidently go to Turner's dorm room, and that they were less than 50 feet from the Kappa Alpha fraternity house in what would have been less than a 30- to 60-second walk from the fraternity house when they slipped on the dirt path.

Kianerci repeatedly spoke of Chanel's penetrating "trauma." But in reality, Chanel's injuries consisted only of superficial abrasions and erythema (redness), which do not constitute trauma. In fact, the medical definition of trauma is "a serious injury to a person's body."[42]

In an attempt to persuade the jury that Turner knew Chanel was unconscious, Kianerci said:

"And we know that at 4:15 a.m., [Chanel] regained consciousness, three hours later . . . And the fact that she was out for so long after that corroborates that he [Turner] knew."[43]

Actually, nobody knew when Chanel transitioned from alertness, to stupor or unconsciousness, or to deep sleep or sleep. Chanel's BAC was back-extrapolated to 0.242 -0.249% -- according to alcohol researcher Dr. Fromme, "a person must reach a blood-alcohol level of .30 and above to pass out from alcohol." This is backed up by other sources. In "How Your Body Reacts to Alcohol," the University of Denver Health and Counseling Center instructions to students states, "BAC .30%: You're in a stupor. You have little comprehension of where you are. You may suddenly pass out at this point and be difficult to awaken."[44] As a point of reference, a BAC of 0.35% compares to the level of consciousness when under general anesthesia.

According to Professor of Law Michael Vitiello, a nationally recognized expert on criminal law:

"the critical issue was not whether the victim was unconscious, but whether Turner believed that she was conscious. He was lying only if he said that he thought that she consented when in fact he knew that she was unconscious. Even if his mistaken view resulted from his high intoxication levels, also largely undisputed, he would not have been lying as long as he honestly believed that she consented. The prosecution failed to address this, and sought to hide this from the jury by the unnecessary inference that 'defendant was lying.' Why, while intoxicated, did Turner waive his Miranda rights and tell police it was consensual? It was because he believed there had been no crime committed."[45]

Witness Lars Peter said that when he had interacted with Turner, "He [Turner] didn't really seem to understand what was happening." This was because Turner believed his actions with Chanel were consensual and he didn't think he had committed a crime.

Regarding Chanel's state of mind in relation to the Kappa Alpha party, Kianerci told the jury:

"her [Chanel's] state of mind that night was not to go hook up with some random college freshman. That was absolutely not her state of mind."

But how did Kianerci know what was Chanel's state of mind, versus facts contained in the record: (1) Chanel had told others she planned to go to the bars in Palo Alto if things didn't work out at the fraternity party, (2) she texted messages to her boyfriend indicating she was apparently trying to make him jealous but would make it up to him, (3) Chanel's group referred to Turner using the name of one of Tiffany's college classmates, (4) she was consensually walking with Turner to his dorm, and (5) Chanel was blackout drunk but functional, and likely willing to engage in sexual risk-taking as is known to occur in alcoholic blackout.

In reference to expert witness Dr. Fromme, Kianerci tried to convince the jury that Dr. Fromme was colluding "with the defense to tailor her testimony." [46] Kianerci based her absurd statement on casual email conservations between Dr. Fromme and Armstrong that had nothing to do with the expert testimony Dr. Fromme presented to the jurors. Dr. Fromme's testimony in court was based solely on science, which Kianerci was unable to dispute and which led her to resort to focusing on irrelevant personal emails and Dr. Fromme's fees for service.

The Issue of Turner Running When Confronted by the Two Swedish Graduate Students

Kianerci asked the jury, "What about the facts of this case that Mr. Turner ran when confronted by two men?"

The facts are that the players bent on discrediting Turner and seemingly using him for their own political and other purposes repeatedly claimed on social media and elsewhere that because Turner ran from witnesses Lars Peter and Carl-Fredrik, this indicated Turner had committed a crime. To the contrary, Turner ran because he feared Lars Peter and Carl-Fredrik would harm him. In fact, when Armstrong asked Lars Peter, "He [Turner] only began to run when you yelled at him, right?" Lars Peter answered "Yeah."[47] Lars Peter not only yelled at Turner, but he yelled obscenities in a threatening manner. Most people would fear for their safety and attempt to escape from two men if one of the men shouted threatening obscenities at them.

In Kianerci's closing argument in reference to when the two Swedes came in contact with Turner, chased him, tripped him, tackled him, restrained him, and held him down, she said:

"This testimony about the shoulder touching, the arm lock, the fact that he broke his wrist, all new information. All new information that he attempts to elicit to you to distract you from the truth, because that information, if it were true, would have been given to Detective Kim."

In truth, Turner had suffered abrasions, his shirt was torn, and Turner's wrist had been broken as evidenced by x-ray and MRI imaging. This information almost certainly would have long been known by both Det. Kim and prosecutor Kianerci. Armstrong knew Turner's wrist had been broken so he should have immediately come forward to refute Kianerci's false statement to the jury. In fact, Armstrong had the opportunity to refute any and all of Kianerci's false statements in his closing argument to the jury that followed, but he did not.

The Trial: The Two Swedish Graduate Students Did Not Witness Turner's Alleged Fingering

Very importantly, it should be emphasized that Lars Peter and Carl-Fredrik observed Turner thrusting on top of Chanel while Turner was fully clothed, but did not observe his touching her. When Armstrong asked Carl-Fredrik, "Did you ever see him [Turner] touch the woman with his hands during this entire evening?" Carl-Fredrik answered "No."[48]

The Trial: The People Did Not Prove Guilt "Beyond a Reasonable Doubt"

Before the jury deliberations began, the jury was instructed by Judge Persky as follows:

> **"The defendant is not guilty of a crime if he actually and reasonably believed that the person was capable of consenting to the act, even if the defendant's belief was wrong. The People have the burden of proving beyond a reasonable doubt that the defendant did not actually and reasonably believe that the woman was [in]capable of consenting. If the People have not met this burden, you must find the defendant not guilty."** [Boldface added]

There were sound reasons to question whether Kianerci had met the "beyond a reasonable doubt" standard: First, Chanel would have appeared to everyone with whom she interacted, including Turner but also others, as being fully functional and not impaired (as discussed elsewhere, a person with alcoholic blackout amnesia would be functional, uninhibited, more likely to engage in sexual risk-taking than when sober, able to perform tasks, but with no memories formed) and could very well have knowingly consented to sexual activity with Turner. Chanel's own sister Tiffany testified that Chanel seemed fine although later gave contradictory testimony. Second, Turner, who himself was impaired due to alcohol consumption, would not have known that Chanel was in a state of blackout drunkenness because as already noted, an observer, even one who is sober, is unable to distinguish blackout drunkenness from sobriety. Third, the two Swedish witnesses, who themselves had been drinking, did not witness the interactions between Turner and Chanel before they were found; they did not witness Turner's alleged fingering. And finally, it was unknown when Chanel had possibly gone to sleep or declined into a state of drunken stupor.

It was for these and other reasons that many lawyers, Stanford alumni, and others who had followed the case believe the prosecution did not meet its essential burden of proof. What observers still can't understand is that, since the prosecution had failed to meet the burden of proof, why Turner's lawyer didn't move for a directed verdict but instead put Turner on the stand and had Turner testify as to items the prosecutor hadn't presented.

The Trial: The Jury Found Turner Guilty of Sexual Assault (not rape)

Despite the lack of evidence and the instructions given at the start and again at the end of the trial, after a two-week trial, the jurors found Turner guilty of three felony counts: (1) assault with intent to rape an intoxicated or unconscious person, California Penal Code section 220(a)(1), (2) sexual penetration when the victim was intoxicated or anesthetized, and this condition was known, or reasonably should have been known by the defendant, California Penal Code section 289(e), and (3) sexual penetration where the victim was unconscious of the nature of the act, and this condition was known, or reasonably should have been known by the defendant, California Penal Code section 289(d). Note that Turner was not convicted of rape. It also seems counts two and three are one and the same, as Chanel was "unconscious" because she was intoxicated—if she hadn't been intoxicated, she would not have been "unconscious."

Turner's convictions carried, in addition to the jail sentence, a devastating lifetime sex offender registration order that will negatively affect almost every aspect of Turner's life for the rest of his life. Note that Turner was convicted of sexual assault, not rape, and he had no intent ever to rape (his clothes were never opened and in fact his DNA wasn't even found on Chanel or Chanel's underwear). Both he and Chanel were engaged in what current generations consider safe sex or not even sex, but that fact wasn't brought out at the trial, either. Given the interactions and the fact that Turner never tried to open his clothing even when he had the opportunity, there was no intent by Turner to engage in what current generations actually consider sex, and certainly no intent to commit rape.

Questions That Anyone Concerned About Justice Needs to Ask

1. **Intent** – What should "intent" mean for purposes of the criminal laws?
2. **Chanel Miller's drunkenness** – Does it make sense that because 22-year-old Chanel was drunk, her consent might be *invalid* under the law? Does it matter that Chanel knew from prior experiences that she blacks out from heavy drinking (meaning she appears perfectly fine to third parties, including to Turner, but hours later she can't remember what she did) but nevertheless had three times the legal limit and then hooked up with Turner, a freshman?
3. **Brock Turner's drunkenness** – Does it make sense that although 19-year-old Turner likewise was drunk, the waiver of his legal rights, including his right to counsel, might be *valid* under the law? Or that he was held to a higher standard than Chanel in determining Chanel's own actions?
4. **Sexual equality** – Women have rightly sought and made significant advances to sexual equality in recent years. What, if any, responsibilities come with that equality?
5. **The lawyers** – In what ways did the Santa Clara County District Attorney Jeff Rosen and Deputy District Attorney/prosecutor Alaleh Kianerci act inappropriately? Likewise, what might Turner's own lawyer have done differently?

Chapter 5

The Pre-Sentencing and Sentencing

The Probation Officer's Sentencing Report

In Santa Clara County, as is the case throughout California, sentencing guidelines are given to the judge after professional officers, usually located in a county's probation department, review the facts of a case, interview the defendant, the accuser, and possibly others, and prepare comprehensive and unbiased recommendations for the court. These procedures were part of progressive reforms years earlier and are meant to eliminate unrelated emotional factors in the sentencing. In Turner's case, the probation officer who conducted the interviews and then prepared the official recommendations to Judge Persky was a highly seasoned and well-respected woman probation officer.

On May 3, 2016, a few weeks after Turner's conviction and a month before Turner's sentencing hearing on June 2, 2016, the probation officer interviewed Chanel about sentencing and other issues. Chanel was quoted in the probation officer's official written report as saying:

"I still feel a lot of anger because of what he put me through at trial. I want him to be sorry and express remorse. He attacked my personal life in whatever way possible and in the end, it didn't work. I don't experience joy from this. I don't feel like I won anything. It was just the anger of hearing what he said it Court. It was devastating. I want him to know it hurt me, but I don't want his life to be over. I want him to be punished, but as a human, I just want him to get better. **I don't want him to feel like his life is over and I don't want him to rot away in jail; he doesn't need to be behind bars.**"[49] [Boldface added]

Chanel also told the probation officer that she wanted Turner to participate in counseling to prevent a similar incident from happening. The probation officer stated in her Case Evaluation that "her [Chanel's] focus and concern was treatment, rather than incarceration." Chanel said Turner made her feel nervous and hoped Turner would not live in the Bay Area. The probation officer acknowledged that Chanel would be forever impacted by Turner's conduct, but noted Chanel's concern was treatment, not incarceration.

The same probation officer interviewed Turner on May 9, 2016. According to the probation officer's official written report, Turner indicated that "At no time did I see that she [Chanel] was not responding. If at any time I thought she was not responding, I would have stopped immediately." Turner described the impact of his conduct, in part, as follows:

"Having imposed suffering on someone else and causing someone else pain—I mean, I can barely live with myself . . . Her [Chanel] having to go through the justice system because of my actions just . . . it's unforgiveable . . . During the trial I didn't want to victimize her at all. That was just my attorney and his way of approaching the case. I didn't want to degrade her in any way . . . I'm sorry for her having to go through this entire process and having to even think about this for a second, all because of my actions that night . . . I can't believe I imposed such suffering on her and I'm so sorry."[50]

The probation officer believed Turner showed "sincere remorse and empathy" for Chanel. Using sophisticated assessment tools, and after interviewing both Chanel and Turner, the probation officer said in her 16-page report that Turner was unlikely to re-offend, and recommended four to six months in county jail, probation, participation of at least one year in sex offender management training, and a list of fees, restitution, and other requirements.

Turner's STATIC-99R report, which was used to predict the likelihood of re-offending, showed a score of "3," indicating a low risk of re-offending. In fact, research findings show that "people convicted of sex offenses are statistically unlikely to reoffend."[51] Turner also underwent a Correctional Assessment and Intervention System (CAIS) evaluation, which evaluates a defendant's risks of re-offending and "needs" concerning risk factors that need to be addressed in order to prevent recidivism. Turner's assessment results identified the needs to resolve internal problems or learn new coping skills, and the need for alcohol abstinence and treatment. Turner's strength was his family history, and because of the severe stress often experienced by family members, family therapy was suggested as a useful intervention.

The probation officer weighed multiple factors in reaching her sentencing recommendations, including the impact of the crime on the victim, the public's safety, Turner's lack of past convictions, his remorse and empathy for Chanel, his young age, Turner's lesser culpability related to his level of intoxication, and the devastating impact sex offender registration would have on Turner's life for the rest of his life.

The hypocrisy of this draconian sex registration requirement is that it is not considered part of a sentence but solely an administrative matter or collateral consequence of criminal conviction that is not appealable, even though it is very much part of a criminal sentence.

Prosecutor Kianerci's Sentencing Packet

The prosecution's sentencing packet included letters from friends, family, and others in support of Chanel. Stanford law school professor Michele Dauber submitted a letter that included sentencing recommendations and emphasized that the offense was all the more egregious because it took place in full view of the public. Prof. Dauber shortly thereafter decided to focus instead on the "behind the dumpster" theme since that apparently would work better for her media campaign. Note also that individuals who spoke at the sentencing hearing, including Chanel, or who contributed supportive letters for Chanel and Turner were not under oath, were not subject to cross-examination, and were not at risk if they were not wholly truthful, even to the point of what could have been perjury if the same statements had been made under oath at the trial itself.

Prosecutor Kianerci's Coordination with Prof. Dauber

Public Records Act disclosures show that Kianerci and Prof. Dauber were coordinating what would be submitted to Judge Persky in connection with Turner's sentencing. For example, in the emails below, Prof. Dauber discussed with Kianerci the letters that were to be submitted to Judge Persky from Stanford students, which implied that the two of them were editing and possibly even ghost-writing the letters from those students, most or all of whom didn't even know Chanel or Turner.

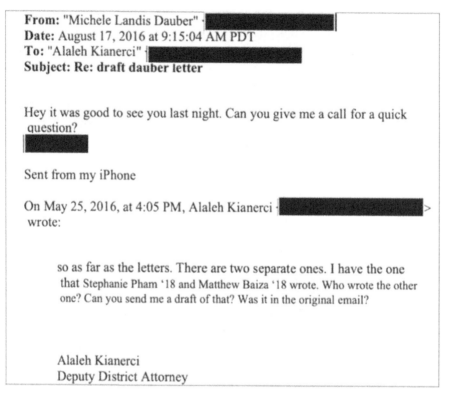

From: "Michele Landis Dauber" ·
Date: August 17, 2016 at 9:15:04 AM PDT
To: "Alaleh Kianerci" ·
Subject: Re: draft dauber letter

Hey it was good to see you last night. Can you give me a call for a quick question?

Sent from my iPhone

On May 25, 2016, at 4:05 PM, Alaleh Kianerci ·   >
wrote:

> so as far as the letters. There are two separate ones. I have the one
> that Stephanie Pham '18 and Matthew Baiza '18 wrote. Who wrote the other
> one? Can you send me a draft of that? Was it in the original email?

Alaleh Kianerci
Deputy District Attorney

Fig. 4. Prof. Dauber and Kianerci discussing student letters to Judge Persky to include in Kianerci's sentencing memorandum.

Additionally, below are email exchanges on May 24, 2016, a week before the sentencing hearing, showing Prof. Dauber and Kianerci discussing, among other things, Prof. Dauber's own sentencing letter to Judge Persky:

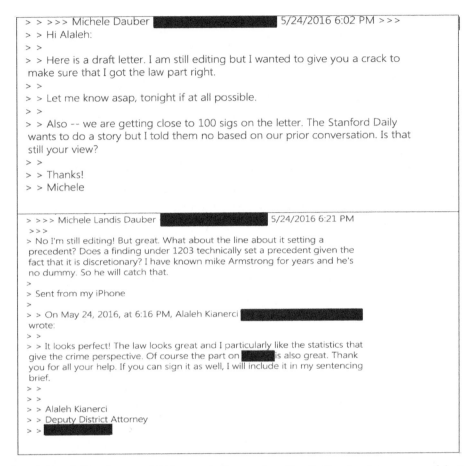

> > >>> Michele Dauber ███████████ 5/24/2016 6:02 PM > > >
> > Hi Alaleh:
> >
> > Here is a draft letter. I am still editing but I wanted to give you a crack to make sure that I got the law part right.
> >
> > Let me know asap, tonight if at all possible.
> >
> > Also -- we are getting close to 100 sigs on the letter. The Stanford Daily wants to do a story but I told them no based on our prior conversation. Is that still your view?
> >
> > Thanks!
> > Michele

> >>> Michele Landis Dauber ███████████ 5/24/2016 6:21 PM
> >>>
> No I'm still editing! But great. What about the line about it setting a precedent? Does a finding under 1203 technically set a precedent given the fact that it is discretionary? I have known mike Armstrong for years and he's no dummy. So he will catch that.
>
> Sent from my iPhone
>
> > On May 24, 2016, at 6:16 PM, Alaleh Kianerci ███████████ wrote:
> >
> > It looks perfect! The law looks great and I particularly like the statistics that give the crime perspective. Of course the part on ███ is also great. Thank you for all your help. If you can sign it as well, I will include it in my sentencing brief.
> >
> >
> > Alaleh Kianerci
> > Deputy District Attorney
> > ███████████

Fig. 5. Prof. Dauber and Kianerci discussing Prof. Dauber's proposed letter to Judge Persky re the judge's sentencing of Turner, and also whether to allow the *Stanford Daily* to report on some developments.

Note that Prof. Dauber says "I have known [M]ike Armstrong [Turner's lawyer] for years and he's no dummy. He will catch that." Under what conditions would Armstrong be reviewing Prof. Dauber's letter to Judge Persky and have any opportunity to "catch that" other than to possibly say something in rebuttal at the sentencing hearing? What were Kianerci and Prof. Dauber concerned about that Armstrong would "catch"?

And on what basis were Prof. Dauber and Kianerci deciding what would and wouldn't be published in the *Stanford Daily*, a student newspaper and where the prosecutor and the DA's office aren't supposed to be making extra-judicial statements or using third parties to do what they aren't allowed to do? The question also arises, was this sort of coordination taking place before and during the trial itself, as well as at sentencing? If so, it would demonstrate that Kianerci and the DA's office were possibly violating the rules of ethics by using Prof. Dauber and possibly others to engage in activities that the DA's office and the prosecutor would not be allowed to do themselves. (See pp. 4, 92, and 99)

What is particularly troublesome is that Prof. Dauber's May 24, 2016 sentencing letter to Judge Persky contained false and exaggerated claims. For example, Prof. Dauber falsely claimed Chanel was found "half-naked with her dress pulled over her head." But Deputy Taylor, who was one of the first responders at the scene said:

> "She was wearing a black, skin tight dress. The bottom of her dress had been pulled up above her hips, and was gathered near her waist."[52] [The dress was not "over her head" as Prof. Dauber falsely claimed.]

Prof. Dauber then made the false statement that:

> "the fact that this sexual assault **occurred in public** and that the victim **was observed being penetrated**..." [Boldface added]

The truth is that nobody observed Chanel "being penetrated," including the two Swedish graduate students. Judge Persky was present for the entire trial and certainly would have been aware of these false statements. It's also shocking that Prof. Dauber, a professor of law, would write statements to a judge that were outright false, and that she apparently assumed Judge Persky would simply accept these types of false statements.

Prosecutor Kianerci's Sentencing Memorandum

In her sentencing memorandum, Kianerci described the evening on January 17, the night Chanel, her sister Tiffany, and the two friends were at the Miller family's home before they left for the Kappa Alpha party. (Although again note, this timeline is contrary to Chanel's statement to

Stanford police when she first woke up in the emergency room, to the effect that Chanel and Tiffany went to the Lagunita Court dorm area at Stanford in the early evening and then to the KA party.) Kianerci said Chanel had four shots of whiskey at home, but Kianerci did not mention the glass of champagne Chanel consumed in addition to the whiskey. Also, Kianerci sidestepped the inconsistency of Chanel telling Stanford police when Chanel first woke up that the only thing she had been drinking was Keystone Light beer, versus what she later told police and others (beer and vodka), likely because Chanel or others realized there were witnesses to what Chanel had consumed that afternoon and evening.

Kianerci went on to describe the paramedics' activities when they arrived at the Kappa Alpha fraternity house. Kianerci said paramedics applied several techniques to rouse Chanel including a "shake and shout" and a "physical pain stimulant," saying none were successful, which is false. In fact, Chanel responded to nail pinching by briefly opening her eyes. Kianerci said Chanel "vomited once, but did not regain consciousness." However, the paramedic at the scene said Chanel was able to move her head and clear her own airway. Kianerci said Chanel's back-extrapolated BAC was 0.22%, "almost three times the legal limit." But according to court records, Chanel's back-extrapolated BAC was 0.242 to 0.249%, more than three times the legal limit. The above examples comprise only some of Kianerci's various statements that were contrary to the publicly available facts.

Kianerci depicted an occurrence prior to the January 17/18 Kappa Alpha incident when Turner allegedly was flirting with a female that the female said made her feel uncomfortable. Kianerci also mentioned an incident prior to the January 17/18 incident when Turner, age 19, was stopped on campus carrying alcohol in a backpack. When Stanford police attempted to speak with the student group Turner was with, the group reportedly ran, but shortly afterwards a member of the group who had been detained by another officer informed police of Turner's phone number. Turner was called by police and instructed to go to the police station, where it was noted Turner had alcohol on his breath. This resulted in charges potentially being brought, but with the provision, as is customary in these types of cases, that the charges would be dismissed if Turner completed specific counseling classes, which he did after which the charges were later dismissed. Kianerci also cited a letter/petition circulated by the Stanford Association of Students for Sexual Assault

Prevention advocating, among other things, against a light sentence for Turner.

Kianerci said Turner was in possession of a fake driver's license, but that statement was as fake as the fake driver's license itself. The fake ID actually belonged to and was in possession of another student and it is hard to believe Kianerci didn't know this. Kianerci also mentioned a "Group Me" image on Turner's phone that read "Whos [sic] tit is that?" implying Turner had taken and distributed the photo (see Chs. 2 and 3). However, Turner was being held down by the Swedes at the time the photo was circulated and he was then in custody and thus could not have taken or distributed the photo. In fact, it was already known who had circulated the photo – and it wasn't Turner.

It's very revealing that Kianerci did not use the GroupMe photo in her arguments before the jury or elsewhere during the trial. This is undoubtedly because Kianerci knew Turner did not take or distribute the photo, leading to the logical speculation that she only mentioned the GroupMe photo and text in her sentencing memorandum for media purposes and because she knew she wouldn't likely be sanctioned or otherwise challenged for engaging in this untruth. Kianerci's false claims about the fake ID and the GroupMe photo were highly prejudicial but were continually and aggressively used in Prof. Dauber's and others' media campaigns against Turner.

Kianerci made the statement, "It is baffling that the [probation officer's] report does not reflect the disingenuousness of the Defendant's 'expression' of remorse, while at the same time continuing to maintain his innocence." However, Turner very clearly expressed remorse (see Turner's letter to the court, Appendix 6) and for Kianerci to deny this information again highlights Kianerci's indifference to the facts and even her willingness to knowingly make false statements to Judge Persky and which then would inevitably be disseminated nationally and worldwide by the media. Moreover, Kianerci's denial of Turner's remorse was sheer speculation and likewise was demonstrably false. In addition, Turner had every right to maintain his innocence if he truly believed the interaction with Chanel was consensual. Furthermore, Turner was no doubt instructed by his attorney that anything he might say could be used against him in the expected appeal. Kianerci knew Turner was under these legal limitations but she exploited this situation nevertheless.

Kianerci's opinion was that the probation department's recommendation of four to six months in county jail was not effective punishment and didn't ensure Turner would not be a danger to the community, notwithstanding that Kianerci had read the probation officer's report and thus knew, as discussed above, the STATIC-99R report showed a low likelihood of re-offending.

According to Kianerci, the punishment didn't "encompass the totality of circumstances surrounding a pattern of behavior by the defendant, and doesn't reflect the impact on the victim or the community, won't deter future crimes, and in this case, sexual assaults on college campuses." Kianerci referred to several California Penal Code provisions that she believed validated her view that Turner should not receive probation or be sentenced according to the probation department's recommendations. Contrary to Kianerci's statements and the media campaign against Judge Persky that ensued, the Commission on Judicial Performance, after looking into the matter, concluded that Judge Persky's sentencing "was within the parameters set by Penal Code section 1203.065(b) and therefore was not unlawful."[53]

In her summation at the sentencing hearing, Kianerci said that:

"This Court should sentence the Defendant to a midterm of six years [in prison] in order to protect society and to punish the Defendant for his multiple sex crimes, to encourage him to lead a law-abiding life in the future and to deter him and others from committing new and similar crimes."

Of course, there were no multiple "sex crimes," as there was one occurrence of alleged digital penetration, which Turner believed was consensual and where in fact he may not even have "penetrated" Chanel when he fingered her. And in reality, the jurors' conviction of intent to commit rape could not rationally be proven. Unless the jurors possessed extrasensory perception or psychic precognition abilities, the concept that Turner intended to rape was contradicted by the undisputed fact that he never opened any of his clothing even when he had the opportunity to do so, and his DNA was not on Chanel nor her clothing. Finally, Kianerci's recommendation of a prison sentence contradicts current research showing sentencing young people to prison, especially for long durations, does not deter crime and in fact does more harm than good.

Kianerci's False "Fake ID" Claim Created Nationwide Toxic Firestorm

In her June 2, 2016 sentencing document to the court, as noted above, Kianerci made the false statement that Turner had been in possession of a fake ID. On the day of sentencing, when the court asked Kianerci if she wished to make any comments regarding sentencing, she admitted:

> **"I made the mistake of stating Mr. Turner, and not another person, was in possession of the fake ID. It was a typo** in the report that I did not clarify, and I apologize for that typo in my papers."[54] [Boldface added]

In other words, Kianerci casually called her false statement a "typo," which it was not – it was a false, and maybe deliberately false, statement. Kianerci's sentencing memo containing the untrue fake ID statement nevertheless was distributed to numerous traditional news and social media outlets; Kianerci evidently did not bother to inform the media of her "typo" because her false statement still appears in numerous traditional news and social media sources to this day.

In fact, shortly after Kianerci's sentencing document became public, Kianerci's "typo" resulted in a toxic firestorm of fake news across the country that further falsely maligned Turner's character. Numerous news sources published Kianerci's false statement that Turner had possessed a fake ID. For example, on June 11, 2016, CNN published the article, "Stanford Rape Case: Inside the Court Documents." Referencing Kianerci's sentencing memo, CNN wrote, "Turner had a fake driver's license in his possession."[55] Numerous other news media followed suit, including the *Los Angeles Times, Palo Alto Online*, KTVU, FOX, Vice, WSIS, *SwimSwam*, and the *Seattle Times* – to name a few. The fake ID falsehood instigated by Kianerci still appears in the various news sites today – neither Kianerci nor any of the above news sites bothered to correct the false information. This is an example of how the mountains of fake news and outright lies against Turner and Judge Persky have been perpetuated in both traditional and social media. And as shown throughout this book, not by accident.

Kianerci Incites Yet Another Media Firestorm – This Time About the GroupMe Photo

In her sentencing memorandum to Judge Persky, Kianerci mentioned the GroupMe screenshot found on Turner's phone that said "whos [sic] tit is that," referencing a photo that had been distributed through the GroupMe messaging app as discussed earlier in this book. Kianerci said that after obtaining a search warrant, Turner's phone was searched by the Santa Clara County Crime Lab (which, by the way and unlike most crime labs and best practices, is not independent but instead is a part of the DA's office itself). Kianerci then said the Crime Lab "learned that when there is a third party application, the images are not stored on the phone and can be deleted by a third party member in the group."[56] Meaning, people besides Turner could add or delete the GroupMe items that were found on the app, yet she still somehow (and wrongly) attributed it all to Turner.

Of significance is that Kianerci *only* mentioned the GroupMe photo in her sentencing memorandum to Judge Persky after the jury had already decided their verdicts and been dismissed. She had not included the GroupMe photo in her list of evidence, did not refer to it at the preliminary hearing, and did not refer to it in her arguments before the jury at the trial – no doubt because it was clear to her and others that Turner had not taken nor distributed the GroupMe photo. Indeed, and as already mentioned in Chapters 2 and 3, Stanford police, Kianerci, and the DA's office knew it would have been impossible for Turner to have taken and distributed the photo because (1) he was being held down by the Swedes at the time the photo was being circulated, and (2) it was already known who had sent the photo – and it wasn't Turner. So why did Kianerci even mention the GroupMe photo in her sentencing memorandum when she had long known it was not taken nor distributed by Turner? This itself is extraordinary prosecutor misconduct, and the question also arises, to what extent was District Attorney Jeff Rosen signing off on these and other inappropriate actions?

In any case, Kianerci's mention of the GroupMe photo in her sentencing memorandum resulted in another media firestorm, which no doubt was intended. One significant example is an article by Ruth Styles published in the *Daily Mail* on June 10, 2016 (eight days after Turner's sentencing) that falsely claimed, "Stanford rapist Brock Turner sent a photo of his victim's breasts to friends after the attack outside a frat house party."[57] Ms. Styles' article included a screenshot of the GroupMe message (p. 22) and that says directly on the screenshot itself "CurtDoge sent a picture to the group." So how could Ms. Styles and the *Daily Mail* claim that Turner sent the photo when the GroupMe screenshot clearly states it was CurtDoge who sent the photo? To add to the falseness of Ms. Style's and the *Daily Mail's* claims, the article later totally contradicts itself by stating that the GroupMe message "was sent by Stanford swimmer Justin Buck, originally of Aberdeen, UK."[58]

Ms. Styles also falsely stated as a fact that "witnesses had told how they saw Turner standing over his victim with his phone and that phone had its light on."[59] But the record shows that no person had ever claimed or testified that they saw Turner standing over Chanel with his cell phone, although it's a possibility that someone else was feeding Ms. Styles false information for her article. Rather, and as already noted, it was in the record that someone other than Turner had stood over Chanel and shone a light on her (and took a photo?) and then fled. Besides Ms. Style's and the *Daily Mail's* false claims of Turner taking and sending the GroupMe photo, Ms. Styles and the *Daily Mail* inappropriately labeled Turner in the article as a "rapist" when in fact Turner was never prosecuted for or convicted of rape. This and many other actions by both Ms. Styles and the *Daily Mail* not only were false, but they were and remain in clear violation of the Independent Press Standards Organisation [sic] standards in the U.K. and for which they continue to have liability if not corrected.

Astonishingly, three years later, Ms. Styles repeated the same falsehoods about the GroupMe photo in a new *Daily Mail* article dated June 6, 2019, carefully timed to appear the same week Chanel's book, *Know My Name*, was announced. Specifically and among other falsehoods, Ms. Styles and the *Daily Mail* again referred to the 2015 GroupMe photo and again falsely stated in the 2019 article that "the swimmer [Turner] sent a picture of her breasts on an encrypted app."[60] It should also be noted that in preparation for this 2019 article, Ms. Styles or others working with her were on site in Ohio (she is based in California) secretly taking photos of Turner at work and elsewhere, attempting to interview his co-workers, and otherwise preparing for their article and the coordinated book launch. Many of these actions constitute still further violations of the requirements of the Independent Press

68

Standards Organisation in the U.K. and for which both Ms. Styles and the *Daily Mail* continue to have liability if not corrected.

Because the GroupMe screenshot and photo were not included in the evidence exhibit indexes, the question also arises, who had forwarded the GroupMe screenshot to the *Daily Mail* and other media sources? How did this false and highly inflammatory story end up in the hands of the press? Was Prof. Dauber involved? Did DA Rosen, prosecutor Kianerci, or others working with them help coordinate this media attack? If so, this also was in violation of the rules of ethics and constituted still additional prosecutorial misconduct.

Still Another "Typo"

Kianerci had also written that it had been two weeks before Chanel was contacted by authorities as to what had happened to her; however, the time interval was actually one week, not two weeks. When this error likewise was brought to everyone's attention, Kianerci said that her having written the wrong number of weeks was another "typo." According to the Merriam-Webster dictionary, a typo is "an error (as of spelling) in typed or typeset material." Kianerci's so-called "typos," including the aforementioned false ID "typo," were a brazen disregard for the facts, not typos.

Mike Armstrong's Sentencing Memorandum

In his case analysis and sentencing memorandum to the court, Turner's lawyer Mike Armstrong told the court that Turner's case was not a prison case, and he asked the court to follow the recommendations of the probation officer, impose county jail for four months, find unusual circumstances to allow probation, and impose probation for three to five years. He requested the court to consolidate counts two and three – penetration of an intoxicated person and penetration of an unconscious person – into one count since there was only one act of alleged penetration. This request was denied.

Armstrong asked to have Turner's previous minor in possession of alcohol citation dismissed, which Armstrong said is done in 99% of cases after the offender completes specific classes, as Turner had done. Armstrong also pointed out, and as already discussed above, that the prosecution's claim that

Turner had been in possession of a fake ID was false in that Turner was not cited for possessing a fake ID, and as a matter of fact, the alleged incident of a fake ID did not involve Turner but another student – still another example where the police, the prosecutor, and possibly even the DA had intentionally made false allegations to Judge Persky and then to the media.

Armstrong reiterated the probation officer's findings, including the probation officer's observations that Turner showed genuine remorse. Armstrong emphasized that only Turner would have known if Chanel had been unconscious when the alleged digital penetration had occurred. Furthermore, Armstrong noted that Turner had no prior record, there were no aggravating factors, and there were four favorable factors warranting probation and possibly not even jail (no weapon, no monetary loss, lack of criminal sophistication, and no taking advantage of a position of trust).

Armstrong cited the prosecution's failure to promptly reveal DNA test results that disproved rape, resulting in a nine-month delay in dropping the rape charges and prolonging Turner's false public label as a rapist. Armstrong said the DA's filing of the initial two rape charges was inappropriate because filing such charges would have required proof beyond reasonable doubt that intercourse had occurred, which was not the case. Armstrong said the false rape charges were "filed in violation of the DA's office policy about when charges can be filed, and were an unethical violation of the prosecutor's power."[61]

Armstrong further pointed out that Chanel had explicitly told the probation officer that she didn't want Turner to be behind bars.

Armstrong's other justifications for probation were that Turner was a good person, he came from a good family, he had a record of accomplishments, but he made poor choices related to alcohol that resulted in the serious incident at Stanford, which cost him his enrollment at Stanford, eliminated the opportunity to compete in the Olympics, and he was soon to be a registered sex offender for life.

Armstrong noted that SB 261, signed by Governor Brown in October 2015, required consideration of parole for youthful offenders who committed their crimes when under age 23 due to their "diminished culpability." While SB 261 concerned parole, the point was that the law recognized that defendants under age 23 had diminished culpability due to their immature

70

neurological brain development and that young people deserve special consideration.

Chanel and Turner Read Their Letters in Court

At the sentencing hearing on June 2, 2016, Chanel read her victim impact statement (see Appendix 5) and Turner read his letter which included his statements of remorse (see Appendix 6).

As discussed elsewhere, Chanel's statement was almost certainly not written on her own. Also, it directly contradicted what she had told the probation officer several weeks earlier, that Turner "doesn't need to be behind bars." Turner's letter was written by him and reflected his true feelings, as expressed by the following example:

"Every day, my mind, my heart, and my body agonize over the suffering and pain I have caused on [Chanel], [Chanel's sister Tiffany], and their entire family and friends. It's unbearable to think that my actions that night have caused these good people so much sorrow and pain. Nobody deserves a single second of what I have caused them to go through. I can never forgive myself for what happened and the consequences that it had."[62]

Turner's Father Presented Character Letter at Sentencing Hearing

When reading the subsequent and again sensationalized traditional news and social media accounts of Turner's father's letter to the court, it would appear that Dan Turner's letter was only about his son's convictions being a "steep price to pay for 20 minutes of action." Nothing could be further from the truth. In fact, after he introduced himself, Dan Turner said:

"Brock is absolutely devastated by the events of January 17, 2015 . . . I can tell you that he [Brock] is truly sorry for what occurred that night and for all the pain and suffering that it has caused for all those involved and impacted by that night."

Dan Turner went on to describe his son as he knew his son while growing up, how his son could be a valued contributor to society, and how the lifetime sex offender registration order will negatively impact his son's life for the rest of his life. Dan Turner was seeking mercy for his son. Any loving father would have done the same. Nevertheless, the propaganda machine being orchestrated by the DA's office and Prof. Dauber took this single phrase totally out of context and spent weeks ridiculing Dan Turner for his defense of his son.

Stanford Swim Team Members and Community Members Showed Support for Turner

After the jury's verdict was announced, some Stanford swim team members, and even members of the Santa Clara County community who didn't know Turner, wrote letters to Judge Persky in support of Turner. Several of the community members had attended Turner's trial and were evidently not influenced by the barrage of fake news and false social media content regularly hurled against Turner, often at the hands of Prof. Dauber and the prosecution.

One of the Stanford swim team members sent a heartbreaking letter to Judge Persky in which he wrote:

"We shared a lane for most pool workouts, which means that we were either chatting or encouraging one or the other for two to four hours a day . . . When Brock first joined the team in September 2014, he immediately stood out from the other freshmen for his level-headedness and easy-going attitude. He opted to quietly learn how the team acted socially, resulting in him being rather quiet, though always smiling and warm, during social gatherings . . . Brock quickly gained a reputation as the responsible newcomer to the team, often spending his spare time with other tamer upperclassmen . . . His comforting demeanor and peaceful outlook were rather infectious, and would often help other teammates to realize when they were being overly rowdy or rambunctious.

"I am worried for Brock himself. Being taken out of society and put into prison could dwindle the fire in his heart until he decides to

douse the flames himself. I'm very scared for my friend, and I hope that his sentence will maximize both the positive effects on society and Brock's rehabilitation and well-being." [Boldface added]

The following is a letter to Judge Persky from a concerned Santa Clara County community member who attended Turner's trial:

"I am not related to, have never met, nor do I have any affiliation with either the defendant or the victim. Neither am I associated with Stanford. I write as a concerned citizen who first learned of the events in the newspaper, and then sat through virtually the entire trial with no predisposition as to guilt or innocence. I heard the testimony of the witnesses for both sides, the summation to the jury, and your instructions to them. Armed with that level of information **I could not have returned a verdict of guilty.**

"Mr. Turner's testimony, which went uncontested, was that the two of them were conversant and ambulatory as they left the party . . . The jury was required to acquit if they accepted Mr. Turner's testimony that in this interval he reasonably believed consent was given for the activity that ensued. Or, the jurors could have rejected his sworn testimony, but would then be left with uncertainty and no known facts as to the sequence of events – **which should have created a barrier to finding guilt beyond a reasonable doubt.**

"Within my community, I can find difference of opinion as to accountability, but sentiment is nearly unanimous that incarceration is not warranted. **Prison time for Brock Turner benefits no one, least of all the community.**

"Ineffable damage to Brock Turner's life most certainly will ensue if the court imposes incarceration. Prison only adds to the loses already suffered by individuals in this matter, and seems an overly harsh, nonproductive penalty for someone not fully yet an adult . . . Direct Mr. Turner to the most positive possible environment so as to enhance the corrective action you deem necessary to take place.

"Please sentence Brock Turner with an eye to the rest of his life, and not the events that occurred one night while a nineteen-year-old." [Boldface added]

Another community member, a Palo Alto resident and mother, wrote the following letter to Judge Persky in support of Turner:

"I have no affiliation with anyone connected with the trial and am not associated with Stanford University . . . I followed the Brock Turner case in the local papers and social media and have real concerns about the outcome. Although I do not condone Brock Turner's actions, I don't think he deserves to carry the full weight of blame for the incident that occurred on the Stanford campus. My impression is that **the university, the fraternity that hosted the party where excessive underage drinking took place, and the intoxicated young women who attended the party, were all complicit in the tragedy of that night**. It seems terribly unfair that Brock Turner, a very young person on the threshold of adult life, is now a registered sex offender for life and destined to spend years in the penal system as a result of a disastrous party on a college campus. As a parent, I find myself particularly distressed that the mother of the young [22-year-old] female victim delivered her daughter to the party on campus knowing that the young woman had already been drinking." [Boldface added]

Still another woman residing in the community wrote the following to Judge Persky:

"I have nieces and nephews attending college and am aware of the "hook up" attitude that seems prevalent today with many of our youth. **I'm disturbed that this young man seems to be taking all the responsibility for an alcohol related situation that got horribly out of hand.** From my perspective, it seems there are many other people and institutions involved who should share in accountability.

"I am concerned for Brock Turner's future, and am hoping that you will consider the most lenient sentence possible. I do not personally know anyone involved in this case. But, I am aware of the burdens of Mr. Turner being labeled a sex offender, surviving in prison and having his life derailed . . . I would hope that society and the legal system could still provide him an opportunity for a future." [Boldface added]

The following letter was written to Judge Persky by a woman who had graduated from Gunn High School in Palo Alto who, like Chanel, had a history of blackout drunkenness. The letter writer provided Judge Persky with a first-hand account of her experiences while blackout drunk:

". . . my behavior changed dramatically when I was blacked out. At those times I was extremely promiscuous . . . **The drinker lives in denial, friends and family are often prone to denial as well, and usually enable the drinker in a number of ways.** The drinker can function shamelessly because they do not remember their inappropriate behavior. In fact, I had many arguments with persons who told me of things I did and I vehemently denied I had done so. The blackout drinker is likely to assume a vastly different personality than when sober.

"My personal experiences came to mind when I followed the narrative in the Brock Turner trial. I not only find it plausible that the blackout drinker gave consent to sexual activity, I believe it probable she did. That would be consistent with the blackout personality. Upon gaining sobriety the drinker then is incredulous that she would have acted thusly and gets support from loved ones who prefer to assess based on her sober state.

". . . if there is doubt to any degree as to consent I think it is more than reasonable to find it was given. The personality that was engaged in that moment is prone to such decisions, but then recedes and becomes invisible in the sobering light of a courtroom. I am not sure the jurors understood this, and urge you to take the above into consideration as regards any discretion you have in the matter of sentencing." [Boldface added]

Another concerned mother and community member wrote the following letter to Judge Persky on Turner's behalf:

"I am writing this letter as a concerned resident of California and as a worried mother of three. I have followed Brock turner's trial and was present in court for several of the sessions.

"I saw significant doubt in the mainstay argument that brock Turner's advances toward the alleged victim were made without her consent. Given that both were intoxicated, she being in a blackout state, and Brock being an eager yet naïve teenager — it stands to reason that Brock's version of her initiative and (possible but not likely misidentified) consent, affords him the benefit of reasonable doubt. Especially in absence of any alternate version on her behalf. Furthermore, his character, clean record, and overall naiveté, combined with inconclusive forensics, amplify the doubt in his guilt.

"**The DA was on a press crusade to get Brock Turner and set him as an example for all long before the trial.** Past experience shows that injustice can be often traced to overzealous DAs on a crusade for 'the greater good' de-jour, the pattern recognized in this case is eerie. The might of the DA office, funded by all of us, put against a nearly bankrupt family, as part of a crusade for a popular 'greater good' . . . Justice tends to be pushed aside in such cases.

"Brock Turner was crushed and turned to dust by the system, in accordance with the law, and in sharp contrast to natural justice and basic common sense. **As a mother, I am terrified to witness how light is the burden of proof required to put a teenager in jail, rob him of his future, and shatter his family to pieces.**" [Boldface added]

Judge Persky Pronounced Turner's Sentence

Before Judge Persky pronounced Turner's sentence, he read a number of passages from Chanel's victim impact statement aloud in court. One wonders if Judge Persky was already aware of the fact that the statement was likely written with the help of others, possibly including with the input of the prosecution. Judge Persky also acknowledged the debilitating impact of the criminal process on people's lives, particularly those of Chanel and her sister Tiffany. Among other factors, Judge Persky considered the Rules of Court, the probation department's recommendation of probation and limited jail time, California law that required judges to consider probation and rehabilitation for first-time offenders, and the consideration that a person who is voluntarily intoxicated is less culpable than a sober defendant with intent to commit rape. Judge Persky also considered Turner's willingness to comply with probation, the adverse collateral consequences on Turner's life resulting from the felony convictions, the devastating effects prison would have on Turner due to his youthful age, the remorse Turner expressed in the letter he read in court, Turner's statement that he was genuinely sorry for the pain he caused Chanel and her family, and the severe consequences lifetime sex offender registration will have on Turner's life.

Judge Persky's final sentencing orders for Turner were (1) six months in county jail (the highest number of months from the probation officer's suggested range of four to six months), (2) three years of probation, (3) participation in a Sex Offender Management program, (4) payment of fees and restitution, and (5) sex offender registration for the rest of Turner's life, a requirement that many prosecutors say is worse than incarceration.

In his response to those who voiced that Turner's sentence was too light, Judge Persky said:

"As a judge, my role is to consider both sides. California law requires every judge to consider rehabilitation and probation for first-time offenders. **It's not always popular, but it's the law, and I took an oath to follow it without regard to public opinion.**"[63] [Boldface added]

The Appeal

An appeal was filed on December 1, 2017. The problem was that many of the most important items could not be raised on appeal because Turner's lawyer at the initial trial had failed to object and thereby preserve the issues for an appeal, let alone possibly affect what was happening in the courtroom.

Months later, virtually all of the key issues in the appeal were withdrawn.

As third parties have observed and most lawyers believe, it is likely that Turner would have prevailed on one or more of those key issues. In that event, there was serious risk that District Attorney Jeff Rosen, Stanford law school Professor Michele Dauber, traditional and social media, and others would demand a re-trial and likewise demand a harsher sentence through another carefully orchestrated media campaign. And the likelihood was high that the many wrongful actions similar to those that occurred during the original trial would be repeated in a new trial.

On August 8, 2018, the California Court of Appeal rendered an opinion rejecting what were the few remaining (and often among the weakest) items that had been raised on appeal.

Chapter 6

Shortcomings by Turner's Defense Lawyer

A review by various attorneys and other volunteers has led to a list of likely failures and shortcomings by Turner's own defense lawyer, Mike Armstrong:

1. Failure to disclose that he had **represented Stanford law school professor Michele Dauber** and/or members of her family on at least two previous occasions. Likewise, failure to disclose that he was **speaking at Prof. Dauber's classes** while preparing for Turner's trial and then again after the trial.

2. Failure at the very outset to **demand that Stanford postpone any Title IX investigations** and hearings because of the likely impact such investigations and hearings would have on the criminal process, and especially if Stanford was turning these materials over to the Santa Clara County DA's office. Years later, it was reported materials of this nature were in fact being provided to the DA's office in various student cases.

3. Failure to pursue the **discrepancies between what Chanel told Stanford police** when she woke up in the hospital emergency room (that she and her sister Tiffany had gone to the Lagunita Court dorm area in the early evening and then to the Kappa Alpha party, and that she only drank Keystone Light beers), versus what she told Stanford police 15 hours later when she went to get her mobile phone (that their mother drove them to the Kappa Alpha party around 11 p.m. that night); also, the **discrepancy that one of the women said they got out of the mother's car** at the Tresidder parking lot and then walked to the party, which would have been a six- to ten-minute walk in the dark, versus a third woman saying they were dropped off in front of the fraternity house. Under oath, Tiffany said she couldn't remember where they were dropped off.

4. Failure to hire an **investigator**. (Chanel stated in her victim impact statement that Turner had hired "private investigators," but that was not true.)

5. Failure to counter the **actions that Stanford faculty and staff were taking** in the media and potentially with the prosecutor from the very outset. At very least, failure to make demands on Stanford that these activities cease, including the improper use of Stanford time and resources.

6. Failure to challenge the **blood and other evidence** that was taken from Turner's body before Turner was even read his Miranda rights. Moreover, informed consents or a warrant were required before taking this evidence, and Armstrong didn't challenge this defect, either.

7. Failure to challenge the **statement Turner gave to Stanford police** while drunk (Turner reportedly fell over one or more times while being examined and was not understanding his Miranda rights once they were finally read to him). At very least, Armstrong should have made this objection to preserve it for appeal, even if some court decisions hold such drunken waivers can be considered valid.

8. Failure to object to the **false rape charges** being left pending for nearly nine months when prosecutor Alaleh Kianerci and District Attorney Jeff Rosen knew there was no evidence of rape from the very first day and weeks (the wet mount evaluation done within hours of the incident showed no sperm, and Turner's DNA likewise was not found on either Chanel or her body). In fact, Kianerci agreed in preliminary meetings that there was no rape, and yet Armstrong failed to insist that the charges be immediately amended to delete all references to rape. By leaving the rape charges pending for nearly nine months, District Attorney Rosen, Deputy DA Alaleh Kianerci, Stanford Prof. Dauber and others all were able to continually call this a rape case for the sensationalized media campaign they were waging, to say nothing as to how this false information ultimately would impact the jury pool.

9. Sending **emails to the expert witness** hired by Armstrong if he knew or should have known he ultimately might turn all of the emails over to the prosecutor.

10. Failure to object when the **prosecutor directly contacted the expert witness** without even the courtesy of giving Armstrong prior notice and an opportunity to object. Note also, prosecutor Kianerci did this only ten days before the trial was to begin, thus depriving Armstrong the time to consider alternatives, especially when he needed to focus on the pending

trial itself. It's hard to believe this timing was an accident, especially since the expert testimony was going to be the most important element in Turner's defense.

11. Failure to assert the **attorney-client and other privileges and doctrines** when Armstrong realized the prosecutor planned to use his communications with the expert witness (see Ch. 7). Armstrong reportedly was acting on the theory that he couldn't assert an attorney-client privilege because Turner had not been copied on the emails, which may or may not have been the case. Even if valid, Armstrong then failed to assert the separate attorney work-product doctrine/privilege even though his communications with the expert were clearly in preparation for the trial and part of his work product.

12. Many or most criminal defense lawyers also question whether any of these items were required to be **shared with the prosecutor**, as opposed to actual written reports and other evidence that Armstrong planned to introduce at trial. It also has been reported that when these email communications between Armstrong and the expert were read to the jury (some at the trial say shouted) by the prosecutor, the expert's credibility was severely damaged and along with it the critical point of the expert's testimony, that is, what alcohol blackout amnesia means (appearing fine to others but not remembering) and the difference between being in blackout, unconscious, or asleep. This was probably the most important element of Turner's defense, on top of the evidence that Stanford police seemed to have hidden or gotten rid of, and testimony about Turner's truthfulness that the judge somehow wouldn't allow. Knowing how important the expert's testimony would be, the prosecutor and District Attorney used questionable techniques to undercut that testimony even though it all was valid and went to the core issue of how Chanel would have come across to Turner, Chanel's ability to consent, and Chanel's actual condition once she passed out or went to sleep.

13. **Failure to challenge the DA's office written response** to him that they didn't have any phone records for Chanel or others. Those phone records would have included the videos and photos Chanel, her sister Tiffany, and others took before and during the party; critically important timelines; GPS location history that could have addressed the conflicting stories Chanel gave to Stanford police about where she was and when;

communications before, during, and after the party including whether Tiffany was even looking for Chanel when Tiffany got home; and communications with others. And the response seems especially wrong since Stanford police had Chanel's phone and possibly other phones in their possession but returned Chanel's phone (and possibly others) the same day as the incident and then subsequently had a few days later what, at their request, Chanel had selectively returned to them. (See pp. 25 and 32)

14. Failure to challenge **other written responses from the DA's office** saying they (or at least Det. Kim) were (a) "not aware" of the license plates in the fraternity parking lot even though Stanford police said they had recorded the license plates, and (b) "no access" to investigations at Stanford even though Det. Kim is employed by Stanford and was in charge of the investigations.

15. Failure to ask Chanel at the preliminary hearing and then at the trial **when did she email or otherwise send back to Stanford police and/or the DA's office photos and other items** on her phone, as she was asked to do by Stanford police when they gave her phone back to her the very day of the incident. Likewise, **failure to ask if she sent all photos, videos, text messages, voice messages, and other items** that were on her phone on January 17 and 18, 2015 or whether she held any back or even deleted any, and if so, what did she hold back or delete? And did anyone advise her what to keep or delete?

16. Failure to **obtain all similar evidence** and other materials from the prosecutor.

17. Failure to ask Chanel, her sister Tiffany and possibly others at both the preliminary hearing and at the trial: Did they have **any communication, directly or indirectly (including through family or others), with Stanford law professor Michele Dauber** before, during, or after the trial? Who else, if anyone, had communicated with them regarding their testimony and/or about the media treatment of the case? Also, whether there were any discussions of a book or other contracts.

18. Failure to object to the **intentional delays in being provided essential evidence** (photos, police reports, etc.) for months when such evidence was required to be produced immediately. This included the time and date stamps the DA and separately the Stanford police had inappropriately

placed on evidence to the effect that the evidence wasn't to be shown to defense counsel or others.

19. Failure to explore what appears to have been **modification of documents** and the Bate stamps that were on them. (Bate stamps are used in litigation to show the continuity of documents and that there was no tampering, which apparently there was here.)

20. Failure to insist on being provided with **the license plate numbers that Stanford police took down** the night of the incident, per the initial official Stanford police reports, and then following up to see if, among other things (a) who might have been able to provide essential facts and thus be called as witnesses, and (b) the possibility, as discussed in other chapters, that Chanel, her sister Tiffany, or their friend Colleen might have driven themselves to the Stanford campus and possibly had done so in the early evening.

21. Failure to pursue the fact that the initial police report said there were **five eyewitnesses**. Likewise, failure to identify the person who had flashed the light over Chanel while she was on the ground and also whether that person had taken any photos at the time.

22. Failure to insist on a **postponement** of the trial when the prosecutor handed Armstrong important evidence not previously seen just as they were walking into the courtroom on the first day of the trial.

23. Agreeing with the prosecutor prior to the trial **not to challenge the tainted DNA lab test**s.

24. At the trial (and possibly in agreement with the prosecutor prior to trial), telling jurors he would **put Turner on the stand** to testify.

25. At the trial, failure to object, on the basis that this was highly prejudicial, when the prosecutor continually referred to **Chanel as "the victim"** and had routinely marked photos and other graphics with the words or letter "victim" or "v." Whether Chanel was a "victim" or not was the core issue of the trial, and failure to object was even worse since there reportedly had been a prior agreement with the prosecutor not to use the word "victim" but instead to use alternative names like Emily Doe, Jane Doe, etc.

26. Failure to object, as discussed in other chapters, when the prosecutor **kept using the word "rape" and the phrase "sexual intercourse"** and in a context implying to the jury that Turner had actually committed "rape"

and "sexual intercourse." None of that was part of the trial, none of that was true, and as also discussed elsewhere, all of this constituted ethical violation by the prosecutor and, if he was involved in these decisions, the District Attorney himself.

27. Failure to object when the **prosecutor told jurors to ignore what they had been instructed**.

28. Failure to object to the photos and prosecutor statements of **Chanel being bandaged, Chanel being lifeless and not breathing, and other melodramatic falsehoods insinuating that Chanel had been beaten or was clinically dead.** Armstrong failed to effectively counter this testimony with testimony that the only bandages and blood on Chanel were from attempts to find a vein for the IV, possibly the minor scratches that may have come from such activities as Chanel urinating in the bushes and then later lying on the ground with Turner, and that Chanel having been found lifeless and not breathing as was claimed by Kianerci was impossible since all those who checked Chanel's breathing status, including the paramedic, noted Chanel was breathing normally.

29. Failure to put on the stand **third parties who could testify** that they saw Chanel and Turner leaving together, consensually. Without those presumably available witnesses, the only such testimony came from Turner himself when he was put on the stand, whereas it was essential to have that testimony also come from credible third parties to corroborate what Turner would say.

30. Failure to object to the prosecutor's early and then continual statements to the jury that Turner and Chanel were **"hidden behind the dumpster"** when in fact they were in full view of passersby and "in front of" the dumpster (technically, Turner and Chanel were in front of a wooden shed that usually housed the dumpster, and the trial exhibits and most of the witnesses in fact described it as a wooden shed, NOT a dumpster).

31. Failure to take and show the jury **photos that nothing happened "behind the dumpster."**

32. Failure to locate the **couple making out nearby** and in full view of passersby, and having them testify.

33. Failure to put on the stand **witnesses the prosecutor once had listed but then didn't call** for testimony, including specifically identified Stanford swim teammates. Is this because their testimony would have supported

Turner and not the prosecutor? Or might have revealed wrongful activities by other members of the swim team?

34. Failure to show **who on the swim team had circulated the GroupMe photo and text message** (described in Chs. 2 and 3). As discussed earlier, shortly after the incident, third parties had circulated numerous false stories that it was Turner who had circulated the photo when it was actually one or more other members of the swim team who had done so, and Turner in fact was already in custody. Worse, it has been reliably reported that one of the swim team members who accused Turner of circulating the photo was in fact the person who circulated it. How could Armstrong not have pursued this issue that was raging in the media and then was referred to by the prosecutor at sentencing? The question also arises, was this the person who held the light over Chanel and then fled the scene? If so, he was a critical witness that both the police and Armstrong should have pursued.

35. Failure to present evidence about the **defects in the DNA testing** (a lab technician's DNA being on the evidence, unidentified third party's DNA being on the evidence, etc.) in addition to the fact that Turner's DNA was not on Chanel's underwear nor any parts of her body.

36. Failure to provide more conclusive **evidence about Chanel's drinking** before going to the fraternity party (during the day and at home) and then at the party, and especially her own longstanding knowledge of and personal experience with blackout amnesia.

37. Failure to explore Chanel's statements to her sister Tiffany that she **might go to bars** in Palo Alto if things didn't work out at the party.

38. Failure to produce evidence of the possible role Stanford law school professor **Michele Dauber** was playing in all that was happening, including with the media and the possibility Prof. Dauber was coordinating with Stanford police/Sheriff's deputies and/or the DA's office on media and other items, coaching witnesses, and helping with the prosecution of the case. As noted earlier, at very least the prosecutor's witnesses should have been asked, who was coaching or otherwise communicating with them?

39. Failure to move for a **directed verdict** when the prosecutor rested her case without producing any evidence that Turner had fingered Chanel, with or without Chanel's consent (there being separate issues about

Chanel's consent). Especially when Turner's DNA was not on Chanel nor her clothing. No third parties had seen the interactions between Turner and Chanel, and Chanel testified she couldn't remember anything. So the only witness was Turner himself, and for unknown reasons, the prosecutor did not introduce, at least at this stage of the trial, Turner's statements made to the Stanford police while drunk.

40. Notwithstanding the above, Armstrong didn't move for a directed verdict but instead put **Turner on the stand to testify as to all of the missing elements,** including that he had fingered Chanel and thereby made the case that the prosecutor hadn't. As already noted, Armstrong also didn't simply ask Turner if he had "fingered" Chanel (which is all Turner had said in his drunken statement at the Stanford police station). Rather, Armstrong phrased his question, "When you say "fingered her, **did you put a finger from your hand into her vagina?"** – meaning, "penetrate" her? Apparently unprepared for how to answer the question, Turner answered "Yes I did."

41. Failure to insist on a **more complete (and correct) answer from the court to a juror's question about criminal intent.** The juror asked whether criminal intent would be negated with respect to Count 3 if the defendant "didn't know or mistakenly believed his act was not penetration." According to lawyers who reviewed the transcripts, the answer to the question should have been "yes," but Armstrong allowed a simple and wrong "no" answer to go back to the jury from the court. Also, realizing this was a critical question to at least some if not all of the jurors, Armstrong should have insisted on a further explanation because, in doing so, he could have forced the judge to realize this was a wrong answer or, even if left as "no," could have provided clarity for the jurors as to what actually was required regarding knowledge, intent, and *mens rea.*

42. Failure to demonstrate throughout the trial, or at least in summation, an itemization of the **testimony that was changed significantly** by Chanel, Chanel's sister Tiffany, and the Swedish graduate students – and pressing the issues about who had coached them to change their testimony. It's interesting that Chanel's apparently long-pending book contract wasn't announced until a few days after the statute of limitations for perjury had expired.

43. Failure to propose **jury instructions on lesser included offenses** (Judge Persky had similar obligations; see Ch. 8).
44. Failure to **object on anywhere from 50 to 100 occasions** when objections were warranted. Worse, Armstrong's failure to make these objections made it impossible to raise these critically important issues on appeal.
45. Although there are many reasons not to invoke a **voluntary intoxication defense** (the burden of proof falls upon the defendant, it can come across to the jury as a defendant being irresponsible, etc.), it may have been appropriate here as a way to help negate the concept that Turner intended to commit rape – especially since this was an important issue before the jury, and was a key theme in the media frenzy being stirred up against Turner. In fact, Judge Persky himself asked Armstrong if he had any questions about involuntary intoxication. Armstrong responded to the judge, "no."[64]
46. Failure to **challenge Chanel's highly charged victim impact statement at sentencing**, including among other things:
    a. How it **changed from what Chanel told the probation department** a few weeks earlier ("he doesn't need to be behind bars").
    b. How and why what was filed with the court on **May 26, 2016** was further revised to what Chanel read in court on **June 2, 2016? And whether that was the same statement that was then immediately distributed via *Buzzfeed* and other media.**
    c. Chanel's Facebook **postings in a bikini** with her boyfriend in Bali and elsewhere after the incident but before the trial were contrary to her statement read in court that she can't stand her body (those postings were subsequently scrubbed).
    d. Chanel's Facebook postings about her doing **comedy club routines** in the months after the incident and before her highly charged statement read in court were also contrary to her statement read in court (those postings also subsequently were scrubbed).
47. At very least, failure to counter the highly sensationalized and **false media campaign** that was being waged by Stanford law school Prof. Dauber and others before, during, and after the trial.

Chapter 7

Inappropriate Actions by the Prosecutor

Failure to Make Critical <u>Brady</u> Disclosures

*W*ikipedia provides a good summary of what are known as <u>Brady</u> disclosure requirements:

"Brady disclosure consists of exculpatory or impeaching information and evidence that is material to the guilt or innocence or to the punishment of a defendant. The term comes from the 1963 U.S. Supreme Court case *Brady v. Maryland*, in which the Supreme Court ruled that suppression by the prosecution of evidence favorable to a defendant who has requested it violates due process.

"Following *Brady*, **the prosecutor must disclose evidence or information that would prove the innocence of the defendant or would enable the defense to more effectively impeach the credibility of government witnesses.** Evidence that would serve to reduce the defendant's sentence must also be disclosed by the prosecution." [65] [Boldface added]

As discussed throughout this book, it appears that Santa Clara County District Attorney Jeff Rosen, the prosecutor Alaleh Kianerci, Stanford Detective Mike Kim, and others regularly failed to meet their obligations under <u>Brady</u>, under rules of ethics, and under other requirements. Given the very strong likelihood all of this was intentional and resulted in the wrongful conviction of Turner, their obligations existed not only then but continue today, including for those who oversee these people and departments in Santa Clara County and at Stanford.

For example, and as discussed more fully in Chapters 3 and 6, Turner's lawyer, Mike Armstrong, requested in writing, approximately two weeks of the incident, a long list of evidence. His request specifically included the license plate numbers that the Stanford police said they had recorded in the fraternity and possibly other parking lots immediately after the incident, everyone's phone records (Stanford police had possession of both Turner's and Chanel's phones and possibly the phones of others), and any investigations done at Stanford. Yet three weeks later, the DA's office responded in writing that Stanford Det. Kim was not aware of the requested items. Some of these important items did not exist because Det. Kim did not bother to obtain or process them, or in some instances (license plates, etc.) the requested items seem to have disappeared.

Obviously, Armstrong's request was for this and other information, no matter who had it, so in some ways it appears that DA Rosen and prosecutor Kianerci were evading the disclosures by only saying that Stanford Det. Kim didn't have the information, which also appears to be an untruth in its own right (see Ch. 3).

It also should be noted, whether or not requested by Turner's lawyer, a prosecutor's obligations to disclose all evidence, including evidence that would undercut the prosecutor's own case and support a showing of innocence, are far more extensive than are the obligations for criminal defense counsel. And because of the official roles Det. Kim and other Stanford police were playing throughout the case, these obligations extend to them and their supervisors at Stanford, including now.

These obligations arise not only from Brady and similar laws, but also from the State Bar rules of ethics that apply to Stanford's lawyers, then and now. These lawyers presumably had knowledge of the missing evidence before and during the trial and continue to have knowledge that would likely show serious prosecutorial misconduct and even a wrongful prosecution and conviction of Turner. Their obligations are heightened by the fact everything took place on the Stanford campus, Turner was a Stanford student at the time Stanford police obtained the evidence that then went missing, and Stanford's own general counsel is the direct supervisor of Stanford's police.[66] These obligations also arise from fundamental concepts of fairness and decency, especially for government officials and for the people who run Stanford.

Improperly Delayed Disclosures

In addition to critically important disclosures not being made and/or with exculpatory evidence possibly being destroyed (the license plate records, phone records, etc.), Kianerci and the DA's office regularly delayed the disclosure of other critically important evidence. This included failing to make timely disclosure of the SART wet mount evaluation for the presence of sperm results (no sperm were found), the SART physical exam results, and the DNA and other forensic lab results related to the alleged assault.

None of this seems to have been by accident. A review of the files shows that a "Do not release for discovery" stamp was placed on materials that were supposed to have been turned over immediately to Turner's lawyer but weren't provided to him until months later.

The legend at the bottom of the Stanford police summary of evidence stated, "Important: The documents listed above should not be included as attachments to reports or listed in the report narrative."

And while walking into the courtroom the first day of the trial, Kianerci handed Turner's lawyer still other important evidence (the EMT written report made 14 months earlier but had not been previously disclosed to him).

Inappropriate Communications with Defense Counsel's Expert Witness

Turner's lawyer, Mike Armstrong, had arranged for an expert witness, Dr. Kim Fromme, a tenured faculty member at the University of Texas, Austin, to testify about the various scientific and medical levels of drunkenness, including memory, motor skills, and when a person is blacked out versus being asleep versus being unconscious (see Ch. 12). This was the only expert Armstrong had planned to use, and her testimony was going to be one of the most important elements if not the most important element of Armstrong's defense of Turner.

On March 4, 2016, a week before the trial was to begin, Kianerci directly contacted Dr. Fromme, apparently without prior notice and without a copy to Armstrong, asking for all of Dr. Fromme's emails and other communications with Armstrong, all of Dr. Fromme's notes, the names of everyone Dr. Fromme consulted, and other information including Dr. Fromme's past testimony in other cases. Criminal defense lawyers note that directly contacting an expert witness in this way is unprofessional even if technically permissible (a question in its own right), shows a prosecutor and a DA's office willing to go up to the line and even over the line of appropriate behavior, and had significant impact on the fairness of Turner's trial.

Armstrong reportedly didn't think his emails and other correspondence with Dr. Fromme were privileged because Turner wasn't copied on the communications (the attorney-client privilege) but without asserting the separate privilege for attorney work product. There's also the question of why Armstrong engaged in these communications if he knew or should have known that he would turn them over to the prosecutor. Many criminal defense attorneys also don't believe these types of communications – especially informal and irrelevant chatter – were meant to be included in the type of "evidence" that is required to be shared with the prosecutor under applicable law. They believe it is only "real evidence" such as a weapon used in the commission of a crime.

As already noted, the issue of what is meant by "blacked out" versus being asleep versus being unconscious was critical at the trial. Chanel herself told Stanford police that when she says she blacks out, she doesn't mean she is unconscious but rather that she doesn't remember what happened but has always been able to function, including getting herself home. Dr. Fromme gave what many observers believed to be very strong testimony, all of which was seriously undercut when Kianerci then read to the jury ("shouted" according to some who were present in the courtroom) selected communications between Armstrong and Dr. Fromme. As already noted, there was nothing wrong with those communications. They showed the normal banter that takes place when preparing for a trial, but they are not the types of communications expected to be shared with a jury.

Given the timing of Kianerci's demand for this material, it can be assumed that both Kianerci and District Attorney Jeff Rosen realized Dr. Fromme's testimony could have been the most damaging part of the defense's presentation, which may explain why they waited until the week before the trial and why they made the demand directly to Dr. Fromme. It appears that they intentionally ambushed Armstrong, although as an experienced defense lawyer, he should have been prepared for this sort of action and he likewise should have invoked privilege or sought a protective order.

Improper Use of Third Parties for Actions Prohibited if Done by the Prosecutor

The rules of ethics prohibit a prosecutor from using third parties to take actions or make statements that the prosecutor may not do directly. Which leads to the question: How much coordination was taking place between District Attorney Rosen, Deputy DA/prosecutor Kianerci and Stanford law school professor Michele Dauber who seems to have been involved throughout the case? It appears that Prof. Dauber was often taking actions that Rosen or Kianerci would have been prohibited from doing. Including making statements to and otherwise coordinating with the media. Among other things, Prof. Dauber appears to have obtained and distributed to the media the GroupMe photo along with the allegation that Turner took and distributed the photo (Ch. 5). She also appears to have helped arrange with *BuzzFeed* and other media for the immediate publication of the victim impact statement that Chanel read at Turner's sentencing (Ch. 14).

Public Records Act disclosures made months after the trial and sentencing also show that Prof. Dauber was coordinating directly with Kianerci in the collection and even the editing of student letters to Judge Persky regarding the proposed sentencing of Turner – and these were students who had no contact with Turner. There also are questions whether Kianerci provided transcripts to Prof. Dauber and/or Chanel so quotes and summaries could be used in the victim impact statement that Chanel then read at Turner's sentencing (see Ch. 9), and there are various reports that Kianerci, Prof. Dauber, and possibly DA Rosen and others played a role in writing, editing, and then disseminating the highly sensationalized victim impact statement that Chanel read in court.

And since the case was attracting constant nationwide and even worldwide media attention, including as orchestrated by Prof. Dauber, it is very likely that the District Attorney himself, Jeff Rosen, was working closely with Kianerci on all aspects of the case. In addition, Public Records Act disclosures made months after the trial and sentencing show that there were in fact ongoing communications among DA Rosen, Kianerci, others in the DA's office, and Prof. Dauber. (See Ch.14. Also see the photos at the end of this chapter.)

At the Trial

Kianerci carried out, in front of the jury, the unethical acts of falsely and continually calling Turner a rapist and labeling his charges as rape when in fact there were no charges of rape and Turner was not being prosecuted for rape. Among other things, Kianerci told the jury, "Now, Brock Turner may not look like a typical rapist."[67] Kianerci's statement that Turner "may not look like a typical rapist" was undoubtedly Kianerci's means of planting with the jury the false concept that Turner was a rapist. She also falsely described the activities as the "rape of an intoxicated person."[68] And Kianerci then said, "Now, the defendant did an act of sexual intercourse."[69] All of these statements were blatantly false. Turner did NOT rape an intoxicated person, nor did he engage in an act of sexual intercourse.

Kianerci went on to say,

"He [Turner] is the quintessential face of campus sexual assault . . . They're [these crimes] committed by men who look exactly like Mr. Turner."

Interestingly, this theme was used for years afterward in the propaganda campaign against Turner, including on posters containing Turner's image and the phrase "The face of campus rape" being placed at campus student unions and then with media coverage about the posters. It was as if the propaganda campaign was being planned ahead of time and with Kianerci's full cooperation.

Kianerci's Deliberate Actions to Confuse and Deceive Jurors

Prosecutor Kianerci employed maneuvers to deliberately confuse and deceive the jurors as to the meaning of Turner's charges by conflating rape with penetration and sexual assault. For example, Kianerci's explanations to the jury of **Count 1** of the charges included the following:

"Count 1 is a failed attempt to complete a rape." [Actually, Count 1 was assault with *intent* to commit rape, NOT a failed attempt to commit rape. Moreover Turner was fully clothed with his zipper up and he had never even started to commit rape, so how could he have attempted to "complete" a rape?]

And:

"So rape of an intoxicated person. Now, the defendant **did an act of sexual intercourse**."[70] [No such thing happened.] [Boldface added]

And in describing **Count 2**, Kianerci said:

"Now, **rape of an intoxicated person** is mirrored and **is very similar to sexual penetration** of an intoxicated person, which is a charge of Count 2 . . . As I mentioned, this mirrors Count 1's rape of an intoxicated person."[71] [There was no charge of "rape of an intoxicated person" and fingering certainly doesn't "mirror" rape.] [Boldface added]

Then in describing **Count 3**, Kianerci said:

"Now, **this is rape of an unconscious person.** So in order to prove to you that when he committed Count 1, assault with intent to commit rape of an unconscious person, again, this mirrors Count 3 . . . Again, mirrors the rape of an unconscious person as it's described in Count 1."[72] [Again, entirely wrong and highly prejudicial.] [Boldface added]

Note that there was no charge of rape in Count 1, and there was no sexual intercourse; in fact, Turner was not charged with any type of rape at all. Kianerci's outrageous and dishonest statements were designed to confuse, deceive, and to sway the jurors into believing Turner had committed rape, which of course, was not true. Kianerci's deceitful actions were at the height of unethical prosecutorial behavior.

Regarding the issue of consent, Kianerci told the jury:

"He [Turner] said he believed that she gave consent. That in and of itself is not enough for the defendant to become not guilty."[73]

In contrast, Kianerci's statement conflicted with Judge Persky's specific instructions to the jury that:

"The defendant is not guilty of a crime if he actually and reasonably believed that the person was capable of consenting to the act, even if the defendant's belief was wrong."

Turner believed Chanel was capable of consenting, as he had readily admitted to police that he had fingered Turner the day of the alleged assault, and Turner's confidence in believing the encounter with Chanel was consensual was further evidenced by the fact that Turner had waived his Miranda rights.

Besides making the above false claims, Kianerci made every effort to repeatedly mention the words "rape" and "rapist" throughout the trial in an apparent and premeditated scheme intended to imprint these words and concepts into the jurors' minds. Kianerci repeated the rape words 37 times when in fact Turner was not even on trial for rape. People familiar with the Turner case still ask how it was possible that Kianerci got away with such brazen prosecutorial misconduct? And again, why didn't Turner's lawyer object?

Kianerci's Questioning Created Juror Confusion and Another National Media Firestorm – This Time About Pine Needles

Another example of when Kianerci seemed to have deliberately confused the jurors occurred when Kianerci questioned the SART (Sexual Assault Response Team) nurse about debris found during the pelvic exam, as follows:

Kianerci: "And you had mentioned some debris that you had located within the vagina?"
SART nurse: "Yes"

[Kianerci intentionally used as a false predicate to her question that the SART nurse had said debris was found in the vagina even though according to the trial transcript, the SART nurse had never said that,[74] and Kianerci would have known from the SART report itself there was no debris found within the vagina. The SART nurse's answer should have been "no" but by the way Kianerci cleverly worded the question, the nurse responded "yes" instead.]

Kianerci: "And can you tell me what People's [exhibit] 59 depicts?"
SART nurse: "That is a picture of the debris that we found during the pelvic exam that was on her vaginal—basically inside the labia minora."

[Because of the likely limited knowledge the jury may have had about female anatomy and nomenclature, the jury may not have known the labia minora are not part of the vagina, thus the jury would have continued to wrongly believe there was debris inside the vagina.]

Court: "We did have one question from one of our jurors. Was the nature of the debris in the vagina determined?"
SART nurse: "No."

[The juror's question about the nature of the debris in the vagina indicated the jurors still wrongly believed there was debris in the vagina, a concept cleverly and falsely implanted by the way Kianerci structured her questions. Because the SART nurse answered "no" when asked if the nature of the debris in the vagina had been determined, this again implied there was debris in the vagina, but that the nature of the debris was unknown. This again would lead the jury to continue wrongly believing there was debris found in the vagina. And again, where was Armstrong in all of this?]

This entire exchange indicates the jury had received – it appears deliberately – confusing information that apparently led them to wrongly believe there was debris found *inside* the vagina when in fact there was debris on the labia minora, not inside the vagina. The presence of the debris in the labia minora area could even have resulted from when Chanel urinated in the bushes. This deliberate action of confusing and misleading the jurors was one of the many dishonest actions Kianerci carried out throughout the trial and that led to the continual tainting of Turner's trial.

What ensued was a sensationalized and widespread fake news and social media frenzy falsely reporting that Turner had shoved pine needles into

Chanel's vagina. As examples, *The Atlantic* quoted Prof. Dauber's false claim that Chanel "had pine needles in her vagina."[75] The *Chicago Tribune* wrote, "it was Turner's fingers, along with dirt and pine needles, that went inside his victim..."[76] *Buzzfeed* reported that "she [Chanel] had dirt and pine needles in her hair and inside her vagina."[77] *OpEdNews* reported that "they had to dislodge pine needles and debris from her [Chanel's] vagina."[78] In describing Chanel's victim impact statement, *USA Today* wrote, "Parts of it were chillingly raw: 'I [Chanel] learned . . . fingers had been jabbed inside me along with pine needles and debris.'"[79] This type of widespread fake news provoked by Kianerci and most likely disseminated with the help of Prof. Dauber continued throughout and after Turner's trial and still persists to this day. None of the news sources have bothered to remove the incorrect information described above from their websites.

This fake news frenzy was later exacerbated by Chanel herself claiming in her widely disseminated victim impact statement that "fingers had been jabbed inside me along with pine needles and debris."

Unfortunately, these types of false and inappropriate statements and activities carried out by Kianerci are what create public mistrust of prosecutors and other government officials.

More Inappropriate Actions

As discussed previously, Kianerci improperly kept the rape charges pending for nearly nine months even though Chanel's wet mount evaluation showed no evidence of rape as early as the day of the alleged assault, and even though Kianerci had DNA lab reports months earlier likewise showing there was no rape. Kianerci only dropped the rape charges on the day of the preliminary hearing, long after she knew there was no probable cause for rape and after months of widespread and sensationalized media coverage saying that Turner was being prosecuted for rape.

Although it was agreed in advance that Chanel would be referred to as "Jane1" and her sister Tiffany as "Jane 2," Kianerci referred to Chanel as "the victim" throughout the trial. In fact, Kianerci used the term "victim" at least 71 times in front of the jury, and likewise marked all evidence with "Victim" or "V." (See also Ch. 4)

Kianerci told the jurors a different standard of what to accept as evidence and as true testimony rather than what is provided under the law. For example, Kianerci referred to Turner's sworn testimony as being under a "magical oath," implying that Turner's testimony was not valid. This was a violation of standard trial protocol and likewise should not have been allowed.

Somehow Chanel, her sister Tiffany and various other witnesses were on a first name basis with the prosecutor ("Alaleh") and the official investigating officer ("Detective Mike") and regularly used those first names in front of the jury.

Many of Kianerci's other inappropriate actions are discussed in various other chapters in this book. These include but are not limited to Kianerci's:

- Repeatedly calling the structure where Chanel and Turner were found a "dumpster" when in fact witnesses called the structure a shed or wooden shed, and trial exhibits of the structure were labelled as "shed" or "wooden shed." The word "dumpster" became a widely used symbol of the Turner case, as no doubt was intended by Kianerci and Rosen and was simultaneously used in the media campaign against Turner before, during, and after the trial and was being orchestrated by Prof. Dauber. (Ch. 3)
- Failing to advise Turner's lawyer, Mike Armstrong, if any of the witnesses who were on her initial witness list but who she did not call to testify may in fact have had exculpatory evidence on Turner's behalf and should have been disclosed to Armstrong. (Ch. 3)
- Falsely describing Chanel to the jury as lifeless, unconscious, and not breathing. (Ch. 4)
- Charging Turner with rape with no probable cause. There were no supporting facts when she (and possibly DA Rosen) brought the charges, by nature of the SART report results that were available within hours of the incident, and as evidenced by the fact that rape charges had to be dropped due to DNA evidence showing no rape had occurred. (Ch. 4)
- Falsely stating that Turner had to be pulled off Chanel by witnesses. In fact, Turner got up on his own and was never "pulled off." (Ch. 4)

- In her sentencing memorandum, falsely claiming that Turner took and circulated the GroupMe photo and, separately, that Turner had a fake ID in his possession when he was arrested (the latter of which Kianerci later claimed was a "typo"). (Ch. 5.) Both false statements resulted in national and international firestorms, but for which Kianerci apparently assumed she could not be sanctioned by making these false statements in a sentencing memorandum versus at the trial.

Again, where was Armstrong in all of this?

California State Bar Ethics Rule 5-110

California State Bar Ethics Rule 5-110. SPECIAL RESPONSIBILITIES OF A PROSECUTOR, provides as follows:

"The prosecutor in a criminal case shall:

"(A) **Refrain from prosecuting a charge that the prosecutor knows is not supported by probable cause. . .**

"(D) **Make timely disclosure** to the defense of all evidence or information known to the prosecutor that tends to negate the guilt of the accused or mitigates the offense, and, in connection with sentencing, disclose to the defense all unprivileged mitigating information known to the prosecutor, except when the prosecutor is relieved of this responsibility by a protective order of the tribunal;

"(E) **Not subpoena** a lawyer in a . . . criminal proceeding to present evidence about a past or present client unless the prosecutor reasonably believes: (1) The information sought is not protected from disclosure by any applicable privilege or work product protection; (2) The evidence sought is essential to the successful completion of an ongoing investigation or prosecution; and (3) There is no other feasible alternative to obtain the information;
"(F) Exercise reasonable care to prevent persons under the supervision or direction of the prosecutor, including investigators, law enforcement

personnel, employees or other **persons assisting or associated** with the prosecutor in a criminal case from making an extrajudicial statement that the prosecutor would be prohibited from making under rule 5-120;

"(G) When a prosecutor **knows of new, credible and material evidence** creating a reasonable likelihood that a convicted defendant did not commit an offense of which the defendant was convicted, the prosecutor shall: (1) **Promptly disclose** that evidence to an appropriate court or authority, and (2) If the conviction was obtained in the prosecutor's jurisdiction, (a) Promptly disclose that evidence to the defendant unless a court authorizes delay, and (b) Undertake further investigation, or make reasonable efforts to cause an investigation, to determine whether the defendant was convicted of an offense that the defendant did not commit." [Boldface added]

A careful reading of these provisions indicates a strong case that Rosen, Kianerci, and others in the DA's office regularly violated these requirements.

As is shown throughout the Turner case, there is an urgent need for prosecutorial reform in the U.S. system of justice. Currently, many prosecutors are out of control; they have unchecked and unrestrained prosecutorial powers and limited, if any, accountability to anyone. Many operate in a culture of unethical behavior with a focus on winning convictions at all costs (it helps with budgets and re-elections) and pushing for retributive punishment devoid of mercy.

Prosecutors also are major contributors to America's distinction as the world's biggest jailer. According to the ACLU:

"They [prosecutors] have almost unlimited power to push for more punishment, often in ways that are largely hidden from public view. This focus on obtaining convictions and securing severe prison sentences, instead of addressing the root causes of crime, is a major driver of mass incarceration that compounds racial disparities throughout the justice system."[80]

Kianerci's actions of delaying and withholding (and it appears in many instances, never revealing) exculpatory evidence, deliberately confusing and misleading the jurors, and engaging in the many other unethical and inappropriate actions delineated in this and other chapters of this book are inexcusable. They highlight a heightened need for an investigation of the entire Santa Clara County District Attorney's office combined with prosecutorial reform in Santa Clara County and statewide. The situation is made worse with the warnings that the recall of Judge Persky intentionally sent to judges throughout the state combined the knee-jerk minimum sentencing laws that were put in place after Turner's trial. These warnings to judges and the enactment of newly restrictive laws have allowed prosecutors to limit or entirely push aside the importance of judicial discretion, giving prosecutors even more and often wrongly used power.

For a discussion of potential reforms, also see Chapter 18.

Turner's Release from Jail

Turner was supposed to be released shortly after midnight or in the very early morning at the end of his jail sentence, which is standard procedure for Santa Clara County and other jails. But his release was intentionally delayed so there could be better press coverage. On top of that, Prof. Dauber appears to have been coordinating the press coverage with District Attorney Jeff Rosen, who was present outside the jail but tried to avoid being noticed. However, when a third party was seen holding a sign regarding Chanel, it is reported that DA Rosen and his press secretary Sean Webby called Prof. Dauber over and arranged for her to remove the sign from the third party while Webby reportedly threw a body block to stop the third party from keeping his sign. Prof. Dauber then reportedly threw the sign into the nearby bushes.

Fig. 6. Michele Dauber and District Attorney Jeff Rosen's press secretary Sean Webby at jailhouse rally the morning Turner was released from jail.

Fig. 7. Michele Dauber carrying the sign she took from a third party without permission, with the DA's office press secretary Sean Webby standing by.

Fig. 8. Santa Clara County District Attorney Jeff Rosen, apparently trying to be incognito at the rally against Turner when he was released from jail.

Third parties say that DA Rosen was coordinating with both Prof. Dauber and Webby about the sign and other actions at the rally.

Chapter 8

Issues Concerning the Jury

The Jury Asked a Critical Question and Received an Exact Wrong Answer

A critical element in the outcome of the Turner trial was the fact that one or more of the jurors raised the fundamental question of intent and received an answer that was the exact reverse of what the answer should have been. The jury's question referred to the *mens rea* component of criminal law (that is, intent to commit a crime, or knowledge that an act would be a crime). Specifically, the question asked was:

> "If the defendant did not know or mistakenly believed his act was not penetration does it mitigate the required mental state to commit the crime under Count 3?"[81]

The answer the jury received was "No" when in fact it should have been "Yes," and it was given without any explanation as to the reason for the answer. Incredibly, Turner's lawyer did not dispute the answer even though the answer was the exact reverse of what it should have been.

To put this critically important issue in context, shortly before deliberations were to begin, the jurors received final instructions which were essentially the same as what they were told at the start of the trial, including:

> **"The defendant is not guilty of this crime if he did not have the mental state required to commit the crime because he did not know a fact or mistakenly believed a fact.**"[82] [Boldface added]

A criminal defense lawyer who has carefully reviewed the transcripts and related materials regarding the Turner case has commented:

104

"This issue was pivotal. In my jury experience, which I estimate consists of 150 jury trials and counting, this question only gets asked because one or more jurors are voting not guilty and the answer swings votes one way or the other. **So this wrong answer very likely changed votes and very likely resulted in changing the outcome from either a hung jury or an acquittal to guilty verdicts.** It is also important to note that this question shows that it is undeniable that one or more jurors believed Turner's testimony on this issue.

"And as for the answer given to the jury in response to the question, it was wrong. What more can I say, the answer was just flat wrong. The instruction on Count 3 as well as other counts says a defendant is not guilty if they believe, even mistakenly, that what they are doing is not a crime. The jury question was worded awkwardly but it basically asked if Turner should be found not guilty if he thought what he was doing was not the element of the crime (in other words, if he thought fingering was not penetration or that penetration only occurs when there is penetration by the penis). According to the clear instructions given to the jury at both the start of the trial and then again before their deliberations, Turner should have been found not guilty under those circumstances because that would negate the *mens rea* required to convict. The answer said exactly the opposite." [Boldface added]

Regarding knowledge, intent, and *mens rea*, it should also be remembered, Turner thought Chanel was functioning fine, as often happens with someone like Chanel in a state of blackout amnesia (see Chs. 2 and 12).

Failure to Instruct Jury on Lesser Included Offenses

Criminal cases often include jury instructions for what are called lesser included offenses. These instructions are especially appropriate where essential elements of an alleged crime might not be present (here, no intent to commit rape) or may not have been proved at the trial. In this case, lesser included offenses conceivably included sexual battery (which would have entailed ten years of sex offender registration, which even Prof. Dauber has publicly said would have been adequate) versus lifetime registration, or even simple battery which would have not entailed any registration.

Given the extreme and longstanding negative media attention directed at Turner for over a year before the trial, Turner's lawyer Mike Armstrong should have considered alternatives if there were a conviction. Even if Armstrong didn't ask for instructions on lesser included offenses at the outset, having seen the inappropriate actions that took place throughout the trial should have caused him to have considered their appropriateness, especially when the critical testimony of the expert witness was sabotaged by the prosecutor regarding Chanel's consent and lack of memory and Turner's own thoughts and intentions. At very least, these are options that should have been explained to Turner but, as best as is known, were not even offered.

In most jurisdictions, judges themselves have obligations regarding instructions on lesser included offenses. Yet here, no such instructions were included in what Judge Persky proposed to both Armstrong and Kianerci.

More Issues

There are indications jury instructions also may have been misunderstood or ignored by the jury, including as shown by the question asked by the jury during their deliberations.

As discussed above, during deliberations, the jury asked a critically important question about the instructions and got an incomplete and actually wrong answer.[83] Compare that with what the jury was told at the start of the trial[84]:

> **"The defendant is not guilty of this crime if he actually and reasonably believed that the woman was capable of consenting** to sexual intercourse, even if that belief was wrong. People have the burden of proving beyond a reasonable doubt that the defendant did not actually and reasonably believe that the woman was capable of consenting." [Note also that there was no prosecution or claims for sexual intercourse, but this instruction was wrongly given to the jury anyway.]

Also:

"The defendant is not guilty of this crime [penetration] if he actually and reasonably believed that the person was capable of consenting to the act, even if the defendant's belief was wrong. **The People have the burden of proving beyond a reasonable doubt that the defendant actually and reasonably believed that the woman was capable [sic -should be incapable] of consenting. If the People have not met this burden, you must find the defendant not guilty.**[85]

Also:

"To prove that the defendant is guilty of this crime [the third count regarding an unconscious person], the People must prove that: One, the defendant committed an act of sexual penetration with another person; two, the penetration was accomplished by using a foreign object; three, the other person was unable to resist because she was unconscious of the nature of the act; and **four, the defendant knew that the other person was unable to resist because she was unconscious of the nature of the act.**"[86] [Boldface added]

The fact that jurors were raising questions during their deliberations also rebuts the anonymous juror letter to Judge Persky a week following the sentencing saying that there were no issues or questions among the jurors. Also, the anonymous juror letter to Judge Persky contained information reportedly never heard by the jury. If true, did someone involved in the trial help write that letter?

The jury rendered an inconsistent verdict. That is, if they found Turner guilty of specific elements, they could not have found him guilty on other elements. Neither Turner's lawyer nor Judge Persky addressed this inconsistency.

Even More Issues

There were also secondary issues including selection of the jury and what happened after the trial. For example, one of the jurors, in the voir dire (that is, the questions asked when deciding who should and shouldn't serve on a jury), said his daughter had been "roofied" recently. He nevertheless was kept on the jury.

Inappropriate Rush to Judgment

It also has been reported by an individual closely following the case that on the first day of their deliberations, one of the jurors told the court that she or he had to leave by 2:30 p.m. the very next day, that is, the second day of the jury's deliberations.

Some obvious questions and concerns arise. First, assuming this happened, when did this juror know of her or his scheduling problem? Among other things, did the juror need to be away for just the rest of that afternoon, for several days, or for a much longer period of time? Second, why didn't the juror tell Judge Persky of this scheduling problem before being allowed to sit on the jury? Third, assuming Judge Persky was advised of this scheduling problem at the very start or end of the first day of the jury's deliberations (that is, on Tuesday, March 29, 2016), why wasn't a substitute juror seated right then and there? And finally, where was Turner's lawyer Mike Armstrong in all of this? Did both Judge Persky and Armstrong actually think it would be acceptable to force the jury into a fast decision on only the second morning of their deliberations, especially when balanced against the fact it would be very easy for a substitute juror to pick up on what was no more than a day of deliberations and especially given the worldwide media sensation that had been orchestrated about the case for the prior 14 months?

As with so many other questions and apparent wrongdoings in this case, somehow both Judge Persky and Turner's lawyer went along with what seems to have been a highly prejudicial rush to judgment in order to meet an arbitrary 2:30 p.m. deadline, and on only the second day of the jury's deliberations.

This is only speculation, but is it possible that the juror who requested to leave early is the same juror who wrote the alleged anonymous letter to Judge Persky a week after the sentencing, discussed below, criticizing the sentence Judge Persky had imposed on Turner and whose letter was somehow disseminated worldwide within hours of its being delivered to Judge Persky? And even more speculation, is it possible this particular juror was one of the two jurors who attended, just two months later, also discussed below, a meeting promoted by Prof. Dauber for a campaign already underway to recall Judge Persky and that included a public reading of Chanel's victim impact statement?

Specifically, disclosures as a result of Public Records Act requests show that two months after Turner's sentencing and while he was still in jail, Stanford law school professor Michele Dauber sent an email to Santa Clara County District Attorney Jeff Rosen about a public reading of Chanel Miller's victim impact statement and noting that two of the jurors had attended as well. How did Prof. Dauber know that? Were these two jurors specifically invited? Were all the jurors similarly invited? Who had the contact information for the jurors? And why would former jurors even consider attending such an event?

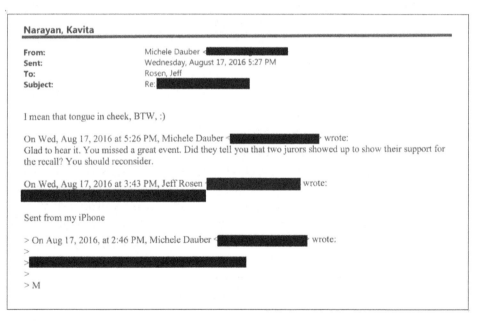

Fig. 9. Email between Michele Dauber and DA Jeff Rosen discussing the odd fact that two jurors showed up for a recall Persky event.

The Anonymous Juror Letter to Judge Persky

Approximately June 11, 2016, nine days after Turner's sentencing, an anonymous juror in the Turner case sent a letter to Judge Persky complaining about Turner's allegedly light sentence. What's interesting is that the letter was immediately and widely circulated to the media and, as discussed below, closely followed the talking points that were about to be used in the campaign to recall Judge Persky, including at times even identical language.

First, there is an obvious question about why a juror would be motivated to send such a letter. If the juror, who was described in a *Palo Alto Online* article as a male, had concerns, he should have contacted Judge Persky and had a direct and confidential conversation. But that wasn't what happened. Rather, the juror and/or whoever was helping orchestrate this event delivered an anonymous letter to the judge and simultaneously assured the letter would have immediate and worldwide media coverage.

Second, it appears the juror was not paying attention as to what Turner was being tried for. Among other things, the juror said that "clearly, there are few to no consequences for a rapist...." But Turner was never tried for rape, and the jury was never asked to convict him of rape, other than DA Rosen and prosecutor Kianerci inappropriately leaving rape charges pending for months prior to the preliminary hearing and with Kianerci then inappropriately using the "rape" word throughout the trial.

Third, contrary to the juror's statement that Turner's sentence should have served as a strong deterrent, a defendant's sentence is not based on deterrence alone. And in fact, sophisticated tests to predict Turner's probability of re-offending showed his probability was very low. Moreover, studies have shown that sex offenders (other than in family and child cases) are extremely unlikely to re-offend, and that the effects of prison on a youthful offender such as Turner do significantly more harm than good.

The juror went on to complain that:

"Mr. Turner is going to appeal the verdict, which not only is a complete waste of taxpayers' money but could mean, if he gets off, that he will not even have to register as a sex offender."

The purpose of a trial is to seek truth, not to satisfy media and mob frenzies. Turner believed he was innocent and he had a constitutional right to appeal what he properly believed was a wrongful conviction. That is a fundamental part of the American system, something this juror, as a new citizen per his letter, hopefully also understood. As a new or even a longstanding citizen, from whatever country this juror came, hopefully he understands the concepts of due process and the presumption of innocence. Moreover, the juror apparently had no inkling of the oppressive and life-ravaging effects that come with a lifetime sex offender registration order.

The juror went on to say Judge Persky "did not accept the jury's findings." That is the sort of thing a lawyer or media consultant might write, not a layperson juror. Contrary to the juror's claim, Judge Persky clearly accepted the jury's verdict and then sentenced Turner strictly within the parameters of the rule of law. In Chapter 5 of this book, Judge Persky is quoted as saying:

"As a judge, my role is to consider both sides. California law requires every judge to consider rehabilitation and probation for first-time offenders. It's not always popular, but it's the law, and I took an oath to follow it without regard to public opinion."[87]

The juror's contention that the sentencing was based on "your [Persky's] own personal opinion" was also seriously flawed. Judge Persky's sentencing was not a personal opinion but rather was based on the written recommendations of a seasoned probation officer whose job was to conduct a thorough investigation of the circumstances of the case and then to make a fact-based and unbiased sentencing recommendation. This process is a fundamental progressive reform and one that a new or longstanding citizen should support, not condemn.

It also is curious that the juror went out of his way to say that the jury "reached a consensus of guilt on all three counts within two days of deliberation" and that it was a "quick and decisive finding." First, the timing was very secondary to the trial. On the other hand, was the sender of this letter also the juror who told the court he had to leave by 2:30 p.m. on the second day of deliberations? Is that why timing was on the mind of this letter-writer? Was this juror also one of the two jurors who attended Michele Dauber's Recall Judge Aaron Persky event two months later, as discussed earlier in this book? Did third parties seek out the juror to write this anonymous letter, or at very least assist the juror in writing and then delivering the letter?

The juror mentioned that Turner "has never expressed sorrow or regret...." This contradicts Turner's 1,916-word letter to the court expressing his remorse. It also contradicts the probation officer's statement that "during the presentence interview, the defendant expressed sincere remorse and empathy for the victim."[88] Apparently these facts didn't matter to the juror, or to whoever helped write the anonymous letter.

The juror referred to a previous Kappa Alpha party when Turner was allegedly flirting with another attendee at the party. Why would the juror even focus on something like this? The juror then described this incident as a "pattern of dangerous behavior," which it was not. It was behavior, assuming it was even accurately described, that unfortunately occurs at virtually all drunken college parties.

At the end of the letter, the juror wrote:

"your concern was for the impact on the assailant. I vehemently disagree, our concern should be for the victim."

Actually, the role of a jury is to determine guilt or innocence of the defendant and has nothing to do with acting on behalf of an accuser. Moreover, at the time of sentencing, a judge is required to consider all parties, not just the accuser. And according to the Commission on Judicial Performance, Judge Persky "performed a multi-factor balancing assessment prescribed by law that took into account both the victim and the defendant."[89] In California, due to prison overcrowding and other factors, judges also are mandated to consider whether probation rather than state prison would be appropriate in sentencing, and to consider the likely impact imprisonment would have on a defendant.

As previously noted, the juror made numerous statements that followed the key talking points that were to be used in the emerging campaign to recall Judge Persky and also mimicked language that lawyers would use, not a layperson juror. For example, the letter contained the statements, "the predominately male jury reached a consensus of guilt," and "the subsequent sentencing memo filed by both sides," and "this case would serve as a very strong deterrent to on-campus assault."

It's also interesting that the juror's letter specifically quoted Judge Persky for something he said at the sentencing hearing:

"During the sentencing you [Judge Persky] said, 'the trial is a search for the truth. It is an imperfect process.'"

But the juror specifically wrote elsewhere in the letter that he "wasn't in the court for the sentencing." Since the trial transcripts were not available to the public at the time the juror wrote and sent the letter, how was the juror able to exactly quote Judge Persky's words?

The wording in the juror's letter also closely mirrors the language and talking points regularly used by Prof. Dauber and others in their various public statements. For example, in her June 8, 2016 *Democracy Now* interview with Amy Goodman,[90] Prof. Dauber said, "those are not unusual circumstances." The juror wrote, "these circumstances are not unusual. Prof. Dauber said, "and it's sending the message." The juror wrote, "what message does this send." Prof. Dauber said, "deterred from coming forward and reporting their crimes." The juror wrote, "less willing to report their attacks." In the same *Democracy Now* article, District Attorney Jeff Rosen is quoted as saying, "The punishment does not fit the crime." The juror wrote, "The punishment does not fit the crime." In other words, the juror's letter seemed to mirror the talking points being used, and even the exact language being used, by Prof. Dauber, prosecutor Kianerci, and DA Rosen. This further reinforces the possibility that Prof. Dauber and/or others may have played a key role in writing and delivering the letter to Judge Persky and circulating it to the media. And if true, everything that happened at the trial and afterwards becomes even more suspect.

Chapter 9

Discrepancies in Chanel Miller's Victim Impact Statement

C hanel Miller read aloud in court prior to Turner's sentencing what is known as a victim impact statement. That statement was immediately distributed to traditional news and social media by the Santa Clara County DA's office and third parties that appear to have been carefully coordinating these activities in advance. Four days after the sentencing, the statement was read in its entirety by Ashley Banfield on CNN, and shortly after that Congresswoman Jackie Speier organized a reading of the entire letter by House members on the House floor and thus also into the House record.

Fig. 10. Ashley Banfield reading Chanel's victim impact statement on CNN.

In response to Chanel's victim impact statement, Vice President Joe Biden issued a widely publicized letter to Chanel stating:

"I am filled with furious anger — both that this happened to you and that our culture is still so broken that you were ever put in the position of defending your own worth . . . Sex without consent is rape. Period. It's a crime."[91]

According to *Buzzfeed*, "Biden wrote the 1994 Violence Against Women Act and was regularly involved in the White House's 'It's On Us' campaign against campus sexual assault."[92]

It is a near certainty that Chanel did not write on her own the victim impact statement that has been so carefully and widely publicized. Among other things, Stanford law school Prof. Michele Dauber reportedly told at least one person that she (Dauber) wrote it. Also, while Chanel, Prof. Dauber, and others initially kept saying Chanel wrote the statement, when questions started to surface in subsequent months, they and their media advisors thereafter carefully said instead "the statement Ms. Miller read" in court.

Recent Public Records Act disclosures also show that the District Attorney's office and the Santa Clara County public relations department carefully said, starting on the very day Chanel read the statement in court, that it was a statement Chanel "disseminated," "read" or similar terms and never that she wrote. The DA's office and others in Santa Clara County government apparently knew the truth from the outset. It should also be noted, there were two versions of the statement, one filed with the court on May 26, 2016 and the one that was "read" in court seven days later. And of course, the statement "read" in court differed dramatically from what Chanel told the probation department weeks earlier when she was interviewed about what she felt should be an appropriate sentence to be imposed on Turner. According to the probation department's official written report, Chanel specifically said "he [Turner] doesn't need to be behind bars."

It also is noteworthy that the statement is riddled throughout with assertions that are factually wrong, intentionally misleading, or raise additional questions about who actually wrote the statement. For example, Chanel said "I had dried blood and bandages on the backs of my hands and elbow." This sentence was used to promote the concept that Chanel had been brutally beaten. In fact, the bandages were due to the paramedic's attempts to insert an IV, which required three attempts, including in the left antecubital vein (inner portion of the elbow) and a final successful IV insertion into the dorsal (top) portion of the right hand.

Chanel seriously downplayed the role alcohol played in the events that happened at the Kappa Alpha party. Near the beginning of her victim impact statement, Chanel said:

"I made silly faces, let my guard down, and drank liquor *too fast* not factoring in that my tolerance had significantly lowered since college." [Italics added]

The issue wasn't that Chanel just drank liquor too fast; but rather, that she drank way *too much* liquor. In fact, she drank four to five shots of whiskey and a glass of champagne at home, then continued to drink beer and multiple shots of vodka at the party, drinking herself to a BAC of 0.242 – 0.249% and into a drunken stupor.

Chanel also said when her sister came to pick her up from the hospital that "she [her sister] did not know that beneath my sweatshirt, I had scratches and bandages on my skin." But that same day when Chanel went to the Stanford police station to pick up her phone, Dep. DeVlugt reported that Chanel did not have any noticeable injuries, she did not have any pain, and "she only had a small bruise from the intravenous needle, which was used on her while she was at the hospital." As already mentioned, the bandages were related to IV insertion attempts, at least one blood draw, and from where an IV had been removed after she was medically cleared.

The morning Chanel returned home from the hospital and SART exam, her boyfriend had called her. Chanel said in her victim impact statement, "That's when I learned I had called him that night in my blackout." Here, Chanel acknowledges she had been in alcohol-induced blackout amnesia, which indicates there were undoubtedly other occurrences at the fraternity party of which she had no memory, such as her interactions with Turner and the possibility or high probability that she willingly left the fraternity party with the intent of going to Turner's dorm and likewise may have consented to kissing and engaging in sexual activity with Turner.

Chanel referred to a specific page number in the trial transcripts in her victim impact statement. But in fact, the transcripts were not available, unless the District Attorney's office or possibly Stanford law school Prof. Dauber had somehow gotten early transcripts prepared and then somehow had given them to Chanel or to whoever drafted Chanel's statement.

Chanel said in her victim impact statement that she was penetrated by a "foreign object." Social and other media then carefully used this phrase from the victim impact statement to give the impression the "foreign object" was a wooden stick or some other inanimate object, when in fact the foreign object was Turner's finger. The wooden stick/inanimate object falsehood was consistently circulated on social media without correction. Chanel also said in her victim impact statement, "fingers had been jabbed inside me along with pine needles and debris." The problem with this claim is that, based on the physical examination, there were no pine needles in her vagina. Nevertheless, news and social media frequently claimed pine needles had been inserted into Chanel, another falsehood that went uncorrected but made for sensationalized media coverage of Chanel's victim impact statement.

The victim impact statement went as far as to imply that Turner had inserted "his hand inside her," which, again, had no basis of fact since (a) Chanel had no memory of her encounter with Turner, and (b) there had never been any such claim. Whoever wrote the statement again was taking inappropriate but sensationalized literary license. Interestingly, Prof. Dauber had written in a tweet (see below), "According to the jury he got his hand inside her. . . . " Besides her statement being completely false (the jury made no such claim), the question arises, did Prof. Dauber write in Chanel's victim impact statement the claim that Turner had inserted his hand inside Chanel? This is asked because nobody else had ever before said Turner had inserted his hand inside Chanel. Furthermore, there was not a shred of evidence indicating that Turner had "intended to rape her [Chanel] with his penis" as Prof. Dauber claimed in at least one tweet, below. To the contrary, Turner's zipper, pants, and other clothing were closed and there was no evidence whatsoever of any such intent or attempt. Furthermore, Prof. Dauber made sure to include the phrase "using a foreign object," which seems to have been included, without clarifying that the "foreign object" was a finger, to imply that Turner had inserted an inanimate object into Chanel, which was how the public, unfamiliar with legal terminology, generally interpreted the phrase "using a foreign object." These types of misleading and false statements are examples of the false and highly inflammatory claims that were regularly published by traditional and social media.

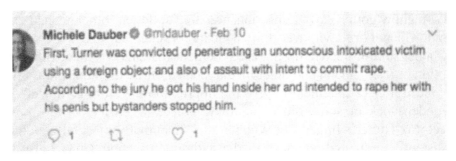

Michele Dauber 🔵 @mldauber · Feb 10

First, Turner was convicted of penetrating an unconscious intoxicated victim using a foreign object and also of assault with intent to commit rape. According to the jury he got his hand inside her and intended to rape her with his penis but bystanders stopped him.

Fig. 11. Prof. Dauber's tweet containing false information.

Chanel's victim impact statement further stated, "I thought there's no way this is going to trial; there were witnesses…." However, the fact is that there were <u>no</u> witnesses to when Chanel and Turner walked away from the fraternity house, when or under what circumstances the alleged fingering had occurred, whether Chanel had consented, and at what point Chanel entered a state of alcoholic stupor. It's possible and even likely that Chanel was in blackout drunkenness and consented to these activities, but in any event, there were no witnesses other than Turner himself.

Chanel said in her victim impact statement that Turner had "hired a powerful attorney, expert witnesses, private investigators who were going to try and find details about my personal life to use against me." But in fact, (a) Turner's attorney worked solo while Chanel's prosecutor for the People had access to assistance from a slew of district attorney office lawyers, support personnel, and the DA himself, (b) there was only one expert witness (Dr. Kim Fromme, discussed in Chs. 4 and 12), and (c) no private investigators had been hired. Also, the motions in limine (that is, procedural motions) prevented the jurors from hearing "any evidence relating to Doe's [Chanel's] sexual history . . . [and] exclude any reference to the victim's [Chanel's] manner of dress as indicative or suggesting of her consent"[93] Furthermore, both Turner and his lawyer reportedly made the decision early on that Chanel was not to be attacked and there would be no attempt to "dig dirt" on her.

Chanel's victim impact statement contains the odd text, "Did your lawyer say some incredulously infuriating, degrading things? Absolutely. He said you had an erection, because it was cold." A careful word search of the police report and trial transcripts, however, shows no such statement was ever made by Turner's lawyer. Moreover, this statement is in direct contradiction to the fundamental scientific fact that cold temperatures cause physiological vasoconstriction, not the necessary vasodilation required for an erect state to occur.

Chanel said in the victim impact statement:

"After a physical assault, I was assaulted with questions designed to attack me, to say see, her facts don't line up, she's out of her mind, she's practically an alcoholic..."

However, virtually all of the questions specifically listed in Chanel's victim impact statement were asked by prosecutor Alaleh Kianerci, not Turner's lawyer, and a number of the other questions specifically cited in her statement were not asked by anyone. It's also curious how Chanel would have such a complete list of the questions that were asked at the trial, although again, all but two or three being asked by prosecutor Kianerci and not Turner's lawyer, and some not even asked:

"How old are you? How much do you weigh? What did you eat that day? Who made dinner? Did you drink with dinner? No, not even water? When did you drink? How much did you drink? What container did you drink out of? Who gave you the drink? How much do you usually drink? Who dropped you off at the party? At what time? But where exactly? What were you wearing? Why were you going to the party? What'd you do when you got there? Are you sure that you did that? But what time did you do that? What does this text mean? Who were you texting? When did you urinate? Where did you urinate? Was your phone on silent when your sister called? Do you remember silencing it? Really because on page 53 I'd like to point out that you said it was set to ring [neither Kianerci nor Armstrong made a reference to p. 53]. Did you drink in college? You said you were a party animal [this was never asked]? How many times did you black out? Did you party at frats? Are you serious with your boyfriend? Are you sexually active with him [this was never asked]? When did you start dating? Would you ever cheat [this was never asked]? Do you have a history of cheating [this was never asked]? What do you mean when you said you wanted to reward him [nobody asked Chanel this question]? Do you remember what time you woke up? Were you wearing your cardigan [not asked]? What color was your cardigan [not asked, but color of cardigan was volunteered by Chanel]? Do you remember any more from that night [not asked]?"

♦ ♦ ♦

Chanel claimed in her victim impact statement that she was asked by Turner's lawyer, "You said you were a party animal?" Actually, the trial transcript shows that Turner's lawyer had asked Chanel if she did a lot of partying in college. Chanel answered, "I did a decent amount. I wouldn't consider myself a party animal." It was Chanel who introduced and used the term "party animal," not Turner's lawyer. Chanel also had told Det. DeVlugt at the police station that while in college, "She did a lot of partying there too."[94]

Chanel said in her victim impact statement:

"Instead of his [Turner's] attorney saying, Did you notice any abrasions? He said, You didn't notice any abrasions, right? This was a game of strategy, as if I could be tricked out of my own worth."

The problem with the above statement is that Turner's lawyer never asked Chanel about any abrasions.

Chanel had also claimed that "the nurse said there had been abrasions, lacerations, and dirt in my genitalia." However, the only reference the SART nurse made to the word "laceration' was in response to Kianerci's question, "And when you're collecting evidence, what types of injuries are you looking for?" The SART nurse responded, "So it could be anywhere from abrasions to tears to lacerations, vegetation, soil, dried secretions, moist secretions." The SART nurse had never testified that Chanel had lacerations in or on her genitalia. Nevertheless, and in a brazen disregard for facts, in a *Daily Mail* article authored by Ruth Styles and published eight days after Chanel had read her victim impact statement in court, Ms. Styles claimed, "an examination on the night of the attack also revealed that Turner 'fingered' the victim so roughly, her vagina was left covered in lacerations."[95] Ms. Styles' sensationalistic statement is, of course, blatantly false and constitutes still another violation of the British Independent Press Standards Organisation

120

rules, yet her article remains online and available to the public without correction of the many inaccuracies the article conveys.

In response to Turner's lawyer's statement that "[Her sister] said she was fine and who knows her better than her sister," Chanel said in the victim impact statement, "You tried to use my own sister against me? Your points of attack were so weak, so low, it was almost embarrassing." In reality, Chanel's sister Tiffany was a main and in some instances the only witness to Chanel's actions at the fraternity party so it was essential to question some of what Tiffany was testifying to.

Chanel made the statement, "I was too drunk to speak English, too drunk to consent way before I was on the ground." Actually, and as already mentioned, Chanel's texts to her boyfriend shortly before her interaction with Turner were spelled correctly, and there were portions of Chanel's voicemails to her boyfriend in which she spoke in clear, coherent sentences. For example, she said to Lucas, "Even though you are so far, I'll reward you . . . I'll reward you by you know what." Lucas said Chanel told him "males were presenting themselves to her but that she liked me."

Chanel said, "having too much to drink was an amateur mistake that I admit to, but it is not criminal." Lest anyone wrongly believes getting drunk in public to the point of alcoholic stupor is perfectly fine, California PC 647f states that if the individual is found so drunk in public that he or she cannot care for his or her own safety, the penalty is jail time and a monetary fine.[96]

Chanel said Turner had stated he intended to "speak out against the college campus drinking culture and the sexual promiscuity that goes along with that." Chanel's response to Turner's statement was:

"Goes along with that, like a side effect, like fries on the side of your order. Where does promiscuity even come into play?"

Actually, promiscuity can come into play when a drinker is drunk and/or experiences alcoholic blackout amnesia, which Chanel said she had experienced herself at the Kappa Alpha party. According to the science, an individual who is drunk or in alcoholic blackout is more uninhibited and more likely to engage in sexual risk-taking than when sober.[97]

Toward the end of her victim impact statement, Chanel told Turner, "Your life is not over, you have decades of years ahead to rewrite your story."

121

Apparently, Chanel didn't understand or wanted to ignore the irreversible damage Turner would endure due to the mostly false and permanent cruel traditional news and social media campaign against him.

Chanel said Turner had been convicted of "violating me, forcibly, sexually, with malicious intent." But there was no force and certainly no malicious intent. She then told Turner to "Figure out how to take responsibility for your own conduct." But shouldn't Chanel take some responsibility for drinking herself to oblivion? Turner erred, but so did Chanel.

Chanel chided the probation officer's report, saying her words were "slimmed down to distortion and taken out of context." However, Chanel's words were unambiguous with a clear frame of reference – there was no distortion of words and there was no evidence that Chanel's words were taken out of context, as is shown here:

> "I want him to know it hurt me, but I don't want his life to be over. I want him to be punished, but as a human, I just want him to get better. **I don't want him to feel like his life is over and I don't want him to rot away in jail; he doesn't need to be behind bars.**" [Boldface added]

The probation officer merely quoted what Chanel had said; the officer actually wrote Chanel's words within quotation marks. Also, in her Case Evaluation, the probation officer said, "her [Chanel's] focus and concern was treatment, rather than incarceration." It is unclear why Chanel would want to deny what she had told the probation officer although others surmise that Prof. Dauber, District Attorney Rosen, Deputy DA Kianerci, and others realized what Chanel had said to the probation officer would undermine the political and financial campaigns they had in mind and were already pursuing.

Chanel said that because Turner "took the risk of going to trial," she and her family underwent a year of "inexplicable suffering," and that Turner "should face the consequences of challenging his crime." But it's clear that Turner didn't believe he had committed a crime, otherwise he would not have admitted immediately after being arrested that he had fingered Chanel. Turner believed he was innocent, and he had a constitutional right to challenge the accusations against him. If Chanel hadn't wanted to undergo the pressures of a trial, she could have insisted that the prosecution negotiate a plea deal – something in fact people say was being discussed but that District Attorney Rosen and Deputy DA Kianerci would not go along with. If true, Rosen and Kianerci had other goals in mind other than Chanel's well-being and that of her family.

Chanel said that Turner "failed to exhibit sincere remorse or responsibility for his conduct." And "he has only apologized for drinking and has yet to define what he did to me as sexual assault." To the contrary, Turner expressed sincere remorse as indicated in his interview with the probation officer and then again in his statement in court. In her article, "The Problem of Punishment," author Judith Levine states, "No defense attorney permits a client to apologize to the victim; that would be an admission of guilt."[98] Ms. Levine embraces restorative justice. However, the current criminal justice system is simply not set up in such a way; rather, it is retributive—that is, an eye for an eye. In Turner's case, however, he genuinely believed his interactions with Chanel were consensual, thus it would have made no sense for Turner to admit guilt when he believed he wasn't guilty.

Also, there was a likelihood that Turner would need to appeal his conviction and sentence, and thus anything he might say to the probation officer or in court could and no doubt would be used against him, in addition to how the media campaign against Turner and Judge Persky would make use of any such statements. And as discussed elsewhere, he did appeal, but most of the key items in the appeal had to be dropped since, if he won on those issues (as most criminal lawyers believe he would have), there was the very high risk that District Attorney Rosen would seek a retrial and a far more serious punishment. Given the media and other frenzies that had been carefully stirred up in Santa Clara County for the 14 months prior to the trial, it would be unthinkable to take such risk for an appeal. Also, many other items that almost certainly would have supported reversal of Turner's conviction could not be raised in the appeal because Turner's defense lawyer for unknown reasons had failed to object to the improper actions that had taken place at the trial. Without the trial record showing that those objections were raised, they were not allowable in an appeal.

Another problem with Chanel's victim impact statement is that she (or whoever helped her write it) repeatedly used the word "rape" when in fact Turner was neither prosecuted for nor convicted of rape. For example, Chanel said "he would try to dilute rape . . . rape is the absence of promiscuity . . . rape is the absence of consent . . . digital rape . . .The seriousness of rape . . . rape is wrong." The frequent and intentional use of the word "rape" in Chanel's statement (no matter who wrote it) likely contributed to the multitude of traditional news articles and frequent social media content accusing Turner of rape and using the word in all of the taglines even if not mentioned in the text itself.

Meantime, Chanel has been applauded by the media worldwide for her victim impact statement. She was named Glamour Magazine's Woman of the Year (Prof. Dauber flew to Los Angeles to accept the award on behalf of Chanel). A year later, Chanel had a book published from which she reportedly had expected to earn millions, and as part of the book's promotion, she was featured at a subsequent Glamour Magazine function.

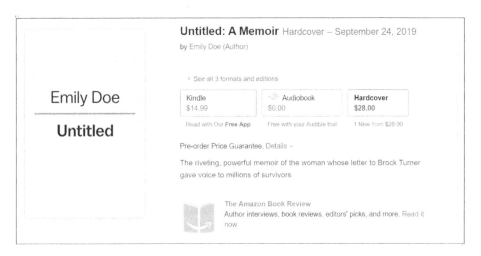

Untitled: A Memoir Hardcover – September 24, 2019
by Emily Doe (Author)

> See all 3 formats and editions

Emily Doe

Untitled

Kindle	Audiobook	Hardcover
$14.99	$0.00	$28.00
Read with Our **Free App**	Free with your Audible trial	1 New from $28.00

Pre-order Price Guarantee. Details

The riveting, powerful memoir of the woman whose letter to Brock Turner gave voice to millions of survivors

The Amazon Book Review
Author interviews, book reviews, editors' picks, and more. Read it now

Fig. 12. Amazon preview of Chanel's book, *Know My Name.*

Apparently as part of the promotion for her book, Chanel also proposed giving a speech at Stanford in early 2020, which required a sum of $40,000 for a speaker's honorarium plus related expenses, and the publisher required that at least 500 copies of Chanel's book, *Know My Name,* be purchased by Stanford at a cost of $8,500.[99] It appears that Chanel has attempted to turn the Stanford incident into a lucrative money-maker for herself and possibly others who have been orchestrating the campaign from the outset.

What is particularly unfortunate is that Chanel apparently held the unfounded belief that the number of months or years Turner spent in jail or prison was somehow a measure of Chanel's self-worth. In her book, *Know My Name*, Chanel describes how she repeatedly had to tell herself, "You are worth more than three months . . . You are worth more than three months."[100] As a matter of fact, Turner's jail sentence was technically six months, and Turner was ordered to register as a sex offender, an oppressive and barbaric punishment – for the rest of his life.

There is no question that Chanel endured suffering and embarrassment; it's heartbreaking. But it was unfair of Chanel to make false and highly inflammatory statements that were then publicized all over the world and elicited unprecedented and unwarranted public scorn and hatred against Turner.

And as Chanel admits, she has no recollection of anything that occurred on January 18 after approximately midnight, including whether she gave consent. Or allegedly of anything else that happened.

Chapter 10

Shortcomings at Stanford

Stanford Failed to Enforce Its Own Policies

Stanford University policies prohibit the serving of alcohol to under-aged students such as Turner. In addition, parties must have monitors. There are no indications they were present at the Kappa Alpha party or, if they were, that they were performing their functions. Party hosts may not serve alcohol to minors nor to attendees who appear to be overly intoxicated. ID's must be checked before serving alcohol to any individual, and special protections must be taken for anyone who appears intoxicated or out of control (for example, Chanel, Chanel's sister Tiffany, and their friends). Stanford took major steps to enforce its rules regarding sexual relationships, but it took no responsibility for its failing to enforce its party and alcohol policies which were meant to protect Stanford students, including an under-aged freshman like Turner.

How Turner Otherwise Was Treated by Stanford

Turner was taken immediately to the Stanford police department. While still drunk and not understanding what was happening (he actually fell over), and before his Miranda rights were even read to him, he was stripped and subjected to an invasive search of his genitalia and other body parts and fluids. This exam was done by the same female technician who then went to the hospital to examine Chanel. When his Miranda rights were subsequently read to him, Turner was still too drunk to rationally comprehend virtually anything. He had no idea about what he was being accused of and in fact he thought the police were protecting him against an attack by the two Swedish graduate students. And regarding the taking of body fluids and other samples, a separate and informed consent or warrant were needed, which didn't happen. Turner then was taken to Santa Clara County jail.

Although Turner had not yet been charged with any crime or other wrongdoing, when he returned to campus from the Santa Clara County jail the next morning:

- He was accompanied then and the following days by two plainclothes officers.
- He was allowed to attend one class but then ordered not to attend any more classes.
- He was allowed to return to his dorm but then suddenly ordered to move to temporary housing elsewhere and ordered not to leave that housing.
- He was not allowed to go to campus dining halls for meals.
- Because police had kept his wallet, money, and phone he had no ID, no money for food or other necessities, and limited means to reach family and friends.
- No one at Stanford offered to assist for any of these basic necessities. And remember, Turner was a Stanford student and to whom they had various moral and contractual obligations.

Title IX Failings at Stanford

Stanford advised Turner it would immediately undertake a Title IX investigation. Stanford, along with other universities, was under pressure at the time as a result of a policy that was adopted by the U.S. Department of Education through its issuance in 2011 of a so-called "Dear Colleague" letter. The use of a Dear Colleague letter allowed the Department of Education to avoid the requirements of the federal Administrative Procedure Act, but because of the threat of the loss of federal funding, virtually all U.S. colleges and universities felt they needed to comply.

The Title IX procedures that Stanford and most other colleges and universities adopted as a result of the Dear Colleague letter lacked fundamental protections about evidence, testimony, and other due process rights. Interestingly, Michele Dauber, the same Stanford law school professor who now was attacking Turner and later headed the recall of Judge Persky, chaired the Stanford committee that adopted its Title IX procedures that lacked these due process safeguards.

It should also be noted, the 2011 Dear Colleague letter was signed by Russlynn Ali, a friend of Prof. Dauber when they were both at Northwestern law school. Various published interviews and resumes show that, a year after Prof. Dauber and her husband Ken Dauber moved to Palo Alto in 2001, Ali had hired Ken Dauber to consult for Ali's nonprofit organization even though Ken Dauber was already employed fulltime at Stanford. When Ali moved to Washington in 2009 to head the Office of Civil Rights in the U.S. Department of Education, somehow Ken Dauber started doing paid consulting work for that department instead, and even though he was now employed full time at Netflix and then at Google. And it was over Ali's signature that the 2011 Dear Colleague letter was issued. This leads to numerous questions as to what roles Michele and Ken Dauber may have played in the 2011 Dear Colleague letter itself as well as the aftermath nationwide.

Since Ali left D.C. in 2012, she has been an executive for a social venture fund based in Palo Alto that is financed and headed by Laurene Powell Jobs, Steve Jobs' widow and who was a Stanford Trustee before, during, and after the Turner case and who also reportedly was a major supporter for the recall of Judge Persky.

With that background in mind, it's curious that starting in early 2020, Prof. Dauber began publicly attacking Laurene Powell Jobs, and even though it's now years after the incident, going out of her way to include a photo of Turner:

Fig. 13. Prof. Dauber's tweets attacking Laurene Powell Jobs.

In any event, the lack of due process safeguards under Stanford's Title IX policies was something that would complicate Turner's defense if a criminal prosecution also were to be brought since any statements and evidence would not have the protections required in a criminal prosecution. It turns out the concerns were real since more recently it has been disclosed that Stanford often did in fact turn over information to the Santa Clara County DA's office gained from Title IX and other campus proceedings.

Stanford also has a policy of non-intervention – that is, it will not intervene in student actions pending in the courts. Most colleges and universities also have policies, whether written or informal, of not allowing college or university resources or personnel to be used in prosecutions without a written agreement and standards. Nevertheless, Prof. Dauber and others at Stanford, based on news and other accounts, appear to have used Stanford resources to assist in the prosecutor's case against Turner and also in the immediately launched and then ongoing media campaign against Turner and later against Judge Persky. As a result, on advice of his criminal defense lawyer and to protect against actions by Stanford that didn't have the protections required for criminal cases yet could have been used against Turner in a criminal investigation and trial, Turner withdrew as a Stanford student.

Other Actions and Inactions by Stanford

A Stanford student services staff member was at the hospital checking on Chanel within hours of her arriving at the hospital. Chanel is not and never has been a Stanford student. No one from Stanford, that night or ever, provided similar concerns or counseling for Turner, the actual Stanford student. As shown elsewhere, the officer in charge of the investigation, Detective Mike Kim, is employed by Stanford's police department. Yet he and others did little if anything to find witnesses or otherwise investigate the matter and, as discussed elsewhere, important evidence that would have been favorable to Turner seems to have been hidden or destroyed.

What Others Think

In the years following the Turner trial and conviction, a growing number of Stanford alumni have been pursuing what in fact happened here. Virtually all are shocked at how the matter was handled by District Attorney Jeff Rosen, prosecutor Alaleh Kianerci, and even by Turner's lawyer Mike Armstrong. They are especially angered, however, by the role Stanford law school Prof. Dauber seems to have played. A fundamental precept of what is taught in law school is the need not to lie at any time, not to distort the truth in legal matters, to adhere at all times to the fundamental ethical obligations of the legal profession, and to assure that judges be protected against inappropriate political pressures and mob opinion.

But in the end, many alumni and others say what they find the most unacceptable has been Stanford's silence throughout the entire matter. These alumni have asked, with so much at stake for a student or former student

(Turner), being aware of the past actions by Prof. Dauber, with the Stanford police being paid by Stanford and supervised by Stanford officials (in recent years, Stanford's own general counsel), and with Stanford apparently being in possession of exculpatory material, how can Stanford possibly justify what it has done and failed to do in the Turner case?

It's a very good question and one that alumni and others should keep asking.

Chapter 11

The Neuroscience of Brain Development, Culpability, and the Law

The Science

Culpability is a key factor throughout the justice system, including in how statutes are written and sentences are determined. In the Turner matter, as is the case with virtually all young offenders, an important issue relates to a youthful defendant's degree of brain development and maturation. It is known that an individual's brain doesn't fully develop until approximately 25 years of age or even later, and the male brain is known to develop more slowly for these purposes than the female brain. When the normal brain reaches maturity, the myelination of the prefrontal cortex and other areas of the brain results in such capabilities as sophistication in the use of good judgment, enhanced executive function, improved rational behavior, skill in planning and predicting outcomes, mature social behavior, impulse control, refined abilities to perceive consequences, and a sophisticated ability to read others' emotions and perceive social cues.

On the other hand, young people, particularly those under the age of 25 and whose brains are not yet fully developed, think mainly with the amygdala portions of the brain (there is one amygdala on each side of the brain), which process emotions, and explains why young people can behave irrationally, act impulsively, misinterpret social cues and others' emotions, and engage in risk-taking behavior. Young people may also fail to consider consequences of their behavior, with their choice of actions also being more susceptible to peer pressure.

There is also the obvious issue that what young people do (meaning all of us when we were young) includes thinking and actions that are very unlikely to be repeated in adulthood. This isn't to excuse wrongful behavior by teens and young adults, but it does say that society needs to consider these issues when we apply the four purposes of our criminal laws – removal from society, retribution, deterrence, and rehabilitation.

The State of California Considers SB 889

As of this writing, the State of California is considering Senate Bill 889, which proposes that due to young people's immature brain development, individuals under age 21 should be dealt with in the juvenile justice system—not in the adult justice system. Brian Richart, president of the Chief Probation Officers of California, said:

"The science says [those] between 18 and 24 have less fully developed prefrontal cortexes . . . Their decision-making is inhibited. They act impulsively and we know this, yet we treat them as if they are fully developed."[101]

Richart continued that he witnessed the impact of prison on a 17-year-old family member even after the individual was released, and that it "informed my own thinking on the more humane way to treat people,"[102]

Brain Maturation Should Be Considered in Culpability

Because of the major developmental differences in the adult brain as compared to a young person's brain, it makes sense for the justice system to judge a youthful offender's culpability in the context of his or her less developed brain maturity as compared to culpability in that of an adult. Brock Turner was 19 years of age at the time of the Kappa Alpha incident, and on top of his immature brain development because of his age, Turner also had severe impairment due to alcohol consumption that occurred shortly before and during the Kappa Alpha party.

It is for these and other reasons that in Turner's case, as in similar cases of teen and young adult behavior, years of incarceration in state prison versus time in county jail would have been inappropriate. And as people who initially advocated sex offender registration are now saying, it makes no sense at all for these teens and young adults to be subjected to the brutal consequences of sex offender registration, especially for life and especially if their offenses had nothing to do with children, which was and is the main purpose for registration. Judge Persky's decision to focus more on rehabilitation rather than severe punishment was the right thing to do.

Intent is a critical element of the criminal justice system. Science, such as neurological development as it relates to young offenders in the criminal justice system, has been missing in guiding criminal justice policy and reform for far too long, especially in the case of teens and young adults. It definitely was missing in the Turner case.

Chapter 12

The Role of Alcohol and Alcohol-Induced Blackout Amnesia

Alcohol Use and Abuse on College and University Campuses

A core issue associated with the Brock Turner case is the rampant use and abuse of alcohol on college and university campuses. This problem has yet to be adequately addressed and mitigated by college and university administrators. According to the National Institute on Alcohol Abuse and Alcoholism, a college freshman's first six weeks of college life, in particular, stand out as a time of harmful alcohol intake and its resultant undesirable effects and events. This is because of "...students' expectations and social pressures at the start of the academic year."[103] Studies show that approximately 50% of student sexual assaults involved alcohol. Of these, 46% of the victims had ingested alcohol, as did 69% of the perpetrators.[104]

Fraternity parties are high-risk settings for alcohol overindulgence and ensuing consensual sexual encounters, and in some cases, sexual assaults. According to researcher A. Abbey, Ph.D.:

"The peer norms for most fraternity parties are to drink heavily, to act in an uninhibited manner and engage in casual sex."[105]

The scene at the Kappa Alpha party, the fraternity at which Chanel Miller and Brock Turner were in attendance, had ample beer and hard liquor for anyone who wanted it, including those under the legal drinking age. Based on Dr. Abbey's research findings, the Stanford Kappa Alpha fraternity party was a likely setting for drunken sexual encounters to occur.

Alcohol-Induced Blackout Amnesia

According to court documents, Chanel had a history of alcohol-induced blackout amnesia. Alcohol-induced blackout, a form of anterograde amnesia, is typically experienced during binge drinking when an individual's blood alcohol concentration (BAC) quickly rises to approximately 0.14 g/dL (0.14%) to 0.20 g/dL (0.20%) or higher through consumption of a large quantity of alcohol in a short period of time. BAC is defined as the amount of alcohol (in grams) in 100 ml of blood. For example, if a drinker has a BAC of 0.10% or 0.10 g/dL, the drinker has 10 grams of alcohol in 100 ml of her/his blood, or one part per 1000 parts blood. Approximately 50% of drinkers have reported experiencing alcohol-induced blackout. [106] Binge drinking is defined as four or more standard drinks in two hours for women, and five or more standard drinks in two hours for men. [107]

In their research, authors Wilhite, Mallard, and Fromme conclude, "It may be that individuals who are predisposed to alcohol-related blackouts engage in riskier, unplanned behavior while drinking, potentially a result of neural differences related to inhibitory processing."[108] The researchers also found that "women who experienced blackouts were at much greater risk of sexual risk-taking behaviors, including unplanned sexual behavior, relative to those without a blackout history."[109]

Risk factors for alcoholic blackout include drinking alcohol on an empty stomach, percentage of alcohol in the alcoholic beverage consumed, Caucasian versus other races, female versus male gender, history of familial alcoholism, history of prior blackout, pre-party drinking, and rapid ingestion of a high quantity of alcohol.

In blackout amnesia, the individual is conscious and has the appearance of normal functioning; for example, the drinker can make decisions, engage in conversation, and can even drive a car (illegally) – but will have no memory (en bloc), or only partial memory (fragmentary) of what occurred during the period of blackout amnesia. Because cognitive and memory impairment takes place before impairment of motor function, a drinker can appear alert and functional, but experience little or no memory formation. According to Boston University School of Public Health chair and alcohol researcher Dr. Richard Saitz:

"A blackout is when you don't remember what happened. You can appear to be completely awake. An observer can't tell when someone is in the midst of not forming a memory."[110] [Boldface added]

The fact that an observer is unable to identify that a person is in blackout amnesia is relevant because Turner was drunk, blunting his ability to decipher Chanel's actions and intentions, and most importantly, Turner would not have known if or when Chanel was in blackout, as she would have appeared functional not just to him but also to third parties.

Blackout can place drinkers at serious risks for motor vehicle accidents while driving, alcohol poisoning, falls, sexual assault, kidnapping, harming others, and a multitude of other hazards. Blackout can induce uninhibited sexual behavior. Extreme alcohol consumption can result in acute alcohol intoxication causing whole-body organ failure and subsequent death.

Alcohol-induced blackout is not to be confused with non-alcoholic blackout (transient loss of consciousness) such as syncope (fainting) due to sudden lack of blood circulation to the brain, abnormal electrical brain activity such as epileptic seizure, or psychogenic blackout due to stress, anxiety, or other psychogenic disorders.[111]

Based on the physiological effects and activities a drinker can carry out during alcohol-induced blackout, Chanel's state of alcoholic blackout during her encounter with Turner can make the case that Turner believed Chanel was coherent and provided consent, then sometime after sexual activity had commenced, Chanel gradually slipped into a state of alcoholic stupor as her BAC continued to rise. A drinker's BAC can continue to rise approximately two hours or more after ingestion of the last drink. Turner may not have noticed if or when – during their consensual sexual encounter – Chanel progressed from consciousness to her ultimate state of stupor. Turner himself was mentally impaired due to his own alcohol intoxication.

Physiology of Alcohol Intake, Metabolism, and Alcoholic Blackout

Women are more susceptible to the toxic effects of alcohol than men, one reason being that women have higher ratios of body fat to water. Women also have lower levels of alcohol dehydrogenase (ADH), an enzyme in the liver and stomach that breaks down alcohol. After ADH metabolizes alcohol into acetaldehyde, a known carcinogen, the enzyme aldehyde dehydrogenase (ALDH2) metabolizes the toxic acetaldehyde into acetate. The acetate is then metabolized into carbon dioxide and water, at which time the carbon dioxide and water can be excreted such as through the breath, urine, and sweat. The above alcohol detoxification method is one of several, and the most common, routes used by the body to detoxify and remove alcohol.[112] Women's innate lower levels of ADH and high fat to water ratios as compared to those of men explain how a woman with the same weight and alcohol intake as a man would experience greater alcohol intoxication than the man.

A recent study conducted at the Medical Research Council Laboratory of Molecular Biology in Cambridge, England showed that acetaldehyde, the carcinogenic byproduct of alcohol metabolism, "broke and damaged DNA within blood stem cells leading to rearranged chromosomes and permanently altering the DNA sequences within these cells."[113] These altered and mis-repaired DNA sequences in stem cells can then cause cancer formation. Alcohol intake is attributed to at least seven types of cancers in both women and men, including breast, esophageal, laryngeal, stomach, mouth, liver, and bowel cancers. Alcohol's estrogenicity is a factor that, even in moderate drinkers, can increase a woman's risk of developing breast cancer by 30% to 50%.[114]

Chanel is of East Asian and Caucasian descent. Approximately 70% of East Asians have a genetic mutation in ALD or ALDH2 that causes ineffective metabolism of acetaldehyde, resulting in the body's accumulation of toxic acetaldehyde. This induces inflammation and symptoms such as feelings of illness, nausea, headache, and facial flushing (Asian flushing syndrome) caused by blood vessel dilation. People with the aforementioned genetic mutation who drink alcohol on a regular basis have a significantly greater risk of developing esophageal and stomach cancers as compared to people with normal ALD and ALDH2 genetics.[115]

In 2011, neuroscientists at Washington University School of Medicine identified the process of alcohol-induced blackout at the cellular level. It was discovered that a large quantity of alcohol consumption interferes with certain brain receptors, resulting in the production of steroids that inhibit long-term potentiation (a process that strengthens the connections between two neurons), ultimately interfering with synaptic plasticity in the brain's hippocampus and inhibiting memory formation. Interestingly, 5-alpha reductase inhibitors such as Proscar, an oral prescription medication for the treatment of enlarged prostate, can help prevent the formation of new steroid hormones and augment hippocampal glutamate neurotransmission, thereby promoting memory preservation in the presence of excessive alcohol.[116][117]

Physiology of Memory Formation

Normal memory formation, which occurs largely in the hippocampus, is a process of transfer encoding of short-term memory into a process of long-term memory. To recall a memory, the memory is retrieved from long-term memory storage and placed again into short-term memory, at which time the memory is re-experienced, and then returned to long-term memory storage.[118] During blackout, alcohol inhibits the normal process of transfer encoding of short-term memory into long-term memory storage, resulting in partial or complete lack of memory formation.

Interpretation of BAC Levels

In California, a drinker is legally intoxicated when a BAC reaches 0.08% or higher. Chanel's back-extrapolated BAC at the time she was found by witnesses was approximated by Alice King, Santa Clara County supervising criminologist, to be 0.242 to 0.249% -- about three times the legal limit.[119] Because the intravenous fluids Chanel had received through ambulance and hospital treatments were not included in calculating her back-extrapolated BAC, Chanel's actual BAC when she was found by witnesses was likely higher than the reported 0.242 – 0.249%. Turner's BAC, back-extrapolated to estimate his BAC at the time Turner and Chanel were found by witnesses, was 0.171%.

The reason a drinker's BAC can continue to rise for two hours or more after ingestion of the last drink is because alcohol still in the stomach undergoes the process of digestion, is absorbed into the intestines, and enters the circulation while it awaits detoxification by the liver. Alcohol circulating in the blood has a propensity to enter high-fluid organs such as the brain. The liver can typically detoxify one standard drink per hour. A standard drink is

12 ounces of beer, or five ounces of table wine, or 1.5 ounces of distilled spirits (e.g., vodka, gin, whiskey, etc.).[120]

Pre-Party Drinking

Pre-party drinking, where an individual drinks alcohol or drinks alcohol to a state of drunkenness before attending a party, can be a significant precursor to alcoholic blackout. Chanel had consumed four shots of whisky and champagne at home (at least under one of her conflicting versions of events) before attending the Stanford fraternity party. According to LaBrie et al.:

> "the current findings showing that drinking shots of liquor when pre-partying increases the likelihood of blacking out hold particular relevance for women's health and well-being."[121]

The typical intent of pre-party drinking is to:

> "create a 'buzz' or level of inebriation that will heighten enjoyment of the event and possibly endure through the event or until more alcohol can be obtained."[122]

This aligns with Chanel's statement to Stanford police that after drinking four shots of whiskey and champagne at home before attending the Stanford fraternity party (again, under one version of her conflicting statements), "She felt kind of buzzed but was coherent and able to function."[123]

The physiological process of alcohol detoxification explains how Chanel could have been in en bloc blackout (appeared alert, capable of performing tasks, but no memories formed) while consensually engaging in sexual activity with Turner, gradually becoming stuporous even after she had stopped drinking, and then had no later memory of what had transpired during blackout, including whether she had given consent. Turner would not have known Chanel had been in alcoholic blackout.

Blacking Out the Evidence of Alcohol-Induced Blackout

Prosecutor Alaleh Kianerci argued that the defense expert witness's testimony on alcohol-induced blackout should be withheld from the jurors (via the motions in limine) because "it has not been established that alcoholic blackouts are generally accepted in the scientific community," and blackout phenomenology should be excluded "because its probative value, if any, is far outweighed by its prejudicial effect of misleading a jury and confuse [sic] the issues.[124]

Contrary to the prosecutor's belief that alcoholic blackout is not accepted by the scientific community, formal scientific research of alcohol-induced blackout began as early as the 1940s by E.M. Jellinek, and numerous peer-reviewed scientific studies describing alcohol-induced blackout can be found in scientific journals and other medical and scientific sources. For example, in the *Journal of Addiction Medicine*, blackout researchers Rose and Grant state:

> **"Cognitive and memory impairment occurs before motor impairment, possibly explaining how a drinker appearing fully functional can have little subsequent memory."[125]** [Boldface added]

In *Frontiers in Psychology*, a respected trade journal that publishes rigorously peer-reviewed psychology research, researchers D. Hermens and L. Lagopoulos state in their article, "Binge Drinking and the Young Brain: A Mini Review of the Neurobiological Underpinnings of Alcohol-Induced Blackout," that alcohol-induced blackout "leads to a failure in forming new explicit memories (i.e., facts and events)."[126] In the article, "Alcohol-Induced Blackouts and Other Negative Outcomes During the Transition Out of College," authors Wilhite and Fromme state:

> **"someone in a blackout is fully conscious and able to actively engage in various activities, which include conversations, driving vehicles, and sexual behavior, but may not remember them later."[127]** [Boldface added]

The Expert Witness Dr. Kim Fromme

In pretrial motions and in limine discussions, prosecutor Kianerci made multiple statements against alcohol-induced blackout expert witness Dr. Kim Fromme in an effort to discredit and prevent Dr. Fromme's testimony. For example, Kianerci opined, "Much of Dr. Fromme's opinion as documented in her report about the specifics in this case, is based on assumptions, speculation, and conjecture."[128] Kianerci continues:

> "Dr. Fromme merely aims to attack the credibility of this sexual assault victim with absolutely no basis for coming to the medical opinion that she was suffering from an alcohol induced blackout and she engages in rank speculating that she 'possibly' could have consented …"[129]

Note that Chanel herself had testified that she was in alcoholic blackout while at the Stanford Kappa Alpha party, and she couldn't recall if she had given consent.

In stark contrast to Kianerci's cynicism regarding Dr. Fromme's expertise on the subject of alcohol-induced blackout, Dr. Fromme is a highly respected Professor of Clinical Psychology at the University of Texas at Austin, which is one of the highest rated universities in the field of psychology clinical studies. Dr. Fromme is nationally recognized as a top researcher on alcohol studies and alcoholic blackout.

According to Dr. Fromme's curriculum vitae and trial testimony, Dr. Fromme has received millions of dollars in research grants including a $2.3 million grant from the NIH/National Institute on Alcohol Abuse and Alcoholism to fund her state-of-the-art GENES study. The GENES study entails collection of DNA samples from subjects in her previous six-year longitudinal study, from which nearly seven million genetic markers will be examined. Dr. Fromme's DNA research will have a profound impact on scientific knowledge of alcohol consumption and its effects on behavioral and psychological outcomes at the genetic level. Among other honors, Dr. Fromme also is on the editorial boards for two scholarly journals, she conducts reviews for 20 to 30 additional scientific outlets, and she serves on grant review boards at the state, federal, and foundation levels where she evaluates other scientists' research. Dr. Fromme was selected as one of only seven scientists in the U.S. to serve as advisory counsel to the National Institutes of Health, a highly prestigious honor.

Dr. Fromme's more than 100 articles have been published in prestigious scientific journals including *Psychology of Addictive Behaviors, Journal of Abnormal Psychology, Alcoholism: Clinical and Experimental Research, Journal of Studies on Alcohol and Drugs, Archives of Sexual Behavior, Developmental Psychology, Journal of Consulting and Clinical Psychology,* and numerous other journals. As an indication of the impact of this work in the scientific community, Dr. Fromme's current Google Scholar citation count is 10,379, meaning her publications have been cited 10,379 times by other scientists. In 2019, Dr. Fromme received the Award for Distinguished Scientific Contributions, APA Division 50 (Addictions).[130] Dr. Fromme even has a university lab that simulates a real-life barroom, one of a few such labs nationally.

Prosecutor Kianerci's attempts to exclude Dr. Fromme's testimony via motions in limine failed, and subsequently led to a <u>Daubert</u> hearing (that is, a trial judge's evaluation of whether or not an expert's testimony and evidence will be admissible). Dr. Fromme's expert testimony was allowed to be heard by the jury with some exceptions. Unfortunately, key scientific findings were excluded from Dr. Fromme's testimony, including Dr. Fromme's pretrial statement that:

"you can't infer from slurred speech that cognition, behavior, decision-making, are necessarily impaired beyond the level in which you could engage in voluntary actions,"

and that:

"it is scientifically possible that she [Chanel] could have engaged in consensual sexual conduct." [Boldface added]

This testimony would have been critical in proving that Chanel's recorded phone calls to her boyfriend demonstrating slurred speech possibly would not have affected Chanel's ability to make decisions and engage in other voluntary actions, including consent to sexual activity.

In cross-examining Dr. Fromme in the presence of the jury, prosecutor Kianerci's very first question directed at Dr. Fromme was "what percentage of your income is derived by testifying in court as an expert witness?" Kianerci further queried, "I'm actually interested in why you charge a different amount for the military?" Another question was, "How much a year [do] you make testifying for the defense?" Kianerci also asked, "Is your opinion being influenced by the fact that you're getting paid $10,000 and are trying to help the defendant?" Kianerci further said to Dr. Fromme, again in front of the jury, "You have a financial bias in your testimony today. You're going to make about $10,000 based on what you say. Is that not true?" Kianerci's harping on Dr. Fromme's income related to her activities as an expert witness went on and on, comprising multiple pages of the court transcript.

Kianerci then focused on private emails between Mike Armstrong (Turner's lawyer) and Dr. Fromme. As discussed in Chapter 7, Dr. Fromme had provided Kianerci with the emails at Kianerci's request. The emails were conversations that had no relevance to Dr. Fromme's testimony in the Turner case. As always, Dr. Fromme's testimony, without regard for which side had hired her, was based on rigorously reviewed scientific research and nothing less. Dr. Fromme asserted:

"My integrity and reputation is the currency of my field," and that her 30 years of research "has been strictly done for scientific reasons, not litigation . . . I'm just here to share my expertise and to educate the jury about blackouts."

It should be noted that Dr. Fromme is paid for her scientific expertise whether the hiring party wins their case or not. Kianerci continued her baseless efforts to refute the science of alcoholic blackout amnesia despite the facts that Chanel testified that she indeed had a history of alcoholic blackouts, and that Chanel often didn't know how she ended up back at home after partying and experiencing alcoholic blackouts, remembering little or nothing.

Prosecutor Kianerci lacked the ability to attack the science regarding alcoholic blackouts, so she instead attacked the scientist.

Chanel Miller's History of Alcohol-Induced Blackout

Chanel acknowledged experiencing alcohol-induced blackouts at previous parties. In fact, she testified in court that she had experienced "four to five" episodes of blackout while in college.[131] In one of the official police reports filed with the criminal complaint, Stanford deputy Carrie DeVlugt stated that Chanel:

> **"described blackout to be where she is still functioning, but not remembering. She usually makes it home even when she blacks out."**[132] [Boldface added]

Deputy DeVlugt further reported that:

> **"She [Chanel] has blacked out before from drinking, but only when she has been continually drinking for a long time, and it is usually at the end of the night when it happens."**[133] [Boldface added]

Of course, this is similar to what had occurred at the Stanford fraternity party. And as noted in an earlier chapter, there are significant discrepancies in Chanel's own account of her activities that afternoon and evening. These contradictory accounts, given within 15 hours one from the other, indicate Chanel may have had memories or selective memories of what occurred after all, even to the point that when she first woke up in the hospital emergency room she went out of her way to (falsely) say she only had been drinking Keystone Light beers.

Chanel's State of Alcoholic Blackout Raised Reasonable Doubt

The likelihood that Chanel was in a state of alcoholic blackout amnesia at the Kappa Alpha party was a key hurdle to Kianerci proving beyond a reasonable doubt that Turner knew Chanel was not capable of consent. Knowing this, Kianerci made every effort to first prevent expert witness Dr. Fromme from testifying via motions in limine, and when that failed, Kianerci then waged personal attacks against Dr. Fromme and disparaged the science

145

of alcoholic blackout amnesia in the presence of the jury. This was carried out despite the facts that Chanel's actions at the Kappa Alpha party exemplified classic alcoholic blackout amnesic behavior, and Chanel herself verified she had been in a state of alcoholic blackout amnesia, during which time she continued to carry out activities such as making phone calls and sending text messages, but then allegedly had no memories of these activities.

The jury never heard these critically essential points.

What Was Learned

The evidence shows that Chanel's drunkenness and self-described alcohol-induced state of blackout did indeed play a major role in her sexual encounter with Brock Turner. The likelihood is that Chanel could have consented to sexual activity with Turner while she was in a state of en bloc alcohol-induced blackout and when the fingering occurred. The two Swedish graduate student witnesses who later came upon Turner and Chanel, and who had also been drinking, only witnessed dry humping with Turner fully clothed; they did not witness the earlier fingering, and for her part, Chanel simply said she could not remember.

In his book, *Talking to Strangers*, Malcom Gladwell makes the point that:

> **"our drunken, blacked-out selves are not the same as our sober selves."**[134] [Boldface added]

After the Kappa Alpha incident, Chanel Miller, while sober, said she was in an exclusive relationship with her boyfriend and would never have voluntarily left the Kappa Alpha fraternity party with another man. But at Kappa Alpha, the record indicates Chanel wasn't the sober Chanel Miller. Rather, she was "Emily Doe," the drunk partygoer whose alcohol-saturated brain led her to behave in classic drunken fashion — impulsive, uninhibited, making poor judgments, inclined to sexual risk-taking — and quite amenable to leaving the party with another man.

Victims of sexual assault cannot be blamed for their assaults. However, they should be held accountable for their own actions if their actions, such as drinking alcohol to a state of drunkenness, resulted in predictable and high risks to both themselves and others. This is not victim blaming or shaming;

rather, it's common sense, raw reality, and it's about preventing sexual assault and other injurious consequences.

As an analogy, nobody can dispute that people who harm or kill themselves and/or others while driving drunk should be accountable for their actions. It's safe to say that if Brock Turner and Chanel Miller had been sober, what happened at Stanford would not have happened.

Chapter 13

Modern-Day Mob Vigilantism and Shaming

Early Historical Mob Vigilantism and Shaming

In this nation's early historical past, citizens engaged in mob vigilantism, mob public shaming, and mob violence against fellow community members through witch-hunts, tarring and feathering with hot wood tar, the use of stocks, lynchings, and other inhumane and abhorrent forms of physical torture, persecution, and public vilification. This inflicted horrendous emotional and physical harm, and often resulted in the targets' deaths. These actions were barred by the 8th amendment to the U.S. Constitution, ratified in 1791, that prohibits the infliction of cruel and unusual punishment. The past history of barbaric violence against alleged wrong-doers ran contrary to the new nation's concepts of moral ethics and integrity. Apparently, U.S. citizens had decided that burning one's neighbors at the stake was wrong, and they thus prohibited such authoritarian bullying as part of the Bill of Rights amendments to the Constitution.

Modern-Day Mob Vigilantism and Shaming

Fast-forward to the 21st Century. Society now has the Internet, which makes it possible for harmful cruelty and hatred to instantaneously reach all four corners of the world. In many ways the Internet, especially through social media, has deteriorated to a new form of mob vigilantism, public shaming, bullying, and mob violence that would have been impossible before the inception of the Internet. It's called cyber mob vigilantism and public shaming and can involve harassment, threats, and false information against the victim. This can inflict severe mental and emotional harm upon victims, even causing symptoms of physical disease. According to New York University professor Jennifer Jacquet:

"The speed at which information can travel, the frequency of anonymous shaming, the size of the audience it can reach, and the permanence of the information separate digital shaming from shaming of the past."[135]

Social media is a powerful weapon in destroying lives through hateful character assassination and malicious public shaming, with compassion, decency, and moral ethics being all but extinct. Regrettably, once a victim has been publicly character-assassinated and/or shamed by social media, little can be done to undo the damage inflicted upon the victim and the victim's reputation. The hateful words are permanent. Victims' families and friends are often painfully affected as well. Social media-ignited character assassination, hatred, and shaming spread like wildfires and are virtually impossible to contain and extinguish.

Brock Turner: A Victim of Mob Vigilantism and Shaming

A recent victim of extreme cruel and relentless Internet mob vigilantism and mob hatred was Brock Turner. And even after more than five years since the Stanford incident involving Turner and Chanel, Turner continues to be the orchestrated target of relentless public shaming and persecution. Here's an infinitesimally small sample:

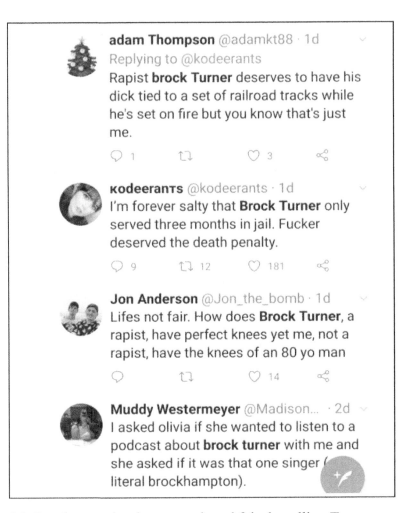

Fig. 14. People tweeting hate speech and falsely calling Turner a rapist.

Fig. 15. Various hateful tweets against Turner.

Internet mob vigilantism and shaming is a dangerous phenomenon in which online mobs can congregate almost instantaneously and swarm to reach millions of people at rapid speed, resulting in often extreme harm upon their victims and others. Mob participants can choose to be anonymous, they're decidedly emboldened, and they can make statements they would likely never say to others face-to-face, including death threats. Even when mob Internet bullies and vigilantes identify themselves, mob participants are emboldened to pass unfounded judgments, regardless of how harmful their words may be, because their statements are rarely fact-checked or confronted; there are few to no consequences to mob participants for their actions. Shaming and punishing through vigilantism directly conflicts with America's fundamental concepts of due process.

Internet vigilante mobs can provoke outrage based on disinformation which then snowballs into dangerously large and uncontrolled mobs out for blood. These mobs engage in unchecked bullying that relies on false hysteria and repeated untruths. Internet mob violence, shaming, and hatred can destroy victims, cause loss of victims' jobs, destroy victims' reputations, ostracize and banish them from society, and can even push victims to suicide. Internet shaming and vigilante mob participation bring out a disturbing savagery in participants that they probably didn't realize they possessed.

The Need for Anti-Cyberbullying Laws

Social media networking sites such as Twitter, Instagram, and Facebook have limited mechanisms available for victims to report harassment, threats, and other offensive and harmful content. While anti-cyberbullying laws are currently in place in the U.S., there are no specific anti-cyberbullying laws at the federal level, and individual states are left to design their own cyberbullying laws, which vary in effectiveness, and often focus primarily on school cyberbullying.[136] However, England, for example, has a number of laws in place such as the Malicious Communications Act, that:

"[prohibits] indecent or grossly offensive communication for the purpose of causing 'distress or anxiety to the recipient' . . . and [prohibits] threats and information which is false and known or believed to be false by the sender of the communication."[137]

Penalties include up to six months in prison and/or fines of over $6,000. The U.S. would benefit from considering similar anti-cyberbullying laws.

Cyber Vigilantism and Shaming as a Means to Silence Free Speech

It is not unusual for cyber bullies and mobs to bully and silence individuals whose ideas don't align with those of the bullies. This happened to individuals who protested the false accusations and cruel treatment of Brock Turner by Internet mobs and traditional news agencies. Readers who made comments opposed to the hordes of false statements against Turner and Judge Persky in both traditional and social media were often shamed or had their comments deleted. As a result, people feared and refrained from expressing their opinions, and avoided starting dialogue about the true facts of the Turner case such as court transcript facts that were in Turner's favor.

Dr. Guy Aitchison, Irish Research Council Postdoctoral Fellow, rightly asserts:

> "As well as the effects on them personally, a culture of shaming imperils public debate as people will be driven to self-censor and avoid controversial topics."[138]

Vigilantism and public shaming also serve as strategies for social control.

Brock Turner and Others as Victims of Prof. Dauber's Public Defamation and Shaming

Internet mob vigilantism, shaming, and violence, in all appearances, served and continue to serve as Prof. Dauber's main tools to attack Brock Turner, Judge Aaron Persky, and others. Prof. Dauber, a Stanford law school professor and a friend of Chanel Miller and her family, used a toolbox that includes disseminating disinformation and outright falsehoods, public shaming, and instructions to others as to how to harm targeted victims. Prof. Dauber's Internet shaming was relentless, and she continued to use it against Turner, Judge Persky, and those who questioned Prof. Dauber's actions or those whose opinions were contrary to hers (an Internet search shows that she did something similar years earlier to her brother Michael Landis).

153

Examples of Prof. Dauber's many toxic tweets against Turner include her label of Turner as "Lying rapist Brock Turner,"[139] and her tweet that "Brock Turner is a lying unrepentant sex predator who never showed real remorse for sexual assault."[140] Prof. Dauber continued to depict Turner as a rapist, even though Turner was convicted of sexual assault, not rape. In fact, he wasn't even prosecuted nor tried for rape.

Fig. 16. Prof. Dauber's tweet mocking Turner's father.

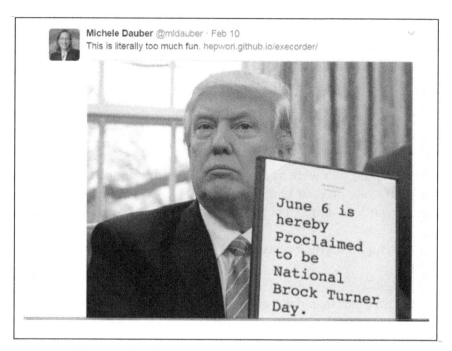

Michele Dauber @mldauber · Feb 10
This is literally too much fun. hepwori.github.io/execorder/

June 6 is hereby Proclaimed to be National Brock Turner Day.

Fig. 17. Prof. Dauber's tweet mocking Turner.

Prof. Dauber's vitriol and hatred towards Turner wasn't limited to tweets. The *LA Times* quoted Prof. Dauber describing Turner as a "calculated, lying, unrepentant sex predator."[141] The *Palo Alto Daily Post* published Prof. Dauber's statement that, "He [Turner] isn't remorseful or accountable and learned nothing, which is exactly why the light sentence was wrong."[142] In contradiction to Prof. Dauber's false statements that Turner showed no remorse, the court documents contain Turner's 1,916-word letter of remorse, including his statement,

"I would give anything to change what happened that night. I can never forgive myself for imposing trauma and pain on [Chanel Miller]. It debilitates me to think that my actions have caused her emotional and physical stress that is completely unwarranted and unfair."[143]

In a PBS *Democracy Now* interview with Amy Goodman, Prof. Dauber said Chanel Miller had been "gravely injured" by Turner.[144] However, the physical assessment conducted by paramedics at the scene showed normal vital signs, no signs of trauma, although as discussed elsewhere, there were skin puncture marks at the two sites where intravenous needle insertions had been unsuccessfully attempted by paramedics, and superficial scrapes from lying in the vicinity of pine trees. In fact, at the preliminary hearing when Kianerci asked Chanel about her injuries, there were no indications of any serious injuries whatsoever as indicated below:

Kianerci: "When you were at the hospital you didn't notice that you were injured in any way on your body, did you?"
Chanel: "I noticed blood on my hands and bandages on my hand and elbows."
Kianerci: "But after you learned the process you realized that was from the IV, right?"
Chanel: "Yes."
Kianerci: "So other than that you didn't notice any injuries on your body?"
Chanel: "Except for a scratch on my neck."

Prof. Dauber also said in her interview with Amy Goodman:

> "Her [Chanel's] clothing was off . . . She was naked . . . She had dirt and pine needles in her vagina . . .She didn't wake up in the hospital . . . The paramedics were unable to revive her . . .the crime scene was totally gruesome."[145]

All of Prof. Dauber's above statements are false. In fact, all of Chanel's clothing was on her body except a pair of underwear, which contained DNA from several individuals, but none of it was Turner's. The SART examination showed no dirt or pine needles in her vagina. Chanel had some superficial abrasions, which would be expected when making out near pine trees, and her body was not contused. Chanel opened her eyes when paramedics pinched her nail, and paramedics observed Chanel move her head and clear her own airway while she vomited. Chanel's Glasgow score was 11, with a score of 15 indicating full awakeness. Chanel woke up in the emergency room after sobering up, and was discharged within hours after she arrived, an implausible scenario for a gravely injured patient.

Nevertheless, Prof. Dauber's false statements in the *Democracy Now* publication, and also in other traditional news and social media where Prof. Dauber grossly and intentionally misstated the facts, were widely disseminated to the public without the public knowing the statements were false, and without the various news media bothering to verify and/or correct Prof. Dauber's false statements. Thus the public came away with a perception of the Turner case that was brazenly distorted and outright wrong – and that caused irreparable damage to Turner's reputation.

In another act of distorting facts and stoking public hatred against Turner, Prof. Dauber said in an interview published in *Mother Jones*, "in this [Turner's] case, you have two eyewitnesses who literally pulled the attacker off the unconscious victim."[146] However, court transcripts show the two witnesses said Turner got up by himself.

On June 6, 2016, the day the Turner trial documents were officially released to the public, Prof. Dauber tweeted a letter written by Turner's childhood friend to the court in support of Turner. The friend, Leslie Rasmussen, is a talented drummer and Good English band member. Of note is that Prof. Dauber's tweet of Leslie's letter is dated June 6, 2016 at 1:21 a.m., that is, apparently before it was publicly released.[147] That same early morning, at 6:50 a.m., in response to a tweet to Prof. Dauber from Gabriella Paiela, a writer for *New York Magazine*, Prof. Dauber tweeted to Gabriella, "...If journo, Email me please."[148] Six minutes later, Paiella responded to Prof. Dauber, "Just emailed, thanks."[149] Later that same day the article, "Brock Turner's Childhood Friend Blames His Felony Sexual-Assault Conviction on Political Correctness," written by Paiella, appeared in *New York Magazine*.[150] According to the *New York Times*:

"Within hours of Ms. Rasmussen's letter being made public by New York Magazine, Good English was removed from a roster of Brooklyn venues where they were scheduled to perform in the coming days, including Rock Shop in Gowanus, Industry City Distillery in Greenwood, Gold Sounds in Bushwick, and Bar Matchless in Greenpoint."[151]

Stemming from Prof. Dauber's tweet of Leslie's letter, young Ms. Rasmussen became the subject of intense cyberbullying and public shaming. Prof. Dauber would have been well aware of the normal innate vulnerabilities in young people who have barely transitioned from teenagers to young adults, as Prof. Dauber's own daughter, Amanda, had committed suicide a few years earlier at age 25. Yet Prof. Dauber apparently had no qualms about her deliberate act to publicly harm and shame Ms. Rasmussen.

Prof. Dauber was quoted in multiple traditional news media articles and TV interviews, where she continued to state false information about Turner, Judge Persky, and those against whom she wished to retaliate.

After Turner's return to his family's home in Ohio, gun-toting vigilantes, including anarchists and people carrying M4 assault and AR-15 rifles, appeared at the family home. Among other things, the vigilantes called for the "castration and killing of rapists" and spoke of Turner's "extremely light sentence."[152] Of course, these people's actions were based on false sound bites and other disinformation continually being presented on a daily and even hourly basis in social media and the press. Prof. Dauber's response to the vigilantes' actions was, "We strongly condemn the armed protesters...We do not support vigilante action of any kind."[153] Yet Prof. Dauber was responsible for disseminating much of the global disinformation against Turner that would incite these fringe groups and others.

Fig. 18. Armed vigilantes posted in front of the Turner home in Ohio.

Prof. Dauber Tweets Hateful Song Against Turner; Advocates Extreme Violence and Suicide

On December 2, 2017, Prof. Dauber tweeted a sick, violent, and hateful song, "F___ Brock Turner."[154] Even though she is a professor of law, Prof. Dauber also went out of her way to attack the fact that Turner had filed an appeal that appropriately raised issues concerning the trial and his conviction. The song, recorded by Melted Crayons at Bliss Studios, apparently located in New Jersey, called for extreme violence against Turner and even encouraged him to take his own life. In her tweet, Prof. Dauber urged the mob to "Please enjoy this song,"[155] likewise advocating for extreme violence against Turner and suggesting that Turner take his own life. Most reasonable people would believe that this is not an example that should be set by a professor, and certainly not a professor of law. Because of the detailed information included in the song, the question also arises, who really wrote the song?

Michele Dauber ● @mldauber · 3d
#BrockTurner appealed his conviction and said it was "all lies" and that he didn't do anything wrong. He isn't remorseful or accountable and learned nothing, which is exactly why the light sentence was wrong. Please enjoy this song. bit.ly/2iF5d3w

Fig. 19. Prof. Dauber's tweet promoting song advocating Turner is harmed and kills himself.

"Here's our song that pays tribute to everyone's favorite scumbag!

"DOWNLOAD SONG HERE: https://meltedcrayons.bandcamp.com/tr... Christian Cordes - Vocals Instagram - @thechristianattrel Twitter - @NextGenCordes Brandon Cordes - Guitar, Bass, Keyboard, Tuba, Glockenspiel, Drums Instagram - @theprincebrandon Twitter - @brandonprincec Written, Recorded and Produced by Melted Crayons At Bliss Studios in Howell NJ Arcade Records – 2016."[156]

(1st Verse)
Brock Turner
You're the definition of scum
Get stepped on like old gum
I hope your face gets kicked in
Brock Turner
Change your freaking last name
Cause Timmy Turners got it claimed
He doesn't need the shame

(Chorus)
I hope you never get a job
I hope you never get the girl
Cause we all know what you'll do
It makes us all want to hurl
I hope you get tossed in a dumpster
Fuck Brock Turner

(2nd Verse)
Brock Turner
You're like a subway cockroach
A thing that no one
will ever want to approach
Brock Turner
You might as well be poop
A thing that needs to be cleaned off
the bottom of my boot

(Chorus)
I hope you live your life
with no fun or joy
with the constant reminder
of the life you destroyed
I hope you fall through a gutter
Fuck Brock Turner

(Bridge)
We should never forget
the two badass heroes of this story
Peter J and Carl A
Swedish super heroes
who deserve all the glory
Hey Brock Turner
I got a question for ya
For the day if you become a father
How ya gonna tell your daughter

that you're a monster

(3rd Verse)
Brock Turner
I hope you enjoyed your song
I hope it was something
that you could sing along too
Not really
I hope you eat a dick
Or choose to take a nosedive
off the top of a cliff

(Chorus)
I hope you never get a job
I hope you never get the girl
Cause we all know what you'll do
It makes us all want to hurl
I hope you get tossed in a dumpster
Fuck Brock Turner

In response to Prof. Dauber's posting of the cruel and violent song, retired Judge LaDoris Cordell, a former Palo Alto councilwoman and former vice provost at Stanford, was quoted in the *San Jose Mercury News* as saying:

"It's truly deplorable . . . I think that the fact that a Stanford law professor who teaches undergraduates and who blatantly and vigorously endorses violence against a young man who is exercising his constitutional right to appeal his conviction is highly disturbing and totally inappropriate."[157]

The *Palo Alto Daily Post* quoted retired Judge LaDoris Cordell's response to the violent song and other acts of hatred towards Turner as follows:

"I am just stunned at the level of violence, vulgarity, the bullying, all this stuff, aimed at this young man . . . He erred. He has been convicted. And so we as a society, we believe in redemption, particularly in young people."[158]

Another tweet sent by Prof. Dauber, which has since been deleted, instructed the mob to continue shaming Turner.

It belies the very core of human moral decency that Prof. Dauber – a resident in a community where high school student suicides were at epidemic levels while her husband sat on the community's school board, and whose own daughter committed suicide – would advocate that a young person commit suicide, and no less encourage others to enjoy this. Many were shocked that Prof. Dauber – a mother, wife, and teacher – would advocate the suicide of a young person as messaged in the above song. Cyber vigilantism, persecution, and shaming are not to be confused with ethical and lawful activism.

Knowing that Prof. Dauber tweeted the aforementioned horrible message advocating violence and suicide, it's ironic that Prof. Dauber and her husband Ken had years earlier launched an organization called "We Can Do Better" in an effort to help stem a rise in student suicides in Palo Alto, California.[159]

Someone also arranged for posters to be placed on college campuses with Turner's picture and captions that referred to him as a rapist or a symbol of campus rape. Here's one that was placed at the student union at Cal Poly, coincidentally the college Chanel's sister had attended:

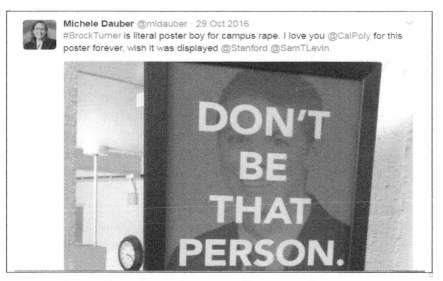

Fig. 20. Prof. Dauber's hateful tweet falsely labeling Turner a rapist.

Even to this day, years after Turner's 2016 trial, uninformed people still believe and spread false statements about Turner.

Turner Appeared in Textbook for High School and College Students

Another cruel and malicious attack against Turner appeared in the 2017 second edition of the textbook, *Introduction to Criminal Justice: Systems Diversity, and Change,* authored by University of Colorado professors Callie Rennison and Mary Dodge. The textbook is used in both high schools and colleges and features a photo of Turner, under which is a caption that falsely states:

> "Brock Turner, a Stanford student who raped and assaulted an unconscious female student behind a dumpster at a fraternity party, was recently released from jail after serving only three months."[160]

Shortly after this second edition was released, someone arranged for a Facebook posting about the newly added section, which then allowed the campaign against Turner to have newspapers around the country run individual but very similarly worded articles about the social media posting and quoting the textbook's language. In other words, another self-generated and fake story.

If the book's authors had actually done their homework and researched the facts of the case instead of relying on social media hearsay and unsubstantiated news reports, they would have learned that Turner was never prosecuted for or convicted of rape. It's disappointing that Turner's family did not sue the professors for libel, as this would have been a valuable learning opportunity for both the professors and their students. The textbook's publisher, SAGE Publications, Inc., was contacted by volunteer alumni and told about the untruths but SAGE insisted on keeping the text. A few months later, however, the publisher issued a press release that it would be revising the text for its third edition, although from all reports still not doing the necessary due diligence about what actually happened and how SAGE and other media were being carefully used in the campaign against both Turner and Judge Persky.

Rape is another example of a crime that has se... sion in its definition over time. While rape has a... crime and considered *mala in se*, how it has been s... has changed. For example, originally, the FBI define... "carnal knowledge of a female forcibly and against h... 2011, the FBI definition was changed to broaden t... that are considered rape: "penetration, no matter h... the vagina or anus with a body part or object, or... tion by a sex organ of another person, without the c... victim." This change included boys and men as vic... behavior beyond the penetration of a vagina by a p... the FBI removed the word *forcibly* from this defini... reflect contemporary understanding of this viole... not necessarily involve force, but it does involve a f... such as when a person is unconscious. A recent hi... example is that of rapist Brock Turner. Turner, a stu... University, was caught in the act, and ultimate... three felony charges: assault with intent to rape... woman, sexually penetrating an intoxicated perso... object, and sexually penetrating an unconscious p... eign object. Turner's victim was unconscious dur... it happened behind a trash container outside of... fraternity house on campus.

Brock Turner, a Stanford student who raped and assaulted an unconscious female college student behind a dumpster at a fraternity party, was recently released from jail after serving only three months. Some are shocked at how short this sentence is. Others who are more familiar with the way sexual violence has been...

Fig. 21. Image of Brock Turner in textbook, *Introduction to Criminal Justice: Systems Diversity, and Change,* containing false rape claim by Profs. Callie Rennison and Mary Dodge.[161]

The News Media, and Rigged Internet Search Engines

A recurrent problem is that traditional news agencies often follow the mobs and publish the mobs' opinions and sentiments with little to no independent fact-checking or investigation. This may be related to the news agencies' fears that if they oppose or question a mob's opinions, the news agencies can stand to lose ad dollars and readership, especially when a mob appears to represent widely accepted popular opinion, even if the opinion is contrary to fact-based evidence. It may also be due to the desperate need for revenue.

For years on end, various media outlets including the *New York Times, USA Today, Daily Mail of London, San Francisco Chronicle, San Jose Mercury News, ESPN,* and many others regularly featured stories using headlines and web taglines calling Turner a rapist and republishing what any investigation would have shown were intentionally false statements about both Turner and Judge Persky.

The local newspaper in Dayton, Ohio even went so far as to feature Turner's face on its entire front page and cleverly covered part of the newspaper's name (*"City Paper"*) with the photo so that it appeared to say, "City Raper."

Fig. 22. Malicious defamation by local Dayton, Ohio newspaper, the *Dayton City Paper.*

Someone also arranged for an artist to convert photos of both Turner and Judge Persky into highly stylized and grotesque images of them, and which then also were featured in various news stories:

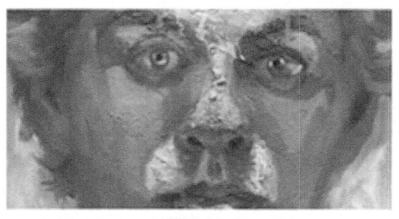
Fig. 23. Cruel distorted picture of Turner published in *USA Today*.

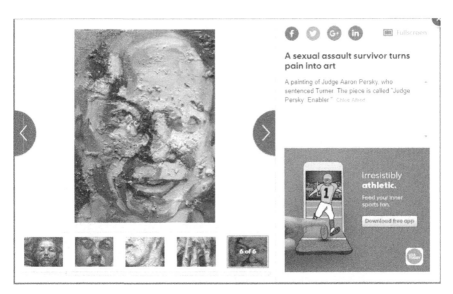

Fig. 24. Cruel distorted picture of Judge Persky published in *USA Today*.

While the recall campaign against Judge Persky was pending, the *Washington Post* and *USA Today* posted at their web sites, a few months one from the other, slightly different two-minute grotesque and hateful videos but with remarkably similar text, photos, and background music. When alumni volunteers contacted both news organizations and questioned the source of the videos, advised them of the factual errors, and showed that the videos likely constituted improper in-kind campaign contributions, both the *Washington Post* and *USA Today* responded that the videos were entirely the work of their reporters and that they stood by what was posted.

Some of the traditional news and social media abuses – probably most of them – also are the response to algorithms at Google and other search engines and social media that increase the chances of being highlighted by use of trigger words such as "rape" and "Stanford." In fact, it appears part of the campaign against Turner was to elevate his name sufficiently so that his name alone could increase the algorithm rankings. And thus the web taglines, even by media including the *New York Times*, *USA Today*, and others, typically used and continue to use the words "rape" in their web taglines, for any stories related to Turner or Judge Persky, and even if the word "rape" appears nowhere in the stories themselves.

In the *Wall Street Journal* article, "How Google Interferes With its Search Algorithms and Changes Your Results," the article states, "Over time, Google has increasingly re-engineered and interfered with search results to a far greater degree than the company and its executives have acknowledged, a *Wall Street Journal* investigation has found." Moreover, "Despite publicly denying doing so, Google keeps blacklists to remove certain sites or prevent others from surfacing in certain types of results. These moves are separate from those that block sites as required by U.S. or foreign law…"[162]

Could it be that Google, headquartered in Santa Clara County, interfered with the June 5, 2018 Santa Clara County election to sway voters to recall Judge Persky? Interestingly, Prof. Dauber's husband, Ken Dauber, has worked as a software engineer at Google since 2007. In an email obtained from the Santa Clara County District Attorney's office via the California Public Records Act, in which Prof. Dauber wrote to Turner's prosecutor Alaleh Kianerci concerning an individual who was broadcasting personal information about Chanel Miller from unredacted court transcripts, Prof. Dauber said:

> "Ken [Prof. Dauber's husband] is working through connections at Twitter we will see what we can do. He [Ken] already got one account taken down but he [the third party] just started using this one."[163]

Trial by Twitter

Intense and extensive public Internet shaming and disinformation against Brock Turner resulted in a mob-initiated court of public opinion "Trial by Twitter" that deemed Turner guilty of rape even before his pre-trial hearing and formal trial. There was so much public hostility and false information circulating against Turner that it became impossible for Turner to receive a fair trial. The 12 jurors in Turner's case would almost certainly have heard the disinformation and public shaming against Turner well before Turner's formal trial, as social and traditional media disseminated disinformation and labeled Turner a rapist almost immediately after the alleged January 18, 2015 hookup. In fact, disinformation and the false description of Turner as a rapist had been spread worldwide for an entire 14 months before Turner's formal trial on March 14, 2016. This lengthy interval of disinformation and false depiction of Turner as a rapist could have engendered juror pre-trial bias against Turner before he even stepped into the courthouse.

As noted earlier, Turner was never tried for rape. Rather, the District Attorney and the prosecutor brought rape charges and left them pending for nearly nine months even though they knew shortly after the incident that there was no evidence of rape whatsoever. Worse, as also discussed elsewhere, Turner's DNA was not found on Chanel nor on her underwear, and the District Attorney and prosecutor also knew that fact not long after the incident.

But the fake rape charges became shaming and a very important tool for the cyberbullying.

The Psychology of Cyber-Shaming

According to clinical psychotherapist and media contributor Dr. Aaron Balick:

"Shame is a difficult and intensely uncomfortable emotion to have, some might say it's one of the worst emotions one can experience."[164]

Cyber-shaming and bullying often have lasting, and even lifetime negative effects on its victims, as victims can experience a variety of medical conditions such as migraines, heart conditions, and gastrointestinal symptoms, and emotional problems such as anxiety, insomnia, depression, eating disorders, loneliness, self-injury, and suicidal ideation. Sadly, cyber-shaming has resulted in victims, many of whom were young people, taking their own lives. Suicide may have been what some cyberbullying/shaming victims believed was their only hope in ending their harrowing emotional pain. Words can't adequately describe how sorrowful and heartbreaking the loss of life due to suicide is to victims' families, who will forever feel the pain, anguish, and despair of the loss of their loved ones.

Very importantly, suicide is not a solution; life is precious, help is available, and problems can be solved. Anyone considering suicide should seek immediate help from appropriate sources, call the **toll-free and confidential** National Suicide Prevention Lifeline (NSPL) at 1–800–273–

TALK (8255), or call 911. The NSPL service is free and available 24 hours per day.

Who Does This?

The actions against Turner and his family have been constant and hardly accidental. What is particularly strange is that the attacks and apparent hatred continue, especially by some individuals, almost six years later.

In addition to the gun-toting protestors that appeared outside the Turner home for several weeks on end after his release from jail, a family friend had tried to raise money to help with the legal fees. Her name and other personal information were posted on the web and she was viciously attacked for weeks thereafter. GoFundMe refused to open an account to help on the basis they don't allow fund-raising for convicted felons, which in other cases seems not to be true. When Turner started working for a landscaping company, the name of his employer was posted on the web as well as locations where they were working, with the admonition that both Turner and the landscaping company should be fired by their clients. Viscous lies and even statements that Turner should die were posted regularly at Facebook, Twitter, and other social media, but when those entities were contacted, they said there was nothing they could or would do.

One of the most recent attacks was a gift shop near the Turner home in Ohio that posted a message on a blackboard outside the store. A photo of the sign was then posted on Twitter by Stanford Prof. David Palumbo-Liu and re-tweeted by Prof. Dauber on August 11, 2020 – this was more than 5-1/2 years after the alleged assault. It's odd that these two older adults – Profs. Palumbo-Liu and Dauber – remain so fixated on a case that happened nearly six years ago and that their views are expressed with such personal vilification. What would Stanford do if a senior staff member behaved this way regarding a former freshman, and worse, from almost six years ago? This is no longer an issue of tenure or First Amendment rights.

In the *HuffPost* article, "Online Shaming: A Virtual Playground for Adults," author Sue Sheff makes the point that:

"What's not normal is that the cyber-attacks are being made by adults. We aren't talking about youth anymore. These are adults that should know better and need to grow up."[165]

Fig. 25. Tweet posted on Twitter by Prof. David Palumbo-Liu and re-tweeted by Prof. Dauber August 11, 2020.

Likewise, student publications at Stanford continue to publish attacks against Turner and anyone who might raise questions and concerns about what actually took place in the case. Moreover, there are numerous reports and actual incidents where it appears that Prof. Dauber and possibly others are allowed to review and edit the student by-lined articles before the articles are published, and sometimes where the headlines and articles are revised even after publication to insert language that is more in line with Prof. Dauber's themes.

People who raise contrary issues are often banned for life from posting any further comments at the Stanford student publications. Who decides what are and aren't acceptable comments, especially in an academic community that seeks diversity of speech and thought and the comments state verifiable facts? And then of all things, the speaker is banned, not the content of their speech. The degree of censorship in these student publications is contrary to the cherished concepts of freedom of expression and sharing of ideas, which university students should encourage, not deter.

Fig. 26. One of several *Stanford Daily* commenters who reportedly are banned for life after posting fact-based opinions on the Turner matter (comment and poster's name redacted).

On August 18, 2020, again more than 5-1/2 years after the alleged assault, and shortly before the 2020 Republican National Convention, Jena Friedman, a standup comedian and former field producer at *The Daily Show*, posted the following false statement on Twitter:[166]

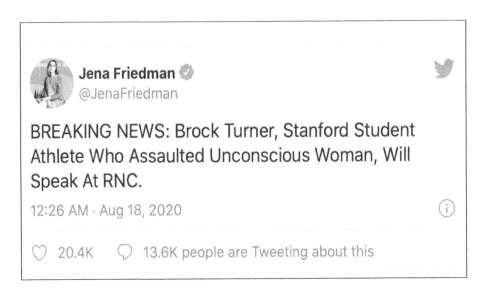

Fig. 27. Cruel tweet by Jena Friedman.

Again, it was strange that a television comedian would somehow refer to Turner by name and so many years later. Apparently, a large number of people on social media believed the false tweet – something that was likely intended – and responded accordingly. Ms. Friedman's tweet also appeared on Facebook. Ms. Friedman later explained that her tweet was meant as "satire." But using cruelty against others for the purpose of entertainment is inexcusable and outright inhumane.

The terrible effects cyber vigilantism and public shaming can have on victims raises the question, who would engage in such destructive and cruel behavior against their fellow human beings – and in this case against someone who was a 19-year-old freshman at the time? According to psychologists, bullies lack empathy, they may have been victims of bullying themselves, and they may have experienced abuse or one or more other traumatic events. Bullying others places the bully at risk for substance abuse and depression. In her article, "Common Characteristics of a Bully," Amy Morin, LCSW states:

"Bullying may stem from underlying psychological issues. Mental health issues, like anxiety, or a behavior disorder, like oppositional defiant disorder, may contribute to bullying."[167]

According to Dr. Balick:

"Shaming says more about the person doing the shaming, than the person being shamed."[168]

Cyber bullies, seated in front of their computer screens inflicting emotional pain and humiliation on their intended invisible victims, don't see their victims' suffering, sorrow, and tears. Shaming and bullying, in any forms, are direct threats to human dignity and highlight the cruel and sadistic elements of the personalities of those who participate in hurting others. Unfortunately, and to the detriment of society, studies show that:

"…given the right circumstances, only a quarter of people have the fortitude to stand up and say, 'I'm not going to participate in this.'"[169]

How utterly sad.

Embrace the Moral Code of Ethics

Brock Turner is in a sense a victim and casualty of the #MeToo movement, which has morphed into an agenda of disparity to the detriment of boys and men. Turner, who was only 19 when the sexual incident with 22-year-old Chanel Miller occurred, has been persistently publicly shamed, cyber-lynched, vilified, lied about, and pictured all over the Internet/news media – far beyond the scope of punishment anyone would deserve. Even cold-blooded mass murderers are treated with more humanity than Turner.

The Internet has served as a major tool for people to bully and attack Turner and Judge Persky even years after Turner's trial and sentencing. According to the nymag.com article, "The Internet Apologizes:"

"the Silicon Valley dream of building a networked utopia turned into a globalized strip-mall casino overrun by pop-up ads and cyberbullies and Vladimir Putin.

"those who built the internet have provided us with a clear and disturbing account of why everything went so wrong -- how the technology they created has been used to undermine the very aspects of a free society that made that technology possible in the first place."[170]

On a more optimistic note, it is hoped all is not lost because there are still members of society who will condemn the types of vicious and cruel cyber and other attacks that permeated the Turner case and others like it. There still are people who have the moral decency and strength of character to take the moral high ground against cruelty and hatred and say, "I will not participate."

It is likewise hoped that, through the material in this book and other sources, there will be people at Stanford, in Santa Clara County, nationally, and worldwide who will finally address the injustices against Turner that have taken place in the Turner case.

Chapter 14

The Recall of Judge Aaron Persky

"The #MeToo movement is – perhaps unintentionally – pushing mercy out of the courtroom and replacing it with spite."[171]

Judge Persky – Another Undeserved Victim

Another undeserved victim ensnared by the #MeToo movement, social media, non-factual news reports, and ongoing attacks by Stanford law school Prof. Michele Dauber was Santa Clara County Superior Court Judge Aaron Persky, who was recalled from the bench due to his sentencing in the Turner case. Judge Persky was recalled largely because Prof. Dauber and the recall proponents falsely claimed, and then highly publicized, that Judge Persky showed bias in favor of privileged White male athletes when in fact virtually all of his past cases that were wrongly criticized involved non-privileged, non-White defendants, and virtually all were plea deals between the defendants and the District Attorney's office. (See Chapter 15 for a detailed analysis of the cases.)

Judge Persky, who had a stellar record during his then-13 years on the bench, was perceived by some as having handed a light sentence to Brock Turner, a 19-year-old first-year Stanford student and star swimmer convicted of sexual assault. In reality, Turner's sentence was by no means light. In fact, Turner was sentenced to six months in jail, three years' probation, sex offender rehabilitation, Alcoholics Anonymous participation, and the most devastating mandate of all, a requirement to register for life as a Tier III registered sex offender – a draconian, oppressive, and life-altering sentence for a young man. Turner's lifelong Tier III sex registration sentence is rarely mentioned by traditional news outlets and social media; therefore, many members of the public are unaware that Turner's sentencing included this requirement that, among other things, mandates him to reregister quarterly, in many jurisdictions post signs at his home on Halloween, not be within specified feet of a school or playground, and if he has children, likely to be under severe restrictions about being at his children's schools or having their friends to the house. And of course, even if he was guilty of what he was charged with (there is mounting evidence he in fact was wrongly charged and convicted, as discussed throughout this book), nothing he did had anything to do with children.

Turner's sentence of three years' probation meant he was required to follow strict rules and regulations that, if breached, could result in his incarceration. Failure to adhere to the terms of Tier III sex offender registration, including appearing in person to reregister every three months up to the end of his life, could also result in incarceration. Probation, felony convictions, and in particular Turner's sentence as a Tier III registrant, are in fact severe sentences. Sex offender registration is in a sense a form of banishment from society.

In other words, the sentence imposed by Judge Persky was hardly a light sentence, but that fact didn't fit the narrative being developed by Prof. Dauber, District Attorney Jeff Rosen, and their associates.

Judge Persky: A Fair and Compassionate Judge

Judge Persky was known as a fair and compassionate judge who was respectful towards all those who stood before him in court. According to Santa Clara County deputy public defender Gary Goodman:

"He [Persky] has high integrity, he follows the law . . . You won't find a lawyer who has been in front of him and says that he hasn't been treated with respect and fairness."[172]

Former Santa Clara County Superior Court Judge Len Edwards, a highly regarded and compassionate judge and founder of various child and family advocacy groups such as Court Appointed Special Advocates for children (CASA), foster youth programs, and the Santa Clara Domestic Violence Council, had similar high praise for Judge Persky, saying:

"Once on the bench, we all recognized Judge Persky as an outstanding judge, both hardworking and fair. In all of his judicial decisions, Judge Persky followed the law, as he did in the Brock Turner case. In that case, he adopted the recommendations of the Santa Clara County Probation Office. That office conducted an extensive investigation of Turner's background and, using sophisticated tests, concluded that Turner should not be sent to prison. Judge Persky followed that recommendation . . . I believe we want our judges to be independent and to rule based on the law, not on public pressure."[173]

In a *Mercury News* letter to the editor titled "Judge Persky is Among Our Most Capable Jurists," San Jose attorney Ronald Meckler said:

"I have appeared before Judge Aaron Persky numerous times in Family Court. I have admired him as one of our most capable and thoughtful jurists. He is the opposite of how the Michele Dauber movement portrays him. If we lose him as a judge, it will be a travesty for our community and a personal tragedy for Judge Persky's family."[174]

In opposition to the recall, Retired Judge LaDoris Cordell, who was the first African American to serve as a Superior Court judge in Northern California, expressed that:

"I believe it [the recall] is a dangerous threat to the independence of the judiciary ... [Persky] has no record of bias or misconduct. And I'm opposed to it because I believe this recall is terrible for racial justice. ... A lot of the defendants are young people, and mostly males, of color — Latino and African-American. They are the ones who are going to receive the sentencings of these judges who are going to be hesitant, if not fearful, to impose a leniency in a sentence."[175]

In the *New York Times*, Santa Clara County public defender Molly O'Neal is quoted as saying she was "alarmed by the hysteria" associated with the Turner sentence:

"The judge is required under California law to consider certain mitigating and aggravating factors...including past criminal records and the presence of alcohol . . . We need to be very careful we're not hanging judges out to dry based on one decision, especially because he is considered to be a fair and even-tempered judge."[176]

Santa Clara County public defender Barbara Muller made the comment:

"My clients are all indigent and most of them are nonwhite . . . I have never seen him [Judge Persky] treat my clients differently than those clients who can afford private attorneys."[177]

Not only was Judge Persky a respected and compassionate judge, but Judge Persky was an active and respected executive committee member of the Support Network for Battered Women, he selflessly worked pro bono for underprivileged women and men, and he volunteered for the Santa Clara County Network for a Hate-Free Community. For his exemplary work on hate crimes, Judge Persky received the California Association of Human Relations Organizations' Civil Rights Leadership Award, and the California State Bar presented Judge Persky with the Wiley Manuel Pro Bono Award for his dedicated efforts in working pro bono for the poor.

Michele Dauber Launched the Recall Campaign

Shortly after Turner's sentencing on June 2, 2016, Michele Dauber, a Stanford law school professor and a friend of Chanel Miller and her family, began a deceitful campaign to smear and ultimately recall Judge Persky, who was the subject of the ballot measure to recall him as a Superior Court judge in the upcoming June 5, 2018 Santa Clara County election. Prof. Dauber carried out a vicious social media attack against Judge Persky by spreading disinformation and slandering, defaming, and bullying the judge and those supporting him. And in the midst of it all, there are indications Google's algorithms were used to give high priority to any postings supporting the recall and to make it virtually impossible to find postings with opposing views including even to find the web site for the committee supporting Judge Persky. Facebook appears to have been similarly used, including monthly payments of $7,000 by the recall committee to Facebook according to required public disclosures of campaign expenditures.

On June 6, 2016, required political disclosures show that some of the initial campaign contributions were made to Washington and Sacramento political action committees for subsequent distribution to the Committee to Recall Judge Aaron Persky. On June 10, 2016, the California Legislative Women's Caucus announced its intent to raise money for the recall campaign. In total, $1.4 million was raised from various sources to recall Judge Persky—many of these sources were from out of Santa Clara County and from other states. Approximately $500,000 of these funds were used to pay signature gatherers to obtain signatures for the petition to place the recall measure on the ballot. On February 6, 2018, the Santa Clara Board of Supervisors approved placement of the recall measure on the June 5, 2018 election ballot.[178]

Public Defenders and Other Lawyers Wrote Open Letter Opposing the Recall

An open letter to the Commission on Judicial Performance in opposition to the recall, dated June 15, 2016 and signed by mostly public defenders and defense lawyers, was written in support of Judge Persky and the concept of judicial independence. The letter was also posted on change.org and ultimately acquired a total of 444 signatures.

Spearheaded by Santa Clara County deputy public defender Sajid Kahn, the letter emphasized that Judge Persky legally applied the laws set before him and lawfully used judicial discretion in a fair and merciful manner and in line with the probation department's recommendations. Furthermore, the supporters weren't aware of any improprieties or complaints against Judge Persky during his 13 years on the bench. The supporters noted that recalling Judge Persky would:

> ". . . deter other judges from extending mercy and instead encourage them to issue unfairly harsh sentences for fear of reprisal. We fear that this shift will disproportionally impact the underprivileged and minorities in our communities and perpetuate mass incarceration."[179]

181

Stanford Law School Graduates Wrote Open Letter Opposing the Recall

On June 25, 2016, the *Stanford Daily* published an article concerning an open letter to Prof. Dauber from 53 members of the Stanford Law School graduating Class of 2016 advocating that Prof. Dauber stop her efforts to recall Judge Persky. The students were concerned that the recall would set a harmful precedent for recalling judges who handed down sentences that the public perceived as too lenient, and that recalling judges would compromise judicial independence. The letter stated in part:

> "As we've learned during our time at the law school, judicial independence is a cornerstone of due process and an essential prerequisite for a fair criminal justice system."[180]

The letter continued:

> "If we demand that Judge Persky immediately hand over his gavel for acting on his empathy for this defendant, how can we credibly assure any other judge that her hand need not waver when the human circumstances of a case seem to call for compassion?"[181]

One of the letter writers, Akiva Freidlin, was quoted in the *Stanford Daily* article as pointing out that recalling Judge Persky:

> "goes against the principles that allow us to have a system where an independent judiciary applies laws that they don't make."[182] The letter concluded with the recommendation that Prof. Dauber pursue other methods of tackling judicial reform such as through "educating future judges and jurors about the realities of sexual assault and pressing for systemic changes in how these cases are handled."[183]

While the letter focused on the critical importance of preserving judicial independence and mercy in sentencing decisions, it's disappointing that the writers questioned Turner's six-month jail sentence, but made no mention of Turner's worst requirement of all, his devastating and barbaric sentence as a lifetime Tier III sex offender registrant. Nor did the law students apparently take the time to learn the details of the case itself. As already mentioned, it's a lifetime scarlet letter the extent of which not even cold-blooded murderers are required to bear. Ironically, even Prof. Dauber was quoted as saying ten years as a sex offender registrant was more than enough. And remember, Chanel Miller told the probation officer that Turner didn't even need to be behind bars and that she didn't want his life ruined.

California Law Professors Wrote Letter Opposing the Recall

In August 2017, over 90 California law professors from throughout California wrote a letter titled, "Law Professors' Statement for the Independence of the Judiciary and Against the Recall of Santa Clara County Superior Court Judge Aaron Persky," in which they stated:

"We write in strong opposition to the campaign to recall Judge Aaron Persky of the Santa Clara Superior Court." They continued that the recall "threatens the fundamental principles of judicial independence and fairness that we all embed in the education of our students,"

and that:

"The mechanism of recall was designed for and must be limited to cases where judges are corrupt or incompetent or exhibit bias that leads to systematic injustice in their courtrooms. None of these criteria applies to Judge Persky."[184]

The law professors continued:

"the defense bar's outpouring of opposition to the recall underscores Judge Persky's reputation for being unbiased against those most harshly disadvantaged by our criminal justice system. A broad range of lawyers who have appeared before Judge Persky have publicly attested to the respect they have for him as a fair and impartial jurist."[185]

Retired Judges' Open Letter Opposing the Recall

While the California Judicial Code of Ethics doesn't allow sitting judicial officers to comment on "pending or impending" issues, a group of Santa Clara County retired judges submitted a letter titled "Open Letter on the Need for Judicial Independence" in which they referenced Judge Persky's decision in the Turner case. The retired judges affirmed that judges' decisions should be based on the facts of each case and applicable laws, not on political or public opinion, and that judges should have the freedom to exercise discretion within the bounds of the law.

The judges stated that recalling a judge due to illegal or unethical conduct is appropriate, but that:

"calls to remove a judge because of a decision, even a very unpopular one, when that judge exercised discretion permitted under the law, is an entirely different matter. The essence of judicial independence is that judges must be able to make decisions without fear of political repercussions."[186]

In relation to the Turner case, the former judges said:

"Judge Persky made his decision after considering all the evidence presented at trial, the statements of the victim and the defendant, and a detailed report from an experienced probation officer. The probation officer [a longstanding female member of the probation department] recommended essentially the sentence that was imposed, including the grant of probation."[187]

The judges' letter concluded with the statement that recalling Judge Persky would:

"set a dangerous precedent and be a serious threat to judicial independence."[188]

Despite the fact that many lawyers, judges, and others associated with the justice system and who are generally more knowledgeable than the public regarding the negative impacts of recalling a judge who followed the rule of law, the recall campaign prevailed. This brings up the issues that voters often may not have adequate knowledge to make informed decisions regarding the recall of a judge, and that the voters, easily swayed, are vulnerable to fake news, deceptive advertising, and the impact of unreliable social media content. The intentional misuse and abuse of social and other media in the Turner case especially exacerbated the situation.

Santa Clara County District Attorney Jeff Rosen Opposed the Recall (sort of)

In Santa Clara County, District Attorney Jeff Rosen issued a letter to the public titled, "I support Emily Doe and oppose the recall." In that letter, Rosen wrote that Judge Persky imposed a sentence that was lawful and concurred with the recommendation of the probation department, but Rosen also said he believed the sentence was too lenient. In other words, Rosen was playing both sides, no doubt for political purposes. If Rosen believed the sentence was too lenient, one wonders why Rosen, as the county's District Attorney, didn't appeal the sentence? According to Erwin Chemerinsky, who is dean of the law school at the University of California at Berkeley, and who strongly opposed the recall:

"Judges should not be punished for following the recommendation of the district attorney and the probation department. If a district attorney thinks the sentence was lenient, they can appeal it, but don't recall the judge."[189]

Rosen further stated in his letter:

"I support the principle of recall, but only in circumstances where a judge has exhibited a pattern of abuse or favor for one group of people over another, is unable to perform his duties, or is biased . . . The findings of our local bar, the State's Commission of Judicial Performance, and my review of Judge Persky's decisions have concluded the same thing: there is no pattern."[190]

Unfortunately, there also were numerous indications that District Attorney Rosen and his staff were simultaneously working with Prof. Dauber in support of the recall.

Michele Dauber's Use of the Santa Clara County District Attorney's Office Resources

Prof. Dauber, who graduated from law school but was never admitted to the bar, and who was not and never was employed by the Santa Clara County District Attorney's office, made extensive use of the DA's office to obtain information regarding Judge Persky's previous cases, which Prof. Dauber subsequently distorted and misrepresented to the public to help support her recall campaign (Ch. 15). Hundreds of emails were exchanged between Prof. Dauber and DA's office employees, including District Attorney Jeff Rosen, Assistant DA Terry Harman, Deputy DA Alaleh Kianerci (Brock Turner's prosecutor), Sexual Assault Unit Director Luis Ramos, Assistant DA Cindy Hendrickson, public relations director Sean Webby, and others.

Cindy Hendrickson ultimately ran for and won Judge Persky's seat in the June 5, 2018 county election. Being neither a DA's office employee nor a member of the bar, Prof. Dauber nevertheless apparently had unprecedented privileges and access to tax-payer-funded DA's office resources, yet the vast extent of these DA's office services used by Prof. Dauber would not have been available to most other, if any other, members of the tax-paying public. This has raised suspicions that Prof. Dauber and the DA's office were acting in collusion to achieve Prof. Dauber's goals of unseating Judge Persky and replacing Judge Persky with Cindy Hendrickson, a member of the DA's office own staff.

Fig. 28. Prof. Dauber's email depicting her use of the District Attorney's office resources, and employing student volunteers for research purposes.

An example of ongoing correspondence (subsequently disclosed via Public Records Act requests) between Prof. Dauber and the DA's office staff is Prof. Dauber's email to Assistant DA Terry Harman stating:

"Can I ask you another favor? I would like to get a list of the cases (names and numbers) heard in Judge Persky's courtroom going back as far as I can but at least the past few years" [email dated 7/7/2016].

These cases, of course, were for the purpose of smearing Judge Persky in an attempt to secure his recall from the bench. Some of Prof. Dauber's emails also discuss arranging phone calls between her and various DA's office staff, including Jeff Rosen.

In an email sent by Prof. Dauber to Assistant DA Terry Harman regarding a case (the Gunderson case) that Prof. Dauber ultimately publicly spun to sway public opinion, Prof. Dauber wrote:

"Please don't share the Gunderson case to anyone due to the press exclusives. Please do keep it between us for another 2 weeks before it comes out" [email dated 8/18/2016, as also shown in subsequent Public Records Act disclosures]. [Boldface added]

It appears here that Prof. Dauber was able to dictate the conditions under which the DA's office could communicate with the media.

Prof. Dauber had long managed to obtain important connections with a number of national and international news outlets including *The Guardian*, *Buzzfeed*, the *New York Times*, the *Washington Post*, the *San Francisco Chronicle*, the *Mercury News*, and *Palo Alto Online*. In fact, *Buzzfeed* reporter Tyler Kingkade had been a guest speaker in at least one of Prof. Dauber's classes. Specifically, Kingkade was a speaker in Prof. Dauber's class on February 27, 2018, approximately three months before the June 5, 2018 Santa Clara County election in which Judge Persky was recalled.

Interestingly, emails obtained through the California Public Records Act indicate that not only had *Buzzfeed* reporter Kingkade been a speaker in one or more of Prof. Dauber's classes, but other key individuals related to the Turner case had strategically been scheduled as speakers as well. For example, Turner's lawyer Mike Armstrong, Deputy District Attorney Luis Ramos (Santa Clara County Sexual Assault Unit supervisor), Stanford Police Chief Laura Wilson, and Lauren Schoenthaler, the Stanford Senior University Counsel who would later approve the $150,000 settlement with Chanel and also agree to posting quotes at a memorial to be built, were all invited to speak at Prof. Dauber's sophomore college class in early September 2015, approximately eight months after the alleged sexual assault.

Fig. 29. Email from Schoenthaler indicating Turner's lawyer Mike Armstrong, Stanford Police Chief Laura Wilson, Deputy District Attorney Luis Ramos, and Stanford's then-Senior University Counsel Schoenthaler would participate in a two-hour session of Prof. Dauber's sophomore college class in 2015.

The class session described in Fig. 29 was scheduled for September 1, 2015, approximately one month before Turner's preliminary hearing. A *Palo Alto Weekly* reporter also was scheduled to attend, apparently to cover the event and not as a speaker.

Fig. 30. Email from Schoenthaler advising the others that the reporter from the *Palo Alto Weekly* would be unable to attend the September 1, 2015 class after all.

Schoenthaler's email (Fig. 30) raises the questions, what is the "major irony" that a reporter wouldn't be covering the session, why would that impact whether Deputy DA Ramos would still be willing to participate even though a reporter wouldn't be present after all, and why are reporters even being allowed to cover an academic class that presumably is not otherwise open to the public or even to other students?

On Sep 6, 2016, at 2:58 PM, Luis Ramos ▮▮▮▮▮▮▮▮▮▮ wrote:

Hi Michele. Thanks for your note. I think it's fine for you to inform the class at the outset that we will not discuss the Turner case. I have no objection to the reporter's presence under the scenario you describe below. Will you please provide the address and/or directions where I need to go tomorrow at 9:00? Thanks, L.

Luis M. Ramos
Supervising Deputy District Attorney, Sexual Assault
Santa Clara County
408.792.2793

▮▮▮▮▮▮▮▮▮▮▮▮▮

>>> Michele Dauber ▮▮▮▮▮▮▮▮▮ 9/3/2016 2:42 PM >>>
Hi All:

This is to make you aware of two things. First, Luis stated to me that he does not want to have discussion of the Turner case. That is fine with me as a groundrule and Mike I assume you feel the same way. Shall I just state that at the outset?

Second, a student reporter from the Stanford Daily would like to attend class that day. I am generally inclined toward openness and transparency and allow reporters and community members to attend all my classes generally speaking. I have told her that she cannot quote anyone in the class other than me without their specific consent, including students and guest speakers (in other words, everything is off the record unless she gets a specific consent after class from the speaker). If you are uncomfortable with her being there even under that rule, please let me know ASAP.

Best,
Michele

Fig. 31. Emails a year later (September 2016) between Santa Clara County Deputy DA Luis Ramos and Prof. Dauber indicating that Ramos would not discuss the Turner case during his speaking engagement in Prof. Dauber's class, but that a *Stanford Daily* reporter would be present in the classroom.

Note that the class session mentioned in Fig. 31 was six days after Turner's release from jail (that is, on September 1, 2016) and where Prof. Dauber had been involved at the jail site in a highly publicized rally against Turner. See also Figures 6, 7, and 8. And again, this class and the class a year earlier were being offered for credit and limited to students especially selected for a given year's sophomore college. It would be quite unusual for any classes, including sophomore college classes, to have non-students attend and especially reporters. Yet Prof. Dauber seems to have an unusual practice of wanting at least some of her classes covered by the media and even though, according to the syllabi she uses and distributes, during the school year she prohibits students themselves from using laptops, cell phones, and other web surfing devices during her classes.

It appears that Prof. Dauber was using her Stanford classes to establish strategic rapport with key individuals at Stanford and in Santa Clara County in addition to reporters as part of her planned and ongoing attacks against Turner and Judge Persky. On the other hand, she apparently prohibits students from checking facts and the backgrounds of speakers during her class sessions and, at least from a review of her syllabi, she doesn't disclose her own role in the 2011 Dear Colleague letter or other materials on which students are expected to comment and will be graded.

The Recall Campaign Was Based on Deception

Through Prof. Dauber's direct discussions with members of the District Attorney's office and by enlisting her students to help research Judge Persky's past cases (note that enlisting students' assistance would be inappropriate under certain circumstances), Prof. Dauber chose six of Judge Persky's past cases to scrutinize, distort, and misrepresent to the public. These cases are discussed in detail in Chapter 15 and represent the core of Prof. Dauber's false recall campaign statements about Judge Persky's record.

Many suspect Prof. Dauber not only used extensive DA's office resources, but she likely made use of Stanford University resources (her office, office supplies, electronics, etc.) to fuel and sustain her campaign to unseat Judge Persky. The records (emails, schedules, etc.) also indicate that Prof. Dauber was working essentially full-time on the recall and not doing other things normally expected of a full-time faculty member.

Stanford Law School Prof. Dauber Promoted the Sale of Merchandise, *"The Shop is Open!"*

Fig. 32. Recall campaign's advertisement for store items promoting recall of Judge Persky.

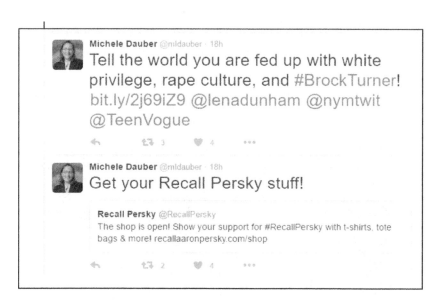

Fig. 33. Prof. Dauber's tweet falsely associating Turner with rape and promoting shop selling Recall Judge Persky items.

The Recall Campaign Took the Low Road, Used Playbook from the Dolphin Group's Notorious Willie Horton Campaign

Fig. 34. The recall campaign's Willie Horton-style attack ad against Judge Persky.

Besides the consistent persecution of both Judge Persky and Brock Turner and the high volume of false information disseminated by the recall campaign against them, the recall campaign took an even lower road and circulated posters and yard signs depicting Judge Persky and Turner in an offensive Willie Horton-style political attack ad campaign.

By way of background, when the notorious Willie Horton ad was first circulated in 1988 by the George H. W. Bush campaign, the purpose of the

194

ad, created by the political consulting firm known as the Dolphin Group, was to associate Michael Dukakis, Bush's Democratic political rival, with Willie Horton, a Black man in prison for murder who was a participant in a controversial weekend furlough program. As the governor of Massachusetts, Dukakis had vetoed a bill that would have prevented prisoners with first-degree murder convictions from participating in a prison furlough program of this nature.[191]

After failing to return to prison during a weekend furlough, Horton raped a White woman, and knifed and inflicted various injuries on her fiancé. The aforementioned ad was intended to frighten White people and give the appearance that Dukakis was soft on crime. Similarly, the recall campaign's Willie Horton-style ad campaign was intended to convince voters that Judge Persky was soft on sex offenders.

The Recall Campaign's Communications Director Was a Dolphin Group Partner

Interestingly, Becky Warren, the Recall Judge Persky campaign's communications director, was a Dolphin Group partner when she started working with the recall campaign. Ms. Warren later left the Dolphin group when that association became an item of discussion and co-founded a Los Angeles-based political consulting firm known as Elevate.[192]

It should be noted, subsequent to the Willie Horton attack ad campaign, the Dolphin Group was involved in numerous other political campaigns, including in California where it is based and where its tactics were regularly questioned by commenters and others. For example, in 1994 the Dolphin Group created an entity called the Californians for Statewide Smoking Restrictions in an effort to pass Prop. 188, a proposition that would, contrary to its name, severely weaken existing smoking restrictions. In other words, Californians for Statewide Smoking Restrictions was actually a deceptive "Trojan Horse" funded by major tobacco companies. According to former State Assemblyman Terry Friedman, the campaign was "the most deceptive campaign in my quarter century of close observation of politics."[193] Years later, when reviewing these and similar political campaigns run by the Dolphin Group, an article in the *Huffington Post* referred to the company as "the Dark Messenger."

Given this background, it was somewhat surprising that in a November 2016 tweet, just as the recall campaign was getting underway against Judge Persky, Prof. Dauber herself made specific reference to Willie Horton, a strange but possibly not coincidental posting given the Dolphin Group's history and their involvement at the time of the posting in the recall campaign against Judge Persky:

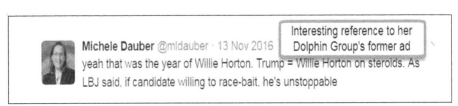

Fig. 35. Prof. Dauber's tweet referencing the Dolphin Group, her campaign manager's former company.

The Recall Campaign Regularly Distorted Facts

The Recall Judge Persky campaign, led by Prof. Dauber, continually distorted the facts and used the "rape" word as often as possible. Note in this fundraising email (Fig. 36, below) dated February 23, 2017, Prof. Dauber distorted the facts from the trial and in the public record and says Turner "dragged [Chanel] behind a dumpster and sexually assaulted her while she was unconscious." Of course, no one ever alleged that Chanel had been carried or dragged anywhere. Because she hadn't been. And as discussed in earlier chapters, everything occurred in front of a wooden shed (not dumpster), in full public view, and with a very high likelihood that Chanel appeared to Turner as fully functioning.

Prof. Dauber's fund-raising email then states Turner was sentenced to "only six months in county jail," omitting the fact that Turner was ordered to register as a sex offender registrant for the rest of his life. And as previously mentioned, Prof. Dauber had in the past indicated that a ten-year, not a lifetime, sex offender registration mandate would have been enough for Turner.

Prof. Dauber then falsely states "this is not an isolated incident for Judge Persky—he has a disturbing history of shielding offenders of domestic and sexual violence from justice." Prof. Dauber's misrepresentations of Judge Persky's cases are debunked in Chapter 15 of this book.

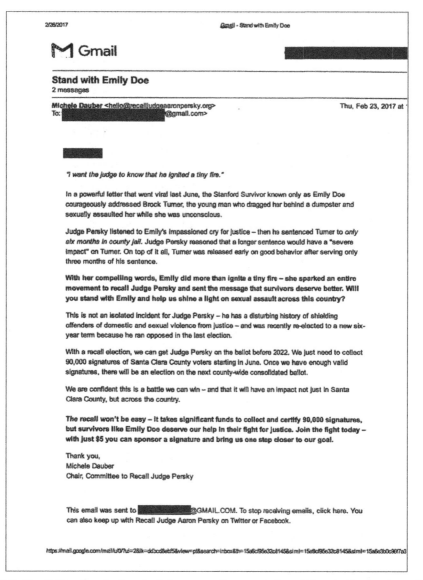

Fig. 36. Prof. Dauber's fundraising email containing false information about Judge Persky and Turner.

The Commission on Judicial Performance and Other Organizations Found No Bias

The Commission on Judicial Performance (CJP) is a state agency and professional organization that investigates complaints of misconduct against judges, and disciplines judges. Contrary to the recall campaign's false claims of Judge Persky's bias in favor of privileged White male athletes, and other falsehoods, the CJP found that:

"[Judge Persky's decisions] do not provide clear and convincing evidence to support the contention that Judge Persky's decisions reflect personal bias in favor of white criminal defendants and/or more privileged criminal defendants, or that he takes crimes involving violence against women less seriously . . . The Turner sentence imposed by Judge Persky was within parameters set by Penal Code section 1203.065(b) and therefore was not unlawful."[194]

The Santa Clara County Bar Association issued the following statement in opposition to the recall of Judge Persky:

"The SCCBA [Santa Clara County Bar Association] opposes the present attempts to remove Judge Persky from the bench based on his sentence in the Brock Turner case. The SCCBA has seen no credible assertions that in issuing the sentence, Judge Persky violated the law or his ethical obligations or acted in bad faith. Nor is the SCCBA aware of any other complaints or allegations of impropriety against Judge Persky during his 13 years on the bench. Seeking to punish a judge under these circumstances presents the very threat to judicial independence that the SCCBA has resolved to condemn.

"Judges have a duty to apply the law to the facts and evidence before them, regardless of public opinion or political pressure. If judges had to fear direct, personal repercussions as a result of their decisions in individual cases, the rule of law would suffer."[195]

The Associated Press, which reviewed 20 of Judge Persky's cases, likewise found no evidence of racial bias or wrongdoing.

Judge Persky Took Night Judge Position

According to the California Code of Civil Procedure and Judicial Ethics Canons, a judge involved in a trial is required to disclose all contributions or loans greater than $100 from a party, individual lawyer, or law office. The disclosure requires listing of the donor's or lender's name, amount and date of contribution or loan, and the cumulative amount of donations or loans from each contributor.

In order to comply with the above requirements, Judge Persky read aloud each of his donors' names before each court session and posted the names of the donors on his court podium. The list was to be updated before each court session. In an interview with the *Palo Alto Daily Post*, Judge Persky said he found the disclosure requirement distasteful. He told the *Palo Alto Daily Post*, "If I get up there on the bench and the ethics rules require me to say, 'That lawyer gave $150 to the campaign and that lawyer gave $200,' it doesn't set, I don't think, the right tone,"[196] The aforementioned disclosure requirement was one of the reasons Judge Persky left his regular court position and instead took an on-call night judge position in the fall of 2017, in which he handled search warrants and emergency protective orders. The disclosure requirement, particularly for Judge Persky who was facing recall, was not only distasteful, but could have resulted in discouraging potential donors from contributing to his campaign.

San Francisco Chronicle and *Palo Alto Daily Post* Opposed the Recall

The *San Francisco Chronicle*, which in 2019 was named by the California News Publishers Association as California's best large newspaper for the fourth year in a row, opposed the recall of Judge Persky. In their endorsement to retain Judge Persky, the *San Francisco Chronicle* Editorial Board wrote in "The Case Against the Recall of Judge Persky":

"Don't blame judges for following their discretion within the law. The recall effort is ill-advised and dangerous. Neither justice for defendants nor the concept of judicial independence is served if judges are guided by their anticipation of public reaction instead of the letter of the law."[197]

The *Palo Alto Daily Post*, considered the Number One newspaper in Palo Alto and the Mid-peninsula, had initially supported the recall, but changed its decision, and on May 10, 2018, the *Palo Alto Daily Post* informed readers that they no longer endorsed the recall, and urged readers to vote "no" on the recall measure. The *Palo Alto Daily Post* editor, Dave Price, surrounded by the recall campaign's forceful and dishonest campaign to recall Judge Persky, had the integrity and courage to closely evaluate the facts and come to his own independent conclusion that the recall effort was wrong. Mr. Price said he had:

"never anticipated that the campaign to remove Judge Persky would result in a lynch-mob movement that threatens the independence of the judiciary."[198]

The *Palo Alto Daily Post* reiterated that Judge Persky's sentencing was lawful, that the Commission on Judicial Performance found no evidence of bias, and that recalling Judge Persky would place judicial independence at risk:

"We don't want judges to be influenced by public opinion. We want judges to follow the law. We don't want them to worry before they make a decision about what people will say about them on Twitter or Facebook."[199]

The *Mercury News* Published its Endorsement of the Recall

In their editorial endorsing the recall measure, "Persky Recall Demands Voters Make Statement on Sexual Assault," the *San Jose Mercury News* editorial board gave the impression that they did not understand the purpose of a judicial recall. The recall process is not for the purpose of making a statement on sexual assault; there are other and better ways to make statements about sexual assault, but not through recall. Instead, the focus should be on important changes such as ensuring rape kits are promptly processed, demanding that colleges and universities take responsibility for controlling alcohol on college campuses, and to change the laws that judges are required to follow, which was later done through passage of A.B. 2888 and A.B. 701. Judges don't make the laws; rather, they follow them in the best interest of the victims and defendants.

The *Mercury News* editorial board praised Judge Persky in that (1) the recall campaign's claims that Judge Persky exhibited a pattern of leniency were actually weak, (2) the Commission on Judicial Performance found no evidence of judicial wrongdoing, and (3) Judge Persky was a "decent man and able judge."[200] The editorial board even went as far as to question whether the recall law should have been written. The *Mercury News'* aforementioned favorable comments portray a judge who should not be recalled. Yet the *Mercury News* editorial board was happy to ruin a fair and well-respected judge's career in order to make a statement, and perhaps appease readers and possibly also Prof. Dauber.

It should be noted that most of the legal community agreed that a recall is appropriate only when a judge shows a pattern of misconduct, incompetence, or engages in illegal conduct, which did not apply to Judge Persky.

The *Mercury News* editorial board said that because Judge Persky's sentencing of Turner failed to make a statement about the seriousness of sexual assault, "he never will again be able to serve as a respected, effective judge."[201] This makes no sense. Judge Persky had a stellar record during his 13 years on the bench, he was considered a fair, intelligent, and compassionate judge, and virtually the entire law community supported him against the recall. The *Mercury News* editorial board somehow decided that because they didn't like one out of Judge Persky's approximately 2000 decisions, he should be the first judge to be recalled in 86 years.

Another erroneous statement made by the *Mercury News* editorial board was, "The judge also failed to take into account the woman's moving statement before delivering the sentence."[202] However, it seems the editorial board missed the part in the trial transcript where Judge Persky said, "And I just want to, before I give my tentative decision, read something from [Chanel's] statement, which I think is appropriate – actually, two things from her statement."[203] Judge Persky then proceeded to read 26 lines from Chanel

Miller's victim impact statement aloud in court, after which he said, "I understand that – as I read – that [Chanel's] life has been devastated by these events, by the – not only the incidents that happened, but the – the criminal process has had such a debilitating impact on people's lives, most notably [Chanel] and her sister."[204]

It should also be remembered, there is substantial evidence that Prof. Dauber, perhaps with Chanel and possibly others, wrote or largely wrote or edited the victim impact statement, and the question arises, did the *Mercury News* know this as well, or at least have suspicions since people in Santa Clara County government, as discussed elsewhere, apparently knew from the very day the statement was read in Judge Persky's courtroom.

As already mentioned, according to emails obtained via the Public Records Act between Prof. Dauber and the District Attorney's office, Prof. Dauber had arrangements with a number of traditional news agencies to which she would send articles, information, and grant interviews on a priority basis. One of these news agencies was the *Mercury News*.

The *Mercury News'* endorsement to recall Judge Persky probably cost Judge Persky his seat on the bench because voters busy with the time-consuming challenges of daily life who lacked the time or interest to research the facts of the recall measure most likely resorted to following the *Mercury News'* endorsement to recall Judge Persky.

San Jose lawyer Ronald Meckler wrote in a *Mercury News* letter to the editor:

> "It was disheartening to read the Mercury News' support of the recall effort as it joins the misguided herd going after Judge Persky's neck. The herd mentality champions slogans over facts; it prefers slick ads over carefully considered justice."[205]

Stanford's Strange Role in the Recall

Public Records Act disclosures now show that in September 2016, the same month as Turner was released from jail and months before the recall was officially announced, Lauren Schoenthaler, at the time a senior lawyer in Stanford's general counsel office, was exchanging emails and using her Stanford general counsel email address to propose lunch for Prof. Dauber,

202

Assistant DA Cindy Hendrickson, and Schoenthaler at Stanford's faculty club. Months later, Ms. Hendrickson announced she was in fact running for Judge Persky's seat and supporting Prof. Dauber's recall efforts.

From: Michele Dauber [mailto███████████████
Sent: Wednesday, September 28, 2016 12:11 PM
To: Lauren Schoenthaler ████████████████████ Hendrickson, Cindy ████████████████████
Subject: lunch meeting

Hi Cindy and Lauren:

Cindy was kind enough to allow me to call and start our conversation over and apologize for the poor communication on my end. We would love to schedule a time for the three of us to have lunch, hopefully week of 10/10 to discuss dating violence and how we can do more to prevent and address it on campus, as well as to educate me further on the problems of DV prosecution in SCC.

Just to get the ball rolling I am good every day that week other than 10/13.

Thanks,

Michele

Fig. 37. Prof. Dauber's September 28, 2016 email pertaining to a lunch meeting with Lauren Schoenthaler and Judge Persky's later successor Cindy Hendrickson.

More recently, it has been disclosed that Schoenthaler was the initially unidentified Stanford lawyer who apparently negotiated the then-confidential settlement with Chanel Miller. Later disclosures of that settlement indicate that Schoenthaler approved a $150,000 payment to Chanel and her sister Tiffany and also committed Stanford to building a memorial (later rebranded as a "contemplative garden") and that Chanel and apparently Prof. Dauber would select quotes from Chanel's victim impact statement to be posted at that site – a statement discussed in other chapters that in fact appears to have been written, at least in part, by Prof. Dauber herself. When Stanford later reneged on the agreement about the quotes, Chanel and Prof. Dauber publicly revealed that Schoenthaler was the Stanford lawyer involved in it all. Further pressures were then brought upon Stanford's senior administration to post the quotes, and the Stanford administration reversed itself still once again and agreed to post the quotes even though they have long known of Prof. Dauber's activities in the Turner and other cases, and even though they knew or had high suspicions that Prof. Dauber had played a role in writing and/or editing the statement that Chanel "read" in court.

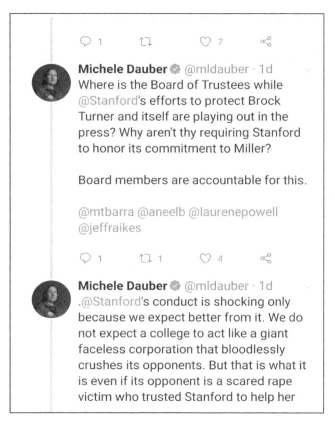

Fig. 38. Prof. Dauber's tweets rebuking Stanford's Board of Trustees.

Sometime after the dispute about the quotes being posted at the "contemplative garden," Google Maps started showing the area as the "Chanel Miller Garden." When senior Stanford administrators were contacted as to whether Stanford had officially named the area as the "Chanel Miller Garden," they responded that Stanford had done no such thing, and that Stanford was unaware as to how the name "Chanel Miller Garden" found its way onto Google Maps. (See Fig. 39)

Someone must have had some authority at Google to place the name "Chanel Miller Garden" onto Google Maps, and since the memorial and posting of the quotes seems to have been largely orchestrated by Prof. Dauber and since her husband Ken Dauber has long worked at Google, the obvious question arises, did Ken or Michele Dauber have a role in getting this name inserted into Google Maps? Most third parties obviously can't get Google to name areas on Google Maps because the third parties want Google to do so, and Stanford alumni and others likewise can't simply name areas on the campus in whatever ways they wish. Also, it is assumed that Google has policies and procedures to assure that names of locations on its maps are officially authorized, and it's interesting that every other name showing at Stanford on Google Maps appears to be a name approved by Stanford.

Fig. 39. Depiction on Google Maps of the Chanel Miller Garden and the very short walking distance (49 ft. and under 1 minute) from the former wooden shed location to the Kappa Alpha fraternity house.

Judge Persky Recalled from the Bench

In what was a dirty and deceitful campaign to recall Judge Persky from his seat in the Santa Clara County Superior Court, Judge Persky lost the election to the DA's office employee Cindy Hendrickson, who was supported and endorsed by the recall campaign.

While the recall campaign boasted that the majority of Santa Clara County voters voted Judge Persky off the bench, that is not actually true. In fact, out of 846,228 total registered voters, only 369,332 votes were cast (43.6%). Of the total 369,332 votes cast, 202,849 voted for the recall, 126,459 voted against the recall, and 40,024 did not vote on the recall measure. Thus, only 23.97% of the total 846,228 registered voters voted for the recall, a small representation of the total number of Santa Clara County registered voters. More than half of all 846,228 Santa Clara County voters (56.4 %) didn't vote at all. It is noteworthy that the cities closest to the facts of the case voted against the recall including Palo Alto, Los Altos, Los Altos Hills, and Stanford (where Prof. Dauber works). Even Prof. Dauber's own precinct in Palo Alto — her own neighbors – voted against the recall.

In response to Judge Persky's recall, Florida public defender and feminist Prya Murad wrote in the *Mercury News*:

"As a public defender, I do not see this as a victory for justice. As a feminist, I do not see this as a victory for civil rights . . . The #MeToo movement is – perhaps unintentionally – pushing mercy out of the courtroom and replacing it with spite."[206]

According to the *Mercury News*, **Turner's prosecutor Alaleh Kianerci did not support the recall of Judge Persky.**[207] And in the CBS News article, "Supportive Email from Assistant DA To Judge Persky Surfaces," it was revealed that prosecutor Kianerci had sent an email to Judge Persky saying:

"Your honor, I am really sorry for any negativity or personal attacks you are enduring . . . I disagreed with your sentence, but I have the utmost respect for you as a judge. You have always been fair to me personally, and it is a pleasure to appear before you."[208]

Interestingly, the CBS News article went on to say, "The email brought up the question of whether there was internal conflict in the Santa Clara County District Attorney's office."[209]

Michele Dauber Sued Judge Persky for Her Campaign's Legal Fees

Prof. Dauber drove the loss of Judge Persky's job as a Santa Clara County judge, resulting in irreparable damage to Judge Persky's career and reputation, and causing extreme stress in the lives of Judge Persky, his wife, and his young children. If that wasn't disgusting enough, Prof. Dauber then sued Judge Persky personally for her committee's alleged costs of litigation in a 2017 legal case against the recall in the amount of $165,000, which was later reduced to $135,000.

The legal costs were the result of Judge Persky's raising an appropriate legal question whether the county registrar was the correct officer under California law to oversee the recall petition process. Judge Persky believed that because judges are state officers, the California Secretary of State, not the county registrar, should have had the aforementioned responsibility.[210] The lawsuit was unsuccessful, and upon petition by Prof. Dauber, Judge Kay Tsenin subsequently ordered Judge Persky to pay the recall campaign's legal fees. Judge Persky said he "pursued the litigation so that Superior Court judges would benefit from the same procedural protections as other state officers who face recall elections."[211] Judge Persky subsequently asked his supporters to help pay for the litigation costs.

Judge Persky Fired from Job as Tennis Coach

In September 2019, almost four years after the Turner trial, Judge Persky was fired from his part-time job at Lynbrook High School in San Jose as a junior varsity girls' tennis coach, a position he held only one day before he was fired, and a job not far from volunteer status with respect to monetary compensation. Judge Persky's firing came shortly after petitions were posted at change.org by several Lynbrook High School students.

One of the students made false statements on Change.org such as, "Turner had raped an unconscious woman," and that:

"Persky's bias towards rapist Brock Turner should be a very compelling reason not to consider Persky to be in a position to coach a public high school sports team."[212]

Another student made a similarly untrue statement saying:

> "[Persky] has a repeated history of allowing severe rape and sexual assault cases to be brushed under the rug."[213]

If the students had actually stuck to the facts – which they either already knew and intentionally disregarded, or which they didn't bother researching, or where their claims may have been encouraged by third parties – they would have known that (1) Turner was not prosecuted for nor convicted of rape, (2) Judge Persky followed the recommendations of the detailed 16-page investigative report written by the female probation officer, as is standard practice, (3) Judge Persky's sentencing was completely legal, and (4) the Commission on Judicial Performance and other organizations found that Judge Persky had shown no bias and had done no wrong. Judge Persky's firing from his coaching job was nothing short of still another hateful witch hunt based on false premises.

Incredibly, Prof. Dauber then blamed some of the issues on Judge Persky's lack of compassion for Asian Americans, as a large number of students at Lynbrook High School were Asian American. Prof. Dauber was ignoring the fact that Judge Persky's wife is Asian and his children are bi-racial, as is Chanel Miller.

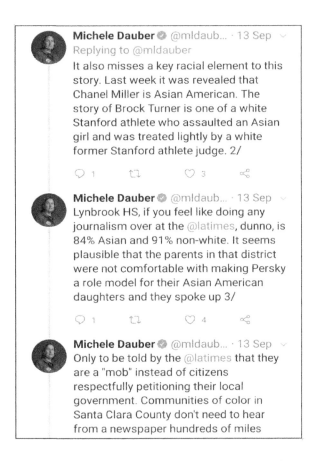

Fig. 40. Prof. Dauber attempting to insert racism into Judge Persky's tennis coaching issue when in fact Judge Persky's own wife is Asian, and Chanel is part Asian and part White.

In the *Los Angeles Times* article, "Firing the Judge in the Brock Turner Sex Assault Case was a Step Towards Mob Rule," the *Times* editorial board wrote:

"Persky's firing as junior varsity tennis coach at Lynbrook High School in San Jose is so ridiculously gratuitous, cowardly and off-base. The action helps turn the quest for justice into mob rule, the law into a popularity contest and the independent judiciary into an endangered species."[214]

In her article, "Judge Persky vs. Mob Rule," author and public defender Rachel Marshall said of Judge Persky's firing from his coaching job:

"It should be obvious: Judge Persky did not commit any crime. He did not condone violence against women. He was simply a judge, and one who showed mercy. Even if one is displeased with the sentence in the Turner case, to suggest that Judge Persky himself is somehow an abuser crosses a line."[215]

What Went Wrong

Judge Persky's past record was never compared by the media or others to those of other sitting judges in Santa Clara County, nor were Judge Persky's cases involving sentencing of women offenders ever examined. Knowing this information could have helped voters make better informed voting decisions. None of Judge Persky's decisions in previous cases ever came into question until Prof. Dauber attacked and distorted Judge Persky's sentencing decisions during the recall campaign. If the recall campaign members truly believed Judge Persky's cases were supposedly so egregious and biased as to warrant removal from the bench, why was there not a single complaint from district attorneys, defense lawyers, prosecutors, victims, or defendants during Judge Persky's 13 years on the bench? There were no complaints because Judge Persky's sentencing was always fair and considerate for both sides.

As the California law professors wrote in their letter in support of Judge Persky:

"The last three elected District Attorneys of Santa Clara County, with 27 years of leadership in that office, are against the recall; surely, they would speak up if they found the judge's record to be improper."[216]

District Attorney Jeff Rosen, who allegedly opposed the recall, said the problem was the law, not Judge Persky, and said there were no other complaints of impropriety during Judge Persky's service on the bench. In reference to Judge Persky's sentencing of Turner, Rosen said "Most of the judges in the state of California would've done the same."[217] Yet, as noted elsewhere, DA Rosen apparently was also coordinating efforts with Prof. Dauber.

Judge Persky was the victim of a massive modern-day lynch mob. And as previously noted, due to California Judicial Code of Ethics regulations, Judge Persky was prohibited from commenting on current issues, including the Turner case, which was awaiting an appeal hearing. This rendered Judge Persky unable to defend himself from the false statements against him. This was akin to Judge Persky fighting in a gun battle without a gun. And Prof. Dauber and her supporters surely knew Judge Persky was under these restrictions.

The vast extent of fake news, dissemination of false information, and intense smearing of Judge Persky's reputation by the recall campaign and others through social media and other means was deplorable and highly unethical. In the article, "The Grim Conclusions of the Largest-Ever Study of Fake News," author and writer for *The Atlantic,* Robinson Meyer, brought up the disheartening point that:

> "Social media seems to systematically amplify falsehood at the expense of the truth, and no one – neither experts nor politicians nor tech companies – knows how to reverse that trend."[218]

The recall vote was tainted by a massive disinformation campaign led by Prof. Dauber. Judge Persky lost his efforts to remain a judge, but it must be emphasized that there simply cannot be a fair or even legal democratic election when the voters are intentionally deceived as happened here.

Chapter 15

Prof. Dauber Misrepresented Judge Persky's Past Cases

"Professor Dauber launched a recall petition against a judge whose sentencing decision she disliked, and whose record she then misrepresented." – U. of Chicago Prof. Brian Leiter [219]

I n order to discredit Judge Persky and convince voters to remove him from the bench, Stanford law school professor Michele Dauber and the recall campaign regularly and publicly misrepresented six of Judge Persky's previous key cases. As previously noted, in this effort Prof. Dauber made regular use of the Santa Clara County District Attorney's office, communicating through ongoing emails and other methods with numerous DA staff members including District Attorney Jeff Rosen, Assistant DA Terry Harman, prosecutor Alaleh Kianerci, and Assistant DA Cindy Hendrickson (Judge Persky's successor after his recall) for the purpose of procuring information to then be used to attack Judge Persky.

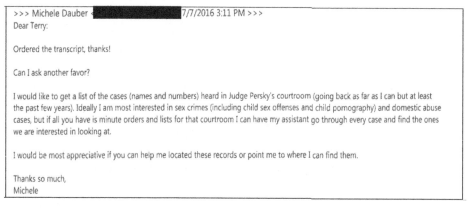

> >> Michele Dauber ▮▮▮▮▮▮▮▮▮▮▮▮ 7/7/2016 3:11 PM >>>
> Dear Terry:
>
> Ordered the transcript, thanks!
>
> Can I ask another favor?
>
> I would like to get a list of the cases (names and numbers) heard in Judge Persky's courtroom (going back as far as I can but at least the past few years). Ideally I am most interested in sex crimes (including child sex offenses and child pornography) and domestic abuse cases, but if all you have is minute orders and lists for that courtroom I can have my assistant go through every case and find the ones we are interested in looking at.
>
> I would be most appreciative if you can help me located these records or point me to where I can find them.
>
> Thanks so much,
> Michele

Fig. 41. Prof. Dauber's email to Assistant DA Terry Harman requesting assistance in obtaining a list of Judge Persky's past cases.

As shown in Public Records Act disclosures, Prof. Dauber also enlisted her graduate student Emma Tsurkov, and possibly other students, to help research Judge Persky's cases. Prof. Dauber subsequently distributed her disinformation to numerous social media and traditional news outlets, claiming Judge Persky showed bias in favor of White, privileged, male college athletes, among other falsehoods. In fact, Prof. Dauber regularly distributed her incorrect renditions of Judge Persky's past cases and other narratives at carefully calculated intervals to her news sources with which she had nurtured favored connections such as the *Mercury News*, *Palo Alto Online*, *The Guardian*, and *Buzzfeed*, in addition to others.

Plea Deals

All of the cases described in this chapter, which are the six cases Prof. Dauber misrepresented to the public via social media, traditional media, and other sources for the purpose of falsely distorting Judge Persky's record, were plea deals with the exception of the De Anza case, which was a jury trial. A plea deal, also known as a plea bargain or plea agreement, is an agreement between the prosecution, the defense lawyer, and the defendant. In the U.S., approximately 90% of criminal cases are handled via plea deals. In a plea deal, the defendant pleads guilty to one or more charges in exchange for lesser charges or sentencing, and at the same time avoids a trial. Sentencing can be negotiated in a plea deal as well. A plea deal can be negotiated with or without a judge, although a judge must approve all plea deals. Unless a plea deal is considered inappropriate with respect to the seriousness of the crime or other factors, judges rarely deny plea deals.

The De Anza Case

In 2007, a 17-year-old female said she was sexually assaulted by members of the De Anza College male baseball team while she was highly intoxicated at an off-campus San Jose party. The victim, identified as Jane Doe for privacy, had consumed approximately 11 shots of vodka and was later found to have a blood alcohol concentration of approximately three times the legal limit. Doe was found in a bedroom by three female members of the De Anza soccer team who were also attending the party. The three soccer players said

214

Doe was unconscious and had vomit on her face and in her hair, and she was allegedly being sexually assaulted by several baseball team members, with six or seven of the men in the room. The women took the victim to a hospital.[220] Doe had no memory of the incident.

After reviewing the evidence in the case, then District Attorney Dolores Carr decided not to prosecute the case, and in 2008, the Attorney General's office said there was not enough evidence to file charges against anyone present at the party.

In a 2011 jury trial presided by Judge Persky, Jane Doe brought a civil lawsuit against the baseball team members, citing emotional and psychological distress (PTSD), and that the 2007 incident had left her "socially phobic and fearful."[221] Most of the defendants already had their cases "dropped, settled [out of court], or transferred their rights to sue their insurance companies for failing to defend them in the lawsuit."[222] According to Jane Doe's lawyer, Doe had received $500,000 to $600,000 in settlement fees from one of the defendants' insurance company, and approximately $50,000 from another defendant.

Doe sought to sue the two remaining defendants for a total of $7.5 million. To disprove Doe's false testimony that the sexual assault incident had left her "socially phobic and fearful," the defendants' counsel wanted to show the jury pictures posted by Doe on Facebook showing her scantily dressed and happily partying. One picture showed Doe in a Halloween costume, and another showed Doe "serving a man a shot of alcohol from her cleavage."[223] The pictures were taken at a different party approximately one year after the 2007 De Anza College incident. Judge Persky allowed the pictures as evidence. It was obvious from Doe's Facebook pictures that she had not been left "socially phobic and fearful." The defense had every right to disprove Doe's false testimony, in which she apparently perjured herself.

According to *BuzzFeed*:

"Dauber described it [allowing photo evidence] as one of the most disturbing examples of bias by Persky; the judge allowed defendants to use a photo of the woman attending a party a year after the alleged assault in a revealing outfit to argue that she did not have PTSD, Dauber said."[224]

Actually, the photos were presented as evidence that Doe did not have "social phobia and fear" as she had claimed under oath. Prof. Dauber left out the part about Doe serving drinks from her cleavage and other disturbing and indecent behavior, and the fact that the evidence went directly to a key issue in Doe's financial claims.

Social phobia and fear, also known as social anxiety disorder, differs from PTSD. Social phobia or social anxiety disorder is a mental disorder that is diagnosed by a qualified mental health professional. According to the National Institute of Mental Health, "The fear that people with social anxiety disorder have in social situations is so strong that they feel it is beyond their ability to control."[225] Symptoms can include sweating, rapid heart rate, rapid breathing, trembling, nausea, limited eye contact with others, tendency to avoid social situations, anxiety before social engagements or performance activities, and fear of demonstrating embarrassing behavior in front of others. The photos admitted as evidence portray Doe as a socially uninhibited and cheerful partygoer, not as the socially phobic and fearful individual she claimed to be.

The jury found the two defendants not liable because they believed that one of the two defendants, from whom the victim sought $2.5 million, had been in the victim's room for less than a second because he left to alert one of the home's residents that the victim was being "gang banged." The jury believed that the second defendant, from whom the victim sought $5 million, had been the first in the room and had been invited in, but left before the other men entered the room.[226] Jury members also believed testimony by the defendants and witnesses that "the girl brought beer to the party, performed a public lap dance and invited them in explicit terms to have group sex."[227] The jurors did not base their verdict on the Facebook pictures allowed at trial.

In the De Anza case, Judge Persky followed the rule of law, the jury found the two defendants not liable, and no money was paid to Jane Doe. Based on the facts described here, both the jury and Judge Persky did the right thing, but apparently not in the opinion of Prof. Dauber.

The Ramirez Case

In November 2014, Salvadorian immigrant Raul Ramirez was arrested after his female roommate reported to police that Ramirez had forcibly digitally penetrated her until she began to cry. Ramirez pleaded guilty to the crime, and he was subsequently charged with felony penetration by force of a conscious person, which carried a mandatory minimum sentence of at least three years in prison. Ramirez' sentence did not allow for probation and a judge did not have legal authority to reduce the sentence. In contrast, Brock Turner's case was a lesser offense that allowed for probation and judicial discretion.

Although Judge Persky, in part, presided over the Ramirez case, the case ended up as a plea bargain negotiated between Ramirez' counsel and the prosecution. Judges rarely decline plea bargains unless in unusual circumstances. According to Akiva Freidlin, a Stanford University law school alumnus who had attended the Ramirez hearings, "A judge typically intervenes [in plea bargains] only if he or she has observed, for example, clearly deficient performance on the part of a defense attorney."[228]

In the *Palo Alto Online* article, "Turner Trial Judge Criticized for Bias in Assault Case," Prof. Dauber said:

> "It seems to be more evidence for the fact that he (Persky) really bent over backwards to give Turner an unreasonably lenient sentence when you compare it to the sentence for this individual [Ramirez], who was not an elite, privileged athlete and didn't get the same level of solicitude from the judge."[229]

In another false statement claiming Judge Persky showed bias against people of color, Prof. Dauber said of the Ramirez case:

> "I think we here have some evidence that he has in fact sentenced Mr. Turner much more leniently than he sentenced this defendant of color."[230]

Prof. Dauber repeatedly made similar false statements about the Ramirez case in social media and various traditional news sources.

Prof. Dauber's statements claiming Judge Persky showed bias were undeniably false, because as already mentioned, the Ramirez case was a plea bargain and the circumstances of the case, a California Penal Code section 289(a) conviction, mandated a minimum sentence of three years in prison, while Turner's conviction allowed probation and judicial discretion. According to the Commission on Judicial Performance:

> "California law explicitly prohibits a downward departure for a violation of Penal Code section 289(a) under any circumstances, whereas the Penal Code sections Brock Turner was convicted of violating permitted (at the time) a downward departure to probation in certain circumstances."[231]

The absurdity of Prof. Dauber's accusations of bias in the Ramirez case is even more glaring knowing that it was Judge Gilbert Brown, not Judge Persky, who handled the final plea bargain. Moreover, Ramirez was never sentenced because he fled the country and prosecutors chose not to pursue him. According to the Commission on Judicial Performance:

> "although Judge Persky handled proceedings earlier in the case, it was not Judge Persky who handled the hearing at which Ramirez entered his guilty plea, but another trial judge; thus, the *Ramirez* case cannot be used to demonstrate disparate treatment in sentencing by Judge Persky."[232]

In other words, the facts proved that Judge Persky was in no way biased, and once again, Prof. Dauber's claims were false.

Despite the fact that Prof. Dauber's claims regarding the Ramirez case were false, numerous traditional news media nevertheless parroted Prof. Dauber's claims without engaging in any efforts to investigate the real facts of the case. For example, the *Guardian* published the article, "Stanford Trial Judge Overseeing Much Harsher Sentence for Similar Case,"[233] *Business Insider* published "The Judge Who Sentenced the ex-Stanford Swimmer to 6 Months in Jail is Expected to Give Latino Man 3 Years for a Similar Crime,"[234] and *Salon* published "Judge in Brock Turner Rape Case Handed El Salvadorian Immigrant 3 Years for Similar Crime."[235] Numerous news media, including the *LA Times*, *HuffPost*, *Vox*, *Vogue*, and others followed suit; that is, they published fake news about the Ramirez case without bothering to learn the facts.

The Chain Case

Robert Chain, a White plumber who was by no means elite, privileged, or an athlete, was arrested in May 2014 for possession of approximately 200 child porn images and a child porn video. One of the victims was an infant. Chain was caught by a San Jose sex crimes investigator who remotely observed Chain downloading child porn content onto his electronic devices.[236] Chain did not produce or distribute child pornography, nor was he suspected of sexually abusing children. Chain was a first-time offender who said he was drinking alcohol while downloading child porn, and that he had been molested as a child.

Chain's defense counsel had asked for a misdemeanor charge, for which Chain could have qualified, but which Judge Persky denied because of the need for what Judge Persky believed was a "more formal period of supervision than misdemeanor probation would afford."[237] Judge Persky ordered a detailed investigative report from the probation department, and the case also had been discussed among the District Attorney's office, Chain's defense counsel, and Judge Persky. The probation department recommended a minimum sentence. Sentencing for child porn can range from zero to 12 months, with the typical sentence being six months.

Besides Chain's felony conviction, Chain was sentenced to three years' probation, four days in jail (including time served), Alcoholics Anonymous participation, sex addiction therapy, counseling, and worst of all, lifetime sex offender registration. The sentencing was considered an "open plea," in which the judge decides the sentencing. Judge Persky indicated that he might be receptive to reducing Chain's sentence to a misdemeanor if, after one year, Chain proved he had adhered to his probation and other sentencing requirements. However, no reduction to a misdemeanor was ever ordered. Because of Chain's remorse and admission of guilt, the prosecutor assigned to the case, Bret Wasley, said that he "did not object [to the sentence] and that his priority was that Chain plead to a felony to ensure a higher level of supervision, rather than get additional jail time."[238] Assistant DA Terry Harman said prosecutors didn't object to Judge Persky's sentencing "because we were satisfied with the felony plea and sex registration in light of the defendant's remorse and admission of guilt."[239] In deciding the sentencing, Judge Persky followed the recommendations of Chain's counsel, the District Attorney's office, and the probation department.

Notwithstanding these facts, however, Prof. Dauber said in a *Palo Alto Online* article that "this 'incredibly lenient' sentencing suggests that the Brock Turner sentence is not an isolated case."[240] On Twitter, Prof. Dauber said "Judge Persky sentenced white middle class Sunnyvale child porn felon Robert Chain to just 4 days in jail."[241] In social media and traditional news media sources, Prof. Dauber regularly described Chain's sentence as "just four days in jail" without any mention of Chain's devastating lifetime sex offender registration requirement, three years' probation, therapy, Alcoholics Anonymous participation, and other requirements.

Public defender Sajid Khan, who actively supported Judge Persky against the recall, said of Chain's sentencing, "while Chain's four-day sentence was 'unusual,' it was within the bounds of the law and actually a 'refreshing' break from the sentencing norm for this type of crime ."[242] In a 2016 email between Prof. Dauber and Assistant DA Terry Harman obtained through Public Records Act disclosures, Harman said Judge Persky's sentence was "quite low," adding, however, that Judge Persky "is not the only judge who has given less than 6 months" in a child pornography case.[243]

According to Chain's attorney, Brian Madden, Chain was an alcoholic whose wife and two young children had left him. Madden added that the future possibility of reducing Chain's conviction to a misdemeanor would "make it easier for the 48-year-old to find future employment, housing and financing because a felony conviction would appear during background checks."[244] According to *Palo Alto Online*, because of his involvement with the Turner case, Judge Persky recused himself from the Chain case in 2016 due to "exposure to publicity that might 'reasonably entertain a doubt that the judge would be able to be impartial."[245]

Robert Chain was in a unique position to turn his life around, which Judge Persky took into consideration. Additional jail time, even six months in jail, would have been a severe hardship and likely would have resulted in Chain losing his employment in addition to other negative impacts to his life, causing Chain to sink even deeper into a life of desperation, possible homelessness, and becoming a burden to society – outcomes that did not fit the crime. Providing Chain with opportunities for redemption such as treating his sex addiction and alcoholism made much more sense than throwing Chain in jail for six months. Judge Persky had the compassion, courage, and foresight to focus on directing Chain towards the right track and preventing recidivism — steps that were beneficial to both society and Chain. The goal of sentencing was not to destroy Chain, who had already lost almost everything; rather, the goal was to return Chain to the community as a decent man -- it's called restorative justice.

The Chiang Case

In October 2014, 35-year-old Cisco Systems software engineer Ming Hsuan Chiang was arrested and charged with felony domestic violence. Chiang allegedly had beaten his fiancé by punching her in the face and on other parts of her body. Chiang had no prior criminal convictions. In April 2016, Chiang pleaded no contest to the charge of battery with serious bodily injury.[246]

Judge Persky delayed Chiang's sentencing until after Chiang was able to renew his immigration visa. District Attorney Jeff Rosen had a "collateral consequences" policy in place which directed prosecutors to "consider immigration and other potential consequences to charges filed."[247] Chiang's plea bargain, negotiated between a prosecutor from Rosen's office and Chiang's defense attorney, resulted in a 72-day jail sentence to be served on weekends, 20 hours of community service, three years' probation, completion of a domestic violence prevention program, and monetary restitution. The probation officer recommended approximately $29,026 in restitution plus other fees. While Judge Persky "presided over one July 2016 restitution hearing . . . Judge Vincent Chiarello signed off on $1,188 in restitution for the victim's medical expenses." [248] Judge Persky was reassigned to another case shortly after the July 2016 hearing.

Prof. Dauber's recall campaign complained that Judge Persky showed bias in favor of Chiang because he postponed Chiang's sentence and gave Chiang the opportunity to work only on weekends. However and as already shown, these actions were for good reasons: Chiang needed his immigration visa so he could work, he was awaiting determination of his restitution costs, he was afforded weekend jail so that he wouldn't lose his job, allowing him to earn money for living expenses and to pay restitution to his fiancé, and this was in accordance with the District Attorney's office policy of not putting anyone's immigration at risk. According to retired Judge LaDoris Cordell, "Mr. Chiang did that [keep his job and pay restitution], and as far as we know, to this day, he has not been rearrested. He is not an athlete nor a privileged white male."[249]

The Gunderson Case

In 2015, Ikaika Gunderson, age 21, was arrested for allegedly choking, hitting, and pushing his girlfriend out of a parked car while engaged in an argument. Gunderson, who was part ethnic Hawaiian and had no criminal record, was charged with felony domestic assault, to which he pleaded no contest. In an effort to help Gunderson attend college in Hawaii and land a possible walk-on opportunity to play football, Judge Persky agreed to delay Gunderson's sentencing for one year to which the District Attorney's office had no objections. Gunderson had family in Hawaii.

Gunderson was also to abide by Judge Persky's directives to participate in a year-long domestic violence program and attend Alcoholics Anonymous or Narcotics Anonymous sessions while in Hawaii. He was to return to Judge Persky's court for sentencing in July 2016. In December 2015, Gunderson was allowed to submit a signed progress report in lieu of traveling to California for an in-person hearing. Judge Persky offered the possibility of lowering Gunderson's felony conviction to a misdemeanor if he complied with the terms of Judge Persky's directives, at which time Gunderson would start three years of probation. The possible walk-on football opportunity never came to fruition; thus Gunderson did not play football.

Upon learning that Gunderson did not attend all of his Alcoholics Anonymous meetings, on March 10, 2016, Judge Persky sentenced Gunderson to "four months of county jail, three years' probation, completion of a certified domestic violence program and payments to a battered women's shelter and domestic violence fund, among other fees."[250] Judge Persky had agreed to delay Gunderson's surrender for three months in order to give Gunderson the opportunity to finish school; however, the probation department instead requested a hearing on March 21, 2016, at which time Gunderson was ordered by a different judge to serve his sentence.[251]

Prof. Dauber was quoted in the *Mercury News* as saying:

> "Once again, Judge Persky has proved that he does not take violence against women seriously and that he will bend over backwards to give special treatment to college athletes who victimize women."[252]

Gunderson's attorney said Gunderson had "physical and psychiatric issues," and welcomed Judge Persky's effort to work with his client. Public defender Gary Goodman referenced the fact that under federal court order, the judicial system was obliged to focus on rehabilitation and not just put people behind bars.[253] Gunderson was arrested again on December 18, 2018 for punching his father while living with his family in Washington. Gunderson's parents sought treatment for their son's psychiatric issues rather than punitive action.

The District Attorney's office, which had not objected to Judge Persky's sentencing for Gunderson, said "The sentence imposed in this case was not unusual . . . the timing was 'unusual, but not unprecedented.'" According to the DA office's public communications officer Sean Webby:

> "It is not unusual for a judge to allow a defendant to serve a jail term in a manner that does not disrupt school or employment."[254]

Judge Persky did his best to help Gunderson get his life together while at the same time handing down appropriate punishment. Furthermore, the victim had told the probation officer:

> "She [the victim] was a forgiving person, they both were intoxicated, he 'wasn't in his right mind' and wondered if counseling, rather than a county jail sentence, would be appropriate."[255]

Prof. Dauber complained that Judge Persky did not comply with the Interstate Compact for Adult Offender Supervision (ICAOS) requirement to notify Hawaii that Gunderson would be in their state. According to *Palo Alto Online*, Anthony Pennella, who oversees ICAOS for the California Department of Corrections and Rehabilitation, said the compact applies to people with deferred sentences. However, Pannella said judges lacked awareness of when the compact's rules should be applied.[256] It should be noted that Prof. Dauber's allegation that Judge Persky did not comply with ICAOS regulations was a technical matter and had nothing to do with bias. There also is a question whether this was Judge Persky's obligation or that of the Santa Clara County probation department which is the county entity that typically handles Interstate Compact arrangements. In fact, Public Records Act disclosures show that the probation department, not Judge Persky or others, handled Brock Turner's interstate transfer including trying to decide on their own if they could force Turner to remain in California for at least a year, and without any apparent reason for trying to do so.

With regard to Prof. Dauber's preferred relationships with certain traditional news media and her ongoing communications with the District Attorney's office, and as noted previously, Prof. Dauber said in an email to Assistant DA Terry Harman:

"Please don't share the Gunderson case to anyone due to the press exclusives. Please do keep it between us for another 2 weeks before it comes out" [email dated 8/18/2016, as shown in subsequent Public Records Act disclosures].

In an earlier email on the same thread, Prof. Dauber told assistant DA Harman:

"I don't want any other press organization to get it, I have given these press orgs exclusives." See below:

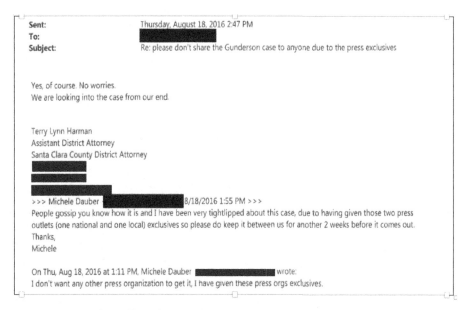

Fig. 42. Prof. Dauber directing assistant DA Harman to withhold information from the media regarding the Gunderson case.

The Smith Case

In 2015, 19-year-old Keenan Smith, an African American, was charged with "felony battery causing serious bodily injury of domestic battery of a witness, felony inflicting corporal injury on a specific person (his girlfriend) and misdemeanor threats to commit a crime resulting in death or great body injury (the second witness)."[257] Smith had allegedly shoved his girlfriend in a parking lot, punched a witness who tried to intervene resulting in unconsciousness, and threatened a second witness. Smith was on the football team at a local community college where he attended classes, and he worked almost full-time as a night-time security guard.

The District Attorney's office had reduced Smith's charges from a felony to a misdemeanor through a plea bargain.[258] A sentence was worked out between the probation department, Judge Northway, and Judge Perky whereby Smith would serve a county jail sentence on weekends (weekend work crew) and attend mandatory domestic violence classes. The goal was to prevent the young man from falling into a cycle of crime that too often befalls young Black and other men. The sentence was not just for the purpose of allowing Smith to play football as claimed by Prof. Dauber; rather, it was to turn Smith's life around by allowing him to incorporate school, work, and football practice around his sentencing and to thereby offer him a chance at success and become a productive citizen. The sentence was compassionate, wholly appropriate, and did not show bias in favor of athletes as was claimed by Prof. Dauber. Smith's sentence also aligned with California's attempt to ameliorate the state's ever-growing problem of prison overcrowding.

Smith was working the night shift four days per week, attending classes at College of San Mateo four hours during the day, attending football practice, and playing in out-of-town football games—an admirable but heavy schedule for anyone to endure. On top of Smith's busy schedule, he was required to perform weekend work at the jail and complete 52 hours of domestic violence classes.[259] Alternate Public Defender Barbara Muller said Smith's opportunity to play football was "Smith's ticket to a scholarship to a four-year college, not just fun and games."[260] Obviously, it makes sense for society to do all it can to help young people, especially young men of color, to succeed in life.

Smith ended up missing three of the domestic violence classes and two months later he had one unexcused absence for his weekend jail work. The unexcused absence was the result of Smith arriving late at the jail work site. Smith came before Judge Persky to address the issue of the missed domestic violence classes, for which Judge Persky gave Smith "one more and probably last chance to complete the domestic violence program."[261] Judge Persky's offer to give Smith one more chance was reasonable and fair and showed Judge Persky's desire to help Smith succeed.

Giving Smith a chance was a much better option than imposing a strict penalty and making life more difficult for Smith, with the possibility that Smith would lose his motivation to work hard and succeed in life.

Prof. Dauber, who had no official role in the DA's office or any other county department, but who seemed intent on tracking down Judge Persky's cases, notified the District Attorney's office about Smith's violations of his probation, at which time prosecutor Alaleh Kianerci – the same Deputy DA who was in regular communication with Prof. Dauber while prosecuting Brock Turner – requested that Smith be immediately locked up.[262] However, Judge Diane Northway instead changed Smith's weekend work sentence to weekend time in jail and ordered Smith to complete his domestic violence classes.

In her response as to whether Judge Persky should have held Smith accountable for violating the terms of his probation, Alternate Public Defender Barbara Muller said "the probation department would typically file a violation to bring it to the judge's attention, which probation did not do in this case."[263] Muller said the District Attorney's office took the "highly unusual" step of requesting a court hearing regarding Smith's violation of his parole terms, which Muller attributed to media attention regarding the case.[264] And as already mentioned, it was Prof. Dauber who had brought Smith's probation violations to the attention of the District Attorney's office.

According to CBS News, Prof. Dauber said:

> "It's clear now that another judge who does not share Judge Persky's bias towards student-athletes has looked at this and now Mr. Smith is getting a stiffer penalty and is now being held accountable . . . We just can't have judges who think football is more important than violence against women."[265]

Fig. 43. Prof. Dauber's tweet misleading readers about the Smith case.

Prof. Dauber blamed Judge Persky for "approving a plea deal that allows Smith to continue playing football at the college of San Mateo."[266] However, according to Alternate Public Defender Barbara Muller:

"When the defense and the prosecution have an agreement, it's very rare that a judge will step in and what-we-call, bust the plea because that would cause court congestion . . . So he did not bust the plea."[267]

As mentioned previously, the plea deal was agreed to by the prosecutor and defense counsel, and the sentence was part of the plea deal based on Smith's young age and lack of a criminal history. The plea deal was intended to allow Smith to attend school, work, and attend football practice and games in order to give Smith a chance at succeeding in life. Everyone benefits when offenders become law-abiding members of society, a goal that the criminal justice system should wholeheartedly embrace. As Ms. Muller rightfully said:

"They want people to remain in pro-social and educational and work environments if at all possible because that really is the only thing that prevents recidivism."[268]

Of importance is that some young people, including some young people of color and the underprivileged, rely on high school or college athletics as a lifeline to improving their life circumstances. Santa Clara University law professor Margaret Russell pointed out that:

"She [Dauber] is ignoring those people of color and those without means who could play college athletics as a means to improve their lives. Judge Persky didn't want Smith to get lost in the prison system."[269]

Gary Goodman, a supervising attorney for the Santa Clara County public defender's office, minced no words when he said:

"When Michele Dauber discusses this [Smith case], she doesn't have a clue what she is talking about."[270]

The Smith case is another example of Judge Persky's constructive efforts to help young people of color and those that are underprivileged, and to avoid the in-and-out of prison cycle that too often befalls young people of color – which flies in the face of Prof. Dauber's baseless premise that Judge Persky favored White, privileged male athletes.

Failure of News Sources and District Attorney's Office to Publicize the Truth

What is disappointing is that it took the *Palo Alto Online* reporters and other traditional news outlets almost two years (25 days before the June 5, 2018 election) to actually investigate Judge Persky's past cases that Prof. Dauber claimed showed bias, giving Prof. Dauber almost two years to peddle her false depictions of Judge Persky's cases. By the time the investigative articles were published, it was too late – the voters had already been misled and the vote was already tainted. The long delay in news reporters' investigative reporting was in itself an act of bias.

District Attorney Jeff Rosen, who began his term as the Santa Clara County District Attorney on January 1, 2011, knew Prof. Dauber was misrepresenting Judge Persky's cases and disseminating the misrepresented cases to social media and traditional news sources in a massive smear campaign against Judge Persky. It is incomprehensible that Rosen made no effort to set the record straight and inform the public of the truth. All of the cases that were skewed and publicly distorted by Prof. Dauber were cases handled by the District Attorney's office while Rosen was in office. How could it be that an election involving the recall of a respected judge – in the 21st Century – was tainted by these types of serious misrepresentations against the judge and that went entirely unchallenged by the District Attorney who oversaw those cases?

Stanford Didn't Stop Prof. Dauber's Inappropriate Behavior

There also remains a significant question: How can Stanford law school, and Stanford itself, condone Prof. Dauber's inappropriate behavior? This is not a question of First Amendment rights nor of academic freedom, as periodically claimed by members of the Stanford administration when pressed on the matter. Members of a faculty, and especially a law school faculty, have obligations to be ethical and truthful and to set an example of proper behavior, including for future members of the bar. It also appears these activities by Prof. Dauber largely took place when most faculty members are expected to be teaching, doing research, and performing other duties for the school.

Summing It Up

Michele Dauber's false accusations of bias arose from nothing more than her intentionally skewed and distorted rendition of Judge Persky's record in order to mislead voters into voting Judge Persky off the bench. What's astonishing is that Prof. Dauber – a member of a distinguished law school faculty, no less – had the audacity to say:

> "Everything we have presented to the public has been thoroughly researched and accurate . . . All of the evidence supports the conclusion that Judge Persky is biased in favor of athletes."[271]

In reality, much of Prof. Dauber's information presented to the public about Judge Persky, and for that matter Brock Turner, was and continues to be inaccurate and outright false.

Santa Clara University law school professor Margaret Russell, who was a co-founder of the Vote No campaign, made it clear that:

> "What you need to know about Professor Dauber is that she says things for six months or eight months until she gets caught - - - and then she has to backtrack because there is absolutely no evidence that Judge Persky is in favor of college athletes."[272]

The recall campaign presented no comparisons of the records of other judges who handled criminal cases in Santa Clara County. In truth, Judge Persky's decisions showed no pattern of bias, and the recall campaign's claim that Judge Persky favored White, privileged, male athletes was simply not true. Retired Judge LaDoris Cordell hit the nail right on the head when she said of the recall campaign:

"I've never dealt with such a dishonest campaign in my life . . . Just flat-out lying."[273] [Boldface added]

In reference to Judge Persky's cases that Prof. Dauber had so seriously misrepresented, Oakland, California public defender and Stanford law school alumna Rachel Marshall observed that:

"the only trend among these cases is that Persky appeared to believe in second chances for young offenders, and was often focused more on rehabilitation than punishment. In general, this is something many Americans now say they want from a justice system that for too long has been overly reliant on incarceration."[274]

As mentioned in the California law professors' letter in opposition to the recall (Ch. 14):

"The mechanism of recall was designed for and must be limited to cases where judges are corrupt or incompetent or exhibit bias that leads to systematic injustice in their courtrooms . . . None of these criteria applies to Judge Persky."[275]

Contrary to Prof. Dauber's claim that Judge Persky favored White, privileged male athletes, Judge Persky actually applied the law in legal and merciful ways to help defendants, many of whom were underprivileged men of color, to return to society with hope for their futures and to become productive and law-abiding citizens, while at the same time considering the needs of victims.

According to the Bay Area's *Mercury News*, defense attorneys praised Judge Persky because he had "a pattern of sparing relatively low-level offenders of color from prison."[276] Retired Santa Clara County Judge LaDoris Cordell, whose distinguished career includes her achievement as the first African American woman to serve as a Superior Court judge in Northern California, said of the defendants in Judge Persky's court:

"These were defendants, young men of color, for whom Judge Persky showed compassion and mixed punishment with mercy ... He

231

cared about young people. Now, thanks to this recall, we're going backward especially in terms of racial justice."[277] [Boldface added]

Chapter 16

Wanted: An Overhaul of the Criminal Justice System

"It is possible to respect the suffering of crime victims AND want criminal justice reforms that treat all humans more like humans."
– Meaghan Ybos

Judge Persky Embraced Criminal Justice Reform

Those in the law community who had ever stood before Judge Aaron Persky knew him as a fair and compassionate judge who focused not only on following the rule of law and considering the victims, but also on crime prevention and reintegration of defendants – especially young redeemable minority defendants – back into society as productive and law-abiding members of the community. Judge Persky treated defendants as human beings. This was demonstrated time and again when Judge Persky gave defendants reasonable incarceration sentences when appropriate, allowed for second chances, and focused on rehabilitation, education, and counseling or therapy to guide people back on track and prevent recidivism.

Judge Persky embraced restorative justice concepts similar to those of some of today's advanced European countries. Ironically, these are also the concepts long espoused by progressive U.S. politicians, law professors, and other commentators of the U.S. criminal justice system. Unlike the current "lock 'em up" philosophy that has taken hold in the U.S. (although now is being dismantled through reforms of sentencing guidelines, revisiting "third strike" laws, and early release programs), countries like Norway treat defendants with humanity and boast some of the lowest recidivism rates in the world.

America's Infamous Incarceration Statistics

It's no secret that compared to other modern industrialized nations, the U.S. now has the highest per capita prison population in the world, even surpassing China and Russia. The U.S. has the further distinction of being the only Western democracy that still imposes the death penalty. Americans live in a nation of mass incarceration, and this distinction has contributed next to nothing towards reducing crime, and in fact has been shown to increase crime.

Our law schools teach that there are four purposes of our criminal laws: removal from society of those who present an ongoing danger, retribution, rehabilitation, and deterrence. America's system of justice has become mainly one of retribution, and it's ineffective.

The United States Department of Justice estimated that in 2017, the number of people behind bars totaled 2.27 million, a figure five and even up to ten times higher than those of other modern industrialized nations. According to the Equal Justice Initiative, one in seven U.S. prisoners are incarcerated for life, with two-thirds of the lifetime prisoners being people of color.[278] It's unfathomable that 2.27 million Americans are locked in cages in a land that prides itself on justice, freedom, and the value of human life.

The U.S. Department of Justice has found that cognitive behavioral programs based on social learning theory helps prevent offenders from returning to jail or prison, but that strict incarceration actually increases recidivism rates. According to Public Safety Canada, "Compared to community sanctions, imprisonment was associated with an increase in recidivism. Further analysis of the incarceration studies found that longer sentences were associated with higher recidivism rates."[279]

Studies have shown that in many cases, offenders, particularly young first-time offenders, can become productive members of society if given opportunities for rehabilitation, counseling, community service, and probation—these measures also help decrease recidivism. According to Regent University researchers Lee Underwood and Aryssa Washington:

"it has become apparent that incarceration and detainment, while necessary for a small portion of juveniles, tends to have more detrimental effects including continued offending and recidivism."[280]

234

It makes sense to treat young offenders' mental health disorders and provide necessary social and other services to put a stop to their criminal behavior while they're still young. The end result would be improved community protection from crime and significant monetary savings.

Americans' Obsession with Length of Incarceration Time

Another problem is the American public's obsession with favoring long incarceration times, some believing that longer incarceration times somehow shorten victims' healing times, which has never been proven. Some people still bemoan Brock Turner's so-called short jail sentence of six months (never mind that he is a sex offender registrant for life); however, a longer sentence would have made no difference in deterrence and recidivism. Turner was considered highly unlikely to reoffend, and sitting in a cage for longer than four to six months would have been futile and would only have resulted in higher taxpayers' costs. As stated by the Public Policy Institute:

> "there is strong evidence that it is not so much the severity of punishment, measured by sentence length, as the certainty of punishment that is most important in deterring crime."[281]

The Alliance for Safety and Justice conducted a survey titled, "The National Survey of Victims Views," from which it was learned that:

> "[Victims of crimes] overwhelmingly prefer criminal justice approaches that prioritize rehabilitation over punishment and strongly prefer investments in crime prevention and treatment to more spending on prisons and jails."[282]

This is in line with Chanel Miller's statement to the probation officer that:

> "I want him [Turner] to know it hurt me, but I don't want his life to be over. I want him to be punished, but as a human, I just want him to get better. I don't want him to feel like his life is over and I don't want him to rot away in jail; he doesn't need to be behind bars."[283]

In her article "Judge Aaron Persky vs. Mob Rule," public defender Rachel Marshall wrote:

"Longer sentences don't protect women, prevent future sexual assault, or lead to rehabilitation; they just perpetuate mass incarceration."[284]

California Enacted A.B. 701 and A.B. 2888

In response to Brock Turner's sentencing, and in typical knee-jerk fashion, California legislators enacted two new sexual assault laws following the Turner trial: California A.B. 701 and A.B. 2888. California rape law had previously defined rape to include unlawful sexual intercourse. Under AB 701, however, the definition of rape now includes all nonconsensual sexual assault. A.B. 2888, written no less by Santa Clara County District Attorney Jeff Rosen, replaced California's previous law allowing probation, under certain conditions, for convictions of sexually assaulting someone who is intoxicated or unconscious. Under A.B. 2888, a conviction of rape or sexual assault requires mandatory prison sentencing. In response to the enactment of the new laws, District Attorney Rosen said, "While prisons are not appropriate for every person convicted of a crime, rapists belong in prison."[285] Never mind that Brock Turner was hardly a rapist, and Rosen knew that.

While the newly enacted feel-good rape/sexual assault laws may have engendered a fresh, albeit false, sense of public safety, there was little talk of potential problems associated with the new laws such as (1) an inherent uncontrolled spike in California's already-overcrowded prison population, (2) increased costs to taxpayers to fund California's massive prison system, (3) racial and economic disparities associated with poor and minority defendants' inability to hire high quality lawyer representation, (4) the inability of judges to impose lesser sentences in questionable cases, (5) the horrors of prison life in a barbaric California prison system, especially for those who are wrongly convicted, and (6) the reality that prison sentences, especially long sentences, often do more harm than good and have little impact on decreasing recidivism; in fact, prison is likely to increase recidivism rates.

Deputy public defender Gary Goodman, who did not support Rosen's new A.B. 2888 bill, said:

"The statutes that are already in place for these types of crimes have been vetted in a slow and careful manner, this [A.B. 2888] is not."[286]

Natasha Minsker, director of the ACLU of California Center for Advocacy and Policy expressed her concerns that those who will be hit hardest by A.B. 710 and A.B. 2888 are poor and minority defendants. According to Ms. Minsker:

"Those who will bear the brunt of this law will be defendants whose parents can't afford to hire the best attorneys money can buy, defendants who take plea deals for a lesser sentence even if they are innocent because they know judges won't have any discretion during sentencing, and defendants who are mentally ill or who themselves suffered from severe sexual abuse."[287]

Add to this the media attention on "victim impact statements," as if a victim who can make a stronger presentation at the time of sentencing should somehow force a judge to impose a harsher sentence than is justified. Worse is when, as happened with Chanel Miller in the Brock Turner case, the victim impact statement appears to have been written by or with the help of third parties including one or more professional media consultants. A more sensible approach would be to allow victims to be heard, but that their statements should play no role whatsoever in sentencing lest those with greater speaking abilities or the money and connections to hire others to help prepare their statements should somehow get "more justice" than someone with less means. As several lawyers have noted, the elements of the crime should be explicitly stated in the statute, and that is what the sentencing likewise should turn on, NOT the sensationalized impact of victim statements.

Consider the following hypothetical scenario: Juan is a young 19-year-old Hispanic male, a college student and part-time employee, who lives in a poor neighborhood. Juan goes to a party, gets drunk, and meets a drunk woman. The two engage in what Juan believes is consensual sexual activity, and the woman is aroused and possibly brought to climax by Juan's fingering her. The next day, now in a sober state, the woman experiences shame and regret and informs police of the encounter. Juan, a first-time offender, is charged with rape per the new A.B. 701 and A.B. 2888 laws, and because Juan's family is unable to afford a lawyer, Juan is assigned to a public defender overloaded with cases. Juan is convicted of rape and starts his mandatory prison sentence. Inside the prison Juan meets hardened criminals, and in a desperate attempt to avoid prison attacks, Juan joins a prison gang. After years in prison, Juan is released and tells his family that he was beaten and raped while in prison. Juan returns to the community as a felon, registered as a lifetime sex offender, and a broken and dehumanized human being. Additionally, Juan is unable to find work. In this case, there's no question that the punishment of prison time and the repercussions thereof as a result of A.B.s 701 and 2888 don't fit the crime – the punishment itself is a crime.

It has been reported that the Santa Clara County probation department, which is the professional unit that recommends sentences, was trying to find a way not to send Brock Turner to jail, let alone state prison, but that the specific crimes involved required some form of incarceration. They recommended four to six months in county jail. As previously discussed, most judges throughout California adopt the professional recommendations of the probation departments. That itself was an important progressive reform years ago. Yet that somehow wasn't adequate for Prof. Dauber who somehow claims being a progressive, nor was it adequate for the media frenzy that Prof. Dauber and others then created.

In considering Turner's sentencing including the professional recommendation of the probation department, Judge Persky expressed his concern that state prison would have a severe impact on Turner, especially since Turner was a youthful offender. Judge Persky's decision was merciful and took courage in light of the massive traditional news and social media disinformation and hatred that had been disseminated against Turner even before the trial. Furthermore, as Julia Ioffe wrote in the *Huffington Post*:

"When he considered the damage a prison term would do to Turner, Judge Persky had been following California sentencing guidelines, which allow lenience for youthful or elderly defendants with no significant criminal record. The state's prison overcrowding crisis also generally motivates judges to seek alternative punishments and minimal incarceration for new offenders."[288]

Much of the language, by the way, that Judge Persky expressed was required to be stated for the record. These were not simply opinions he wanted to make up or to get some media praise for making. Rather, he had to create a record to support what the probation department itself had recommended to him.

Our Broken Prison System: A National Disgrace

U.S. prison conditions are extremely harsh; in fact, our prison system is broken. Prisons are frequently overcrowded, and prisoners have said they are treated like animals. Prisoners are caged in small spaces, they are forced to adhere to strict schedules, they must protect themselves from violence inflicted by other prisoners and even guards, and they have essentially no privacy. Beatings and rapes among prisoners are not uncommon, as are suicides and suicide attempts. Homicides are not unheard of, and in many states, healthcare and mental health services for prisoners are wholly inadequate. In fact, according to the Marshall Project, nurses at an Arizona prison "repeatedly ignored his [a prisoner's] desperate pleas for help...even after open weeping lesions on [his body] were swarmed by flies."[289] The prisoner eventually died several days after admission to a hospital.

Recently, inmates in an Oregon prison filed a lawsuit claiming they were fed food labeled "not for human consumption." However, the case was thrown out; the judge presiding over the case ruled that while the inmates claimed the food was rotten and covered in mold, the food only caused "occasional illness but no other adverse health impacts."[290] In another case, the food service company John Soules Foods, Inc. "accidentally" sold dog food to prisons. What may have been even more disgraceful was that "nobody could even tell that it was dog food. It tasted the same as everything else prisoners are served."[291]

America's Abuse of Solitary Confinement

The U.S. has the reprehensible distinction of being the only Western industrialized nation that subjects prisoners to long-term solitary confinement, a horrifying punishment of sensory deprivation under brutal conditions that can cause severe and often permanent mental and emotional harm and can lead to prisoners resorting to physical self-harm and suicide. Long-term solitary confinement is defined as confinement for more than 15 days. Solitary confinement beyond 15 days is considered a form of torture, yet some prisoners have been kept in solitary confinement for years or even decades. Prisoners in solitary confinement are housed in tiny cells, often without windows, and with very little human contact. Approximately 80,000 – 100,000 prisoners are held in solitary confinement in the U.S. on any given day.[292]

Norway's Model Prison System

Norway's prison system is considered a model system for the rest of the world to follow. The system focuses on rehabilitation rather than retribution or punishment. There is no death penalty. Prisoners are housed in single-bed rooms with furniture and a small bathroom. This applies even to rooms in the country's high-security unit. Security personnel treat prisoners with dignity and respect. Norway has done away with life sentences, their sentences averaging eight months. In contrast, U.S. prison sentences average 2.6 years and prisoners can be sentenced to life in prison and even death.

In the *Huffington Post* article, "How Norway Is Teaching America To Make Its Prisons More Humane," the basis of the Norwegian prison system is described as follows:

"Taking away someone's freedom is the punishment; prison itself needn't be cruel and it shouldn't be if we want to release good neighbors back into the community. In fact, Norway seeks to make the experience as normal as possible."[293]

Prisoners receive training and take classes to help them reintegrate back into society upon their release. The prisons' security personnel view their jobs as serving the community and changing prisoners for the better.

Norway's prison system is working; their recidivism rate is 20% for those released within two years whereas America's recidivism rate after three years is 68%.[294]

There is no sane reason for U.S. prisoners to be treated with cruelty and disdain. In fact, our Constitution prohibits cruel and unusual punishment. As humans, our prisoners deserve a safe prison environment where their basic needs are met. Security personnel need to treat prisoners like humans and perceive their jobs as helping prisoners to get better. An effective prison system requires that inmates realize they are paying the price for their infractions by losing their freedom, and redeemable prisoners must be helped to learn social and career skills so they can successfully re-enter the community as law-abiding and productive citizens. While prisoners deserve to be treated with humanity, a reasonable balance must be struck. Showering inmates with excessive comfort loses focus of the fact that inmates are in prison because they caused harm. In fact, if prisons become too comfortable, people will break down prison doors—to get in.

Judge Persky's decision to sentence Brock Turner to county jail rather than state prison was merciful and based on the fact that today's broken and barbaric prison system can have disastrous effects on the lives of young people – effects that no young person deserves. It should not be forgotten that the massive false information carefully orchestrated against Turner before, during, and after the time of the trial grossly misrepresented what had actually happened. As discussed in detail in earlier chapters of this book, Turner believed Chanel was properly functioning, would not have known of her prior history of alcohol-induced blackout amnesia, and had no intent to cause harm. What was to be accomplished by Prof. Dauber's cruel insistence on a prison sentence of six years or even more? If Prof. Dauber truly believes herself to be progressive, perhaps she could devote her time and talents to fixing an extraordinarily broken prison system in California and throughout the U.S.

Chapter 17

National Sex Offender Registration: A Failed Social Experiment

Sex Offender Registration Is a Form of Merciless Ancient Banishment

Sex offender registration is nothing short of draconian and oppressive banishment from society and is a form of cruel and unusual punishment. In fact, many believe sex offender registration is unconstitutional. According to Santa Clara County public defender Gary Goodman:

> "After death and life without parole, having to register as a sex offender is the worst punishment."[295]

Many people don't realize that Brock Turner was ordered to register as a Tier III sex offender for life. This fact is regularly omitted from traditional news and social media publications and broadcasts, most likely for the purpose of creating sensationalism and fostering the false belief that Turner was only sentenced to six months in jail. Even Prof. Michele Dauber at Stanford, who led the campaign against Turner and then against Judge Persky, was quoted as saying ten years would be adequate in Turner's situation, and that "No one should be defined for the rest of their life by their worst moment." [296]

Many if not most of the sex offender restrictions apply to pedophiles, yet many sex offender registrants, even if the registrant was convicted of sexual assault between adults, must adhere to restrictions designed for pedophiles, which makes no sense. Due to the often-extreme restrictions as to where registrants are allowed to live, many registrants become victims of homelessness, the very serious problem the U.S. has so far been unable to solve. Many registrants likewise are unable to obtain meaningful employment and find affordable housing.

The severe restrictions assigned to registrants and the subsequent detrimental effects on their families and children bring to mind the "Three Generations of Punishment" rule in North Korea, a form of collective punishment whereby three generations of family members of an individual who committed a crime, including a "political" crime, are jailed for life. Collective punishment was also imposed during the Nazi era.

What Sex Offender Registration Entails

In 1947, California became the first state to establish laws requiring those who committed sex offenses to register with their local police departments.[297] Congress enacted the Sex Offender Registration and Notification Act (SORNA) in 2006, which mandates that those handed down sex offender registration orders are also required to appear on the National Sex Offender public website and update their registration according to their tier level assignments. For example, Tier I registrants are required to register every 12 months, Tier II registrants must register every six months, and Tier III registrants must update their registration every three months for life. All registrants must appear in person and have their pictures taken with each update visit. Registrants must also update their registration when they move to a new location.

Depending on the laws of the state in which the sex offender registrant resides, registrants may be restricted as to where they can live, work, attend school, who they can visit, and where they can visit or be present. Many registrants are forbidden to be in or near a location where children congregate. Sex offender registration adversely affects not only the registrants, but also their innocent children, spouses, friends, and other family members. There are currently approximately 106,916 sex offenders registered in California alone, and up to one million nationwide, requiring excessive amounts of funding from taxpayers, many of whom are already subject to exorbitant taxation, to fund the high administrative costs of sex offender registration. While many countries have sex offender registries accessible only to law enforcement and other authorities, the U.S. is one of the few countries where sex offender registrants' information is accessible to the public.

Hardships associated with updating registration will be particularly grueling when lifetime sex offender registrants' ages reach near the ends of their lives. Imagine being required to register every three months in person at age 95, especially when the original offense occurred when the registrant was 18 or 19 years old – or even worse, if the registrant had been wrongly convicted in the first place. These scenarios exemplify the absurdity of sex offender registration. Very troubling is the fact that registrants risk being victims of vigilante justice. Registrants have had their property damaged, have suffered beatings, and have even been murdered by neighbors or others who found the names and locations of registrants on the national sex offender website.

Sex Offender Registration and Requirements Vary by State

One of the major hypocrisies of the sex registration system is that in most states, the requirement to register is not considered a criminal sentence but solely an "administrative" matter or collateral consequence of criminal conviction. Thus, sex offender registration is exempt from all the laws and standards about sentencing including whether a requirement or procedure is "cruel and unusual." The right to review and appeal this "administrative" action is also virtually non-existent.

A person's sex offender registration sentence continues long past the time when the offender would have completed his or her incarceration, probation, and other sentences. A Tier III sex offender registration sentence, for example, never ends.

People often automatically believe that a registrant is on the list because of a sex offense against a child, which is not necessarily true because sex offenses that qualify for sex offender registration can range from sex offenses against a child, to two under-aged kids engaged in unlawful sex, to sex offenses between adults. Even youths "playing doctor" have been placed on the sex offender list.[298] Sex offender registration is particularly tragic for the many individuals that have been wrongly convicted.

Twenty-nine states require teens who engaged in consensual sex to register as sex offenders, and 40 states require juvenile offenders to register as sex offenders. Some of these offenses include indecent exposure or other minor infractions. Even urinating in public can land people on the sex offender list. In other states, registrants are banned from living with their own children.[299] Restrictions as to where registrants can live, work, or be present can range from 300 feet to 2,500 feet from schools, parks, libraries, churches, shopping malls, airports, school bus stops, or any other areas where children may congregate. Such severe restrictions have led to situations whereby the only places sex offender registrants may live or be present are under bridges or areas outside of cities or towns.[300]

Sex offender registrants who are homeless or transients have even more restrictions; in most states they are required to update their registration every seven to 30 days, but in North Dakota, for example, the homeless or transients are required to register every three days.[301] These are extreme restrictions, as many homeless or transient individuals may not have the resources to travel to the agencies where they are required to update their locations, let alone keep track of the days of the week.

What is particularly cruel is that in some states, registrants are banned from accessing state-run emergency shelters during crises such as earthquakes, fires, or severe weather conditions. For example, "Some jurisdictions in Florida prohibit sex offenders from seeking safety at public shelters during hurricanes."[302] The Agricultural Act of 2014 signed by President Obama prevents some sex offenders from receiving food stamps.[303] Many homeless shelters and soup kitchens prevent registered sex offenders from accessing their services. Surely these actions of depriving registrants from receiving food and shelter, especially emergency shelter during such catastrophes as hurricanes, are not only malicious, but must be unconstitutional.

Many states hand down severe punishment for registrants who fail to register or update registration. For example, sex offenders residing in Georgia can land in prison for one to 30 years for failing to register.

Sex Offender Registration Is Ineffective

Studies have repeatedly shown that restricting where sex offender registrants may work, reside, go to school, and the many other restrictions and requirements applied to sex offender registrants do not decrease recidivism or improve public safety; instead, the severe restrictions make re-entry into society mostly out of reach. Eli Lehrer, president and co-founder of the R Street Institute think tank in Washington D.C., observed that:

> "virtually no well-controlled study shows *any* quantifiable benefit from the practice of notifying communities of sex offenders living in their midst."[304]

According to the Illinois SOSOR Task Force:

> "Research has shown residency restrictions neither lead to reductions in sexual crime or recidivism, nor do they act as a deterrent."[305]

Sex offender recidivism rates are among the lowest of all crimes committed nationally, yet sex offender registration is one of the most destructive and demeaning punishments of all, rendering offenders as social outcasts and making employment, education, and affordable housing extremely difficult to obtain, even resulting in homelessness for many. Melissa Hamilton, who is a University of Houston Law Center professor and nationally known expert on sex-offender recidivism, places sex offender recidivism rates in the "low single digits."[306] The ramifications of sex offender registration are extreme punishments in a system that doesn't work.

Over 90 percent of victims of sexual abuse know their abusers, 95 percent of sexual offenses are first-time offenses, and most sexual assault crimes occur in private residences by family members or friends of the victims.[307] Therefore, it is rare to find registered sex offenders lurking around schools, daycare centers, parks, and other places where children unknown to the registrants would congregate.

Oakland, California public defender Rachel Marshall has said her clients prefer jail rather than sex offender registration. As stated by Marshall:

> "We know that the proven methods of protecting public safety involve moving away from monitoring and shaming those who have committed past offenses, and focusing on ways to prevent sex crimes on the front-end, and on meaningful reentry programs that assist people coming out of prison to get jobs, housing, and support . . . They may not provide the

quick-fix satisfaction that politicians love to sell – but they are the only thing proven to work."[308]

Patty Wetterling, whose 11-year-old son was molested and murdered in 1989, succeeded in helping to establish the first sex offender registry program in Minnesota. Her efforts also resulted in the establishment of the nationwide Jacob Wetterling Crimes Against Children and Sexually Violent Offender Registration Act, which President Bill Clinton signed into federal law in 1994. That law requires all states to establish their own sex offender registries. Ms. Wetterling, however, now believes sex offender registration laws have gone too far:

"We've cast such a broad net that we're catching a lot of juveniles who did something stupid or different types of offenders who just screwed up. Should they never be given a chance to turn their lives around?"[309] [Boldface added]

Sex offender registration, which can span 10 or more years and even a lifetime, entails punishing people now, without due process or presumption of innocence, for crimes they have not yet, and probably never will, commit in the future. This makes no sense.

Sex offender registration is a failed social experiment based on the ancient practice of banishment from society that has gone on for far too long and has no place in modern society. It is vengeance—and nothing less.

Worst of all, the extremely destructive requirements and the negative stigma of sex offender registration results in the horrific ruination of the lives of the many individuals that have been wrongly convicted. Including, as shown throughout this book, Brock Turner.

Chapter 18

Correcting the Wrongs, Enacting Reforms

The extensive research undertaken in writing this book has revealed extraordinary wrongs that were intentionally inflicted upon individuals, significant organizational failures, and major systemic defects all of which need correction. Summarizing them here may facilitate the needed actions.

Correcting the Wrongs Against Brock Turner

In light of what actually happened, as discussed in detail throughout this book, the imposition of lifetime Tier III sex offender registration upon Brock Turner is nothing short of outrageous. Turner's defense attorney never revealed his prior and continuing relationship with Prof. Michele Dauber and members of her family. That fact should have disqualified him from being allowed to represent Turner. Another concern is that the defense attorney had left his law firm after accepting the Turner case and thus was now functioning as a solo practitioner in a battle against the full resources of the Santa Clara County District Attorney's office and a carefully orchestrated worldwide media campaign against his client.

This book also details the apparent wrongdoing by both the Stanford police and the Santa Clara County District Attorney's office. These failings alone should be sufficient to justify vacating the most draconian part of Turner's sentence – the imposition of lifetime sex offender registration requirements.

Stanford University is one of the world's finest universities. It should have done much better than what it has done in the Turner case.

Stanford's first shortcoming was Stanford's treatment of one of its own students immediately following the incident. At the Stanford police station, Turner's due process rights were blatantly violated. That night and the next day, Stanford provided counseling to an individual, Chanel Miller, who had never been a Stanford student. Stanford not only failed to do the same for its own student (Turner) who was left in county jail overnight, but it then immediately expelled Turner from his student housing and access to meals, and without so much as giving him money to buy food and other necessities or his cell phone to call home.

The second major shortcoming was Stanford's silence in everything that followed. As discussed in detail throughout this book, Stanford's police department recorded but then seems to have gotten rid of the license plate numbers of the vehicles parked in the Kappa Alpha parking lot and that would have allowed the police and Turner's lawyer to interview witnesses. Unless there was an explanation that hasn't been disclosed, the Stanford police and DA's office then misrepresented the facts about what had happened and claimed in writing they knew nothing about the license plates.

As also discussed in detail in prior chapters, Stanford's police returned Chanel's cell phone and simply asked Chanel to send back whatever Chanel decided was relevant. And then they told Turner's lawyer a few weeks later they had no such phone records.

Likewise, and as again discussed in detail throughout this book, Stanford police wrote down two completely contradictory statements made by Chanel – statements made 15 hours of one another and on the very same day as the incident – about when Chanel had gone to Stanford, what she had been drinking, and what else she and others had been doing that day. Both statements were written and signed by Stanford police and attached to the criminal complaint filed with the court, apparently with no attempt to reconcile the contradictions.

The Stanford police reported and still report to senior officers at Stanford (in recent years, the university's general counsel), so Stanford bears full responsibility for the wrongdoing by the police. During and following Turner's trial, Stanford also was aware of other problems in the case as well as current and prior actions by Prof. Dauber. An open letter from Stanford law school graduates and letters from judges and law faculty throughout California were further red flags, yet Stanford still did nothing to address the ongoing abuses of Turner and then of Judge Persky and including what seems to be improper use of university time, personnel, and resources.

It is not possible to correct all of the past and wrongful abuses to which Brock Turner has been subjected. The least Stanford must do is to alleviate the impact its failings have had on Turner and his family. That includes supporting vacating the lifetime sexual registration requirements imposed on him, providing equal or even greater financial restitution as was provided to Chanel Miller and her sister, fully funding a college education to which Turner is qualified and entitled, whether at Stanford or some other college or university of his choice, and helping assure there are no impediments on his transcript or otherwise that would stand in the way of Turner's continued education. Stanford also must commit to institutional corrections as are delineated below.

Correcting the Wrongs Against Judge Aaron Persky

For following the law and having the courage to do so despite the almost certain negative public reaction that would be stirred up by the District Attorney's office and Prof. Dauber, Judge Persky was recalled from office. The laziness of traditional media nationwide and worldwide, including their willingness to be co-opted by "special access" to information being orchestrated by Prof. Dauber, were also critical factors. The recall of a highly ethical and highly competent judge who followed the law sent a horrible message to other sitting judges, and unless that wrongful message is addressed, it bodes badly for California's courts.

It is urged that the California Attorney General and other state officials conduct a special investigation of the events covered in this book. Such an investigation will likely conclude with findings parallel with those in this book. Through this process, California would go a long way toward correcting the wrongful actions against Judge Persky as well as the judiciary as a whole, including by offering Judge Persky an appointment to a court of appeal or similar position appropriate for someone of Judge Persky's abilities and qualifications.

Stanford Must Address the Following Issues

- Correct the blatant alcohol abuse in its various athletic programs and campus wide.
- Defer Title IX and any related on-campus proceedings while a criminal or similar prosecution is pending against a student.

- Revise its other procedures for dealing with students in situations like this.
- Critically review all other facets of its conduct in the Turner case and clarify its policies and procedures for how it will act in the future.

Larger System Reforms

Cyber-shaming has become a new form of cruel and unusual punishment and a tool to silence free speech. It cannot be allowed to continue. Unfortunately, these tools of worldwide abuse largely stem from Silicon Valley.

A consistent and rational national policy with respect to sex offender registration must be developed, and it must reduce its coverage to only those who are likely to be truly recurrent serial predators. For those less likely to reoffend, registration must not extend beyond the length of sentencing and periods of probation.

The juvenile justice system must be reformed to take into account the science of brain development, alcohol use and abuse, and alcoholic blackout. Emphasis should be on rehabilitation. California's pending SB 889 proposal is a good start.

The criminal justice system must be overhauled. Nations like Norway are a good example to start with.

California should establish a Commission on Prosecutorial Conduct. Such a commission should be a part of currently-contemplated policing reforms as related to racial discrimination, as well as general wrongful prosecution. Unequal justice is a problem from policing through prosecution and then to sentencing. In light of the comment of Stanford officials that District Attorney Rosen had in the past routinely refused to prosecute matters of this kind, consider the possible motivations other than justice underlying the prosecutor's conduct in the Turner case. Is it an accident that District Attorney Jeff Rosen was up for re-election, and might have seen teaming up with Prof. Dauber as a political opportunity? Is it an accident that Prof. Dauber would choose to make an Olympic-hopeful student-athlete the "poster child" for the emerging #MeToo movement? With so much at stake in the success of the DA's prosecution of Turner, is it an accident that Deputy District Attorney and prosecutor Alaleh Kianerci committed so many

251

ethically-dubious actions before the trial and then in the courtroom? Is it an accident that an Assistant District Attorney in Rosen's office, Cindy Hendrickson, succeeded to Judge Persky's judicial position in the same election in which Persky was recalled? Is it an accident that Chanel Miller's victim impact statement was so skillfully written and presented that a lucrative book deal was at least one result? The point of asking these questions is indicative of a much broader set of pressures that appear to have led to prosecutorial misconduct, and not limited solely to matters of race. The problem is truly systemic.

New York State recently tried to address these types of problems by creating an independent commission to review alleged prosecutorial conduct. For wrongful actions by prosecutors, the commission could publicly censure or even recommend to the governor removal of a prosecutor from office. By deterring this type of misconduct, such a commission in California could go far in advancing the fair administration of justice statewide. The New York law was set aside based on separation of powers arguments unique to the State of New York. The basic concept, however, has considerable merit and should be pursued.

Chapter 19

Closing Words

"If I were to remain silent, I'd be guilty of complicity."
– Albert Einstein

As noted at the outset of this book, the events surrounding the Brock Turner case and the recall of Judge Aaron Persky were closely followed and thoroughly researched by 50 to 100 volunteers, and including information from people at Stanford and Santa Clara County. The resultant findings depict a shameful time in recent history when traditional news and social media — led and fed by a Stanford professor and drawing upon the #MeToo movement — engaged in an unprecedented worldwide campaign of bullying, shaming, and falsification of facts. The campaign's leaders understood that theories don't stir up crowds, so the campaign was personalized, using a 19-year-old freshman and a respected judge as the targets of uncritical and unfounded hatred.

In his article "A Terrible Shame," author Eric Posner states:

> "shaming occurs in the absence of due process. While it is triggered by a perceived act of wrongdoing, **no one takes responsibility for establishing what happened** …. The upshot is a reaction that looks a lot like mob rule."[310] [Boldface added]

This book was written to "establish what happened" through a presentation of the truth and facts in the Turner case and Judge Persky's recall from the bench. Mob rule was the unfortunate result of a carefully orchestrated campaign of disinformation.

The purpose for writing this book was to shine a light on the injustices that occurred in the Turner case and that involved the citizens of Silicon Valley and the leadership at Stanford. Hopefully, what has been presented here will serve as a useful lesson to people everywhere not to fall into a similar mob frenzy but instead, check the facts and ask, who is spearheading this frenzy and for what purposes?

It is with urgency that the good citizens of Santa Clara County and the leadership at Stanford must finally correct the wrongs that were done to Brock Turner and former Judge Aaron Persky. Enough is enough.

APPENDICES

1. Timeline of Events

2. Letter to Michele Dauber from Members of the Stanford Law School Graduating Class of 2016 in Opposition to the Recall of Judge Persky

3. Open Letter on the Need for Judicial Independence [Signed by Santa Clara County judges and retired Judges]

4. Law Professors' Statement for the Independence of the Judiciary and Against the Recall of Santa Clara

5. Chanel Miller's Letter to the Court

6. Brock Turner's Letter to the Court

SEE ALSO

1. "Choices Have Consequences" by Tom Lallas, https://helpsaveoursons.com/essay-by-stanford-law-alum-choices-have-consequences-chanel-miller-brock-turner/

2. "Know the Truth" by Tom Lallas, https://helpsaveoursons.com/wp-content/uploads/2019/09/2019-09-23-Know-the-Truth-Chanel-Miller.pdf

3. "Brock Turner, Sorting Through the Noise" by Michael Vitiello, https://scholarlycommons.pacific.edu/cgi/viewcontent.cgi?article=1181&context=uoplawreview

4. "Putting it in Perspective," https://helpsaveoursons.com/wp-content/uploads/2019/09/Putting-It-in-Perspective-Full-Version-5-with-photos.pdf

Appendix 1

Timeline of Events

Saturday, January 17, 2015	
Late afternoon or early evening	Under the initial accounting Chanel Miller gave to Stanford police when she first woke up in the emergency room on Sunday morning, Chanel and her sister Tiffany go to the Lagunita Court dormitory area at Stanford to meet with friend Julia and later go to the party at the Kappa Alpha fraternity house. Chanel also tells police she only drank Keystone Light beers.
Between 10:00 p.m. and 10:45 pm	Under an accounting Chanel gave to Stanford police 15 hours later, although still on Sunday, between 10:00 p.m. and 10:45 p.m. Saturday night, Chanel, her sister Tiffany, and two friends Colleen and Trea engage in pre-party drinking at home. Chanel drinks four shots of whiskey and one glass of champagne before leaving home for the Kappa Alpha party where they meet up with Julia.
Between 10:45 p.m. and 11:00 p.m.	Under the second accounting, Chanel's mother drives Chanel, her sister Tiffany, and the two friends to the Kappa Alpha fraternity party at Stanford. Chanel says they were dropped off at the Tresidder Student Union parking lot, one friend says they were dropped off in front of the fraternity house, and Chanel's sister says she can't remember where they were dropped off. It's a six- to ten-minute walk, in the dark, from the Tresidder parking lot to the fraternity house, so it's hard to believe one or more didn't remember this walk.
11:30 p.m.	Turner arrives at the Kappa Alpha party with friends. Turner had consumed five beers and one whiskey drink at an earlier party.
Sunday, January 18, 2015	

12:00 a.m.	Chanel, her sister Tiffany, and friend Julia leave the party to urinate in nearby bushes. They return to the party approximately 10 minutes later, where they continue to drink in the patio area with three males.
12:16 a.m.	Chanel calls boyfriend, leaves voicemail. When boyfriend listens to voicemail, he can "understand parts of the message but other parts are unintelligible."
12:17 a.m.	Chanel's sister Tiffany leaves with friend Colleen to bring drunk friend Trea to Julia's dorm room via Uber. According to Stanford police, "When she [Tiffany] left Kappa Alpha, her sister [Chanel] appeared to be fine, so she was not worried about leaving her [Chanel] there" (PR 048).
12:19 a.m.	Chanel's boyfriend calls her, has 10-minute conversation. Chanel's speech described by boyfriend as "rambling."
12:29 a.m.	Chanel attempts to call her sister.
12:30 a.m.	Turner and Chanel leave the party to walk to Turner's dorm. They slip on the dirt path and start making out.
12:55 a.m.	Two Swedish graduate students observe Turner and Chanel near the basketball court a mere 49 feet from the Kappa Alpha fraternity house and in full view of passersby.
1:05 a.m.	Stanford Police Deputy Jeffrey Taylor arrives at the scene.
1:12 a.m.	Paramedics (Palo Alto Fire Department) arrive at the scene.
Approximately 1:20 a.m. and for hours thereafter	Turner, drunk, is taken into custody by Stanford police. At Stanford police station, he is stripped and body parts examined and fluids taken without prior Miranda warning and without a warrant. Turner is then read and waives his Miranda rights, believing no crime has occurred since he believes the encounter with Chanel was fully consensual. Turner is then taken to San Jose jail, a few hours later posts bail, and is released from jail.
January 19, 2015	Paramedic report states Chanel's LOC (level of consciousness) is "11" on Glasgow Scale. The highest score is a 15 (fully awake and aware) and the lowest is 3

257

	(deep coma or brain death). Chanel later admits she can't recall whether sexual incident was consensual. Click Here
January 20, 2015	Stanford bans Turner from campus for life (two days after the incident and before investigation by Stanford, Stanford's police, or others). (https://en.wikipedia.org/wiki/People_v._Turner)
January 20, 2015	Police report is submitted to Santa Clara County District Attorney Jeff Rosen. Rape is charged without any DNA evidence. Police report also states Chanel admits to a history of drunken blackouts, including her saying she has suffered blackout amnesia in the past, meaning she functions fine but can't remember what she did.
January 26, 2015	The *Fountain Hopper*, a Stanford student publication, breaks the story that an athlete had been arrested eight days earlier and had left Stanford two days later. Two years after that (December 7, 2017) the *Fountain Hopper* publishes a detailed summary of shortcomings by Stanford police in their investigations of various sexual assault cases and also that pages in Stanford police logs periodically were "stolen" by unknown persons and then replaced, that other police log pages have been re-dated and otherwise tampered with, etc. This 2017 story also contains the mysterious sentence: "(The Brock Turner story also started with a suspicious log entry.)"
January 27, 2015	*Los Angeles Times* publishes, "Former Stanford swimmer accused of raping unconscious woman on campus." Newspapers and other media nationwide and worldwide carry similar stories, and for weeks and months on end.
January 29, 2015	The *Fountain Hopper* publishes full 53-page felony complaint against Turner.
February 2, 2015	Turner is arraigned, pleads not guilty.
February 3, 2015	The *Stanford Daily* publishes "Police report: Brock Turner admits sexual contact, denies alleged rape."
Ongoing	Defamatory misinformation and smear campaign continues in traditional and social media worldwide, including

	branding of Turner as a rapist despite DNA evidence disproving rape.
October 5, 2015	Preliminary hearing takes place.
October 7, 2015	The two rape charges are dropped after DNA testing from nine months earlier disprove rape (www.apnews.com/962a8de554994637afce94a22afb78e9).
March 7, 2016	People's Motions in Limine, key barriers to Turner receiving a fair trial, are filed by District Attorney Jeff Rosen and prosecutor Alaleh Kianerci. Among other limitations, the jury is to be prohibited from hearing evidence regarding Turner's honesty and character (even though he ultimately will testify in his own defense) and the impact of the pending trial (e.g., character references, forfeiture of a promising swim career, etc.). Also to be prohibited is evidence regarding Chanel's extrapolated BAC of 0.24%, expert toxicology and blackout phenomenology testimony, and Chanel's history of drinking and blackout amnesia. In the police report, Stanford deputy Carrie DeVlugt states Chanel "...described blackout to be where she is still functioning, but not remembering. She usually makes it home even when she blacks out." (PR 045). Also: "She has blacked out before from drinking, but only when she has been continually drinking for a long time, and it is usually at the end of the night when it happens." (PR 045). Nevertheless, the police reports and other pre-trial evidence are to be deemed "hearsay." In the People's Motions in Limine, the District Attorney and prosecutor also claim, "it has not been established that alcoholic blackouts are generally accepted by the Scientific community," which is contrary to countless scientific studies and journals.
March 4, 2016	Prosecutor Alaleh Kianerci, without prior notice to Turner's lawyer and only ten days before the trial is to begin, contacts Turner's only witness, Prof. Kim Fromme, and demands all of Prof. Fromme's notes, emails, and other materials not

259

	only regarding the Turner case, but other cases as well. For some reason, Turner's lawyer goes along with it.
March 14, 2016	Turner's criminal trial begins at the Santa Clara County Superior Court in Palo Alto, with Judge Aaron Persky presiding. Turner faces three charges of felony sexual assault.
March 17, 2016	Opening statements are heard at trial.
March 30, 2016	After a two-week trial, the jury finds Turner guilty of three counts of sexual assault.
May 3, 2016 (Chanel) and May 9, 2016 (Turner)	Chanel and Turner are separately interviewed by the Santa Clara County probation department in order for the department to make their official recommendations to Judge Persky as to a proper sentence. Among other things, Chanel is quoted by the probation department as saying, "he [Turner] doesn't need to be behind bars."
May 26, 2016	Chanel's initial version of her victim impact statement is filed with the court. Somehow it differs from what she reads in court seven days later.
June 2, 2016	Chanel reads her revised victim impact statement aloud in court. The victim impact statement contains numerous but significant erroneous statements (see Ch. 9). Chanel continues to assert that she has no memory, however, of what actually happened. For several months, the statement is publicized worldwide as the statement Chanel wrote, although from the very first day, Santa Clara County officials never say Chanel wrote the statement but only that she "read" it or "disseminated" it. Six months later, as evidence mounts that others wrote or significantly edited the statement, the media campaign thereafter carefully says it is the statement Chanel "read" in court.
June 2, 2016	Turner is sentenced to six months in jail, three years' probation, rehabilitation, and a lifetime requirement to

	register as a sex offender even though the purpose of these statutes is largely regarding children.
June 2, 2016	District Attorney Jeff Rosen at a post-sentencing and apparent pre-election campaign press conference states, " [Turner's] punishment does not fit the crime...Campus rape is no different than off-campus rape. Rape is rape. We will prosecute it the same." (sccgov.org, 6/2/16). DA Rosen repeats the word "rape" multiple times, ignoring the fact that Turner was neither tried for nor convicted of rape.
June 3, 2016	The victim impact statement is published online by *Palo Alto Online* and *Buzzfeed*, promoted by Stanford law school Prof. Michele Dauber via Twitter/Facebook, and made a worldwide event.
June 4, 2016	Prof. Dauber tweets Turner's father's "20 minutes of action" statement. That also becomes a worldwide news story.
June 6, 2016	First financial contributions are made to Washington and Sacramento political action committees for distribution to the Committee to Recall Judge Persky.
June 6, 2016	Prof. Dauber tweets about a letter to the court written by Turner's childhood friend, Leslie Rasmussen, one of approximately 30 letters submitted by Turner's family, friends, and others in support of Turner. Shortly after that, Leslie loses her job as a waitress and opportunities for music performances for her band as a result of social media shaming.
June 6, 2016	CNN anchor Ashley Banfield reads the entire victim impact statement on the air, live. CNN continually refers to this as the "Stanford rape survivor's letter to her attacker" and "it was her words." (But see Ch. 9)
June 9, 2016	Vice President Joe Biden writes an open letter to Emily Doe (Chanel) praising her letter.
June 9, 2016	Joe Trippi and John Shallman (Democratic political consultants) join the Recall Judge Aaron Persky campaign

	team. Also included as the communications director is Becky Warren of the Dolphin Group, the same political entity that had invented the notorious Willie Horton campaign years earlier.
June 10, 2016	The California Legislative Women's Caucus announces intent to raise money for the recall campaign. By the time of the June 5th election in 2018, the Recall Persky campaign raises approximately $1.4 million from various sources.
June 10, 2016	Santa Clara County officially releases court documents to the public. Yet somehow Leslie Rasmussen's letter and other materials were in the hands of Prof. Dauber and her media team hours or days earlier.
August, 2016	A public event is held about Turner and the recall. Two jurors attend.
September 1, 2016	Turner is released from jail.
November 18, 2016	Actress Sharon Stone does a reading at Santa Clara University of Chanel's victim impact statement.
December 19, 2016	Judge Persky is cleared of misconduct by the Commission on Judicial Performance.
June 26, 2017	Notice of intent to recall Judge Persky is submitted by the recall campaign committee.
December 1, 2017	Turner files appeal.
December 7, 2017	Prof. Dauber tweets hateful and violent song and invites people to "enjoy" the song's lyrics, which advocate violence and death against Brock Turner (http://padailypost.com/2017/12/07/blowup-over-brock-turner-song/).
February 6, 2018	Santa Clara County Board of Supervisors approves the recall measure for the election ballot in June 2018 even though Judge Persky will be unable to defend himself per California judicial ethics restrictions associated with Turner's pending appeal.

March 26, 2018	California State Appellate court denies Judge Persky's request to move jurisdiction over the recall from Santa Clara County to the California Secretary of State on the basis his judicial office is a state and not county office.
May, 2018	Turner's appeal is amended to remove the most important items, reportedly because had Turner succeeded on one or more of these items (which most attorneys believed he would), there would be high risk that District Attorney Jeff Rosen and prosecutor Alaleh Kianerci would seek harsher penalties if they won in a retrial. There also were fears about the impact the ongoing media campaign against both Turner and Judge Persky during the prior three years would have on a jury, and also any judges willing to hear the case.
June 5, 2018	Voters approve the removal of Judge Persky from office. Palo Alto, Stanford, Los Altos, and Los Altos Hills vote NO on the recall. Prof. Dauber's own precinct votes NO on the recall.
July 24, 2018	Oral arguments for Turner's remaining items on appeal are submitted to the Sixth District appellate court.
August 8, 2018	The Sixth District appellate court denies the appeal to reverse Turner's three felony convictions and also denies a new trial.
October 24, 2018	The recall campaign sues former Judge Persky for their legal costs opposing Persky's prior lawsuit as to what was the proper jurisdiction to oversee the recall (California Secretary of State versus county officers). Judge Kay Tsenin orders ex-Judge Persky to pay $161,825.68 to cover legal fees the recall campaign says they incurred in defense of ex-Judge Persky's legal challenges. The order is later reduced to $135,000.00.
September 4, 2019	Chanel Miller's book, *Know My Name*, in which she reveals her real name, is scheduled to be released on September 24, 2019. Coincidentally, this is only a few days after the statute of limitations for perjury has expired.
September 6, 2019	The *Daily Mail of London* publishes a multi-page article about Chanel's pending book. The article includes photos of

	Turner secretly taken in prior weeks as well as attempted interviews with his co-workers. Apparently the *Daily Mail* was part of the planned media campaign for Chanel's book, and whose publisher is based in the UK. https://www.dailymail.co.uk/news/article-7436027/Stanford-rapist-Brock-Turner-seen-time-victim-Chanel-Miller-revealed-herself.html
September 22, 2019	CBS broadcasts a highly publicized interview with Chanel on "60-Minutes." Several weeks prior to the broadcast, the producers were advised by various sources that there were major questions about who actually wrote or helped Chanel write the victim impact statement that would be the centerpiece of their broadcast. They also were provided with information showing major discrepancies in the statement as well as inappropriate actions involving Turner's prosecution and conviction. Even though Chanel reads some of the more sensationalized language of her statement in the broadcast, she is not asked, at least on camera, who wrote or helped write the statement and who has been coaching her?

Appendix 2

Letter to Michele Dauber from Members of the Stanford Law School Graduating Class of 2016 in Opposition to the Judge Persky Recall

Dear Professor Dauber,

We are members of the graduating Class of 2016, and we were inspired to write this letter because of your leadership in responding to the Brock Turner rape case. As we bid farewell to the Stanford community we've been privileged to be a part of over the last three years, we can't help but take note of those events and the discussion surrounding it, and we feel compelled to apply what we've learned at SLS to weigh in on an aspect of that discourse we find troubling.

First, we are proud of your leading role in advocating for reform of how society responds to sexual violence. Rape and other forms of sexual assault are urgent problems that are too often neglected or obscured by euphemisms, silence, and shame. The best scholars use their expertise to shine light on pressing civic issues like these: they articulate their visions of a more just society, and they engage with policymakers and the public to spur and shape reform. We've been privileged to learn at a place where faculty like you take up that mantle.

We'd also like to emphasize our agreement with your goals. We, like you, believe that members of the Stanford community — indeed, of every community — should be doing all we can to confront the problem head on, by preventing sexual violence in the first place, ensuring that those who experience it receive support and healing, and insisting that those responsible face consequences that reflect the seriousness of their actions. We, like you, are disturbed by the six-month jail sentence that Turner received, which appears lenient when measured against the relevant sentencing guidelines, the much-longer sentences many thousands of Americans are serving for less-serious crimes, and the trauma that the target of his assault so bravely described at Turner's sentencing hearing. And we, like you, are especially troubled by our suspicion that race and privilege explain those discrepancies. Accountability means little when we demand it only from the already-disenfranchised, and the transformative power of mercy is diminished when we reserve it only for the privileged.

At the same time, one aspect of your recent advocacy troubles us: the nascent campaign you have championed to recall Judge Aaron Persky, who sentenced Turner. We have deep reservations about the idea of a judge — any judge — being fired over sentencing decisions that the public perceives as too lenient.

As we've learned during our time at the law school, judicial independence is a cornerstone of due process and an essential prerequisite of a fair criminal justice system. Judges are entrusted with immense power over the life and liberty of criminal defendants from all walks of life, and they need latitude to exercise that power judiciously. After decades of mass incarceration driven by mandatory minimums and other punitive sentencing regimes, we believe that judicial leniency is already too scarce, even though we strongly disagree with how it was applied to Turner. And in a world where judges believe they are one unpopular sentencing decision away from an abrupt pink slip, it will only grow scarcer. A high-profile campaign to recall Judge Persky because he showed too much solicitude for a defendant convicted of odious crimes would evoke an ugly chapter of California's history: when three justices of our state's highest court were recalled from the bench because they voted to oppose the death penalty, in accordance with the dictates of justice and the constitution as they understood them. Though the values underlying that effort were different from the ones animating the current recall debate, the chilling effect on judicial independence would be the same.

To be clear, our hesitation about a recall campaign does not stem from a belief that Judge Persky's decision to give Turner a below-guidelines sentence was correct or that his stated justifications for doing so were sound. Many of us, like you, believe that justice called for a stiffer sentence in his case. But we think humility requires us to recognize that we won't always be able to distinguish between legitimate and illegitimate exercises of judicial mercy. If you or we claim the power to make that decision, how can we credibly deny it to anyone else? If we demand that Judge Persky immediately hand over his gavel for acting on his empathy for this defendant, how we can we credibly assure any other judge that her hand need not waver when the human circumstances of a case seem to call for compassion?

This is not an abstract concern: many of us count our work with Stanford's Three Strikes Project as one of the most powerful experiences we had at SLS. Through the project, we represented clients serving life sentences for non-violent felonies as they petitioned for early release under Propositions 36 and 47 — transformative ballot measures championed by your Stanford colleagues, which have begun to roll back

266

the worst excesses of California's punitive sentencing laws. In that role, we had to ask county judges like Aaron Persky to grant early release to men and women serving life in prison because the people of California once believed that our clients' mistakes made them irredeemable. Even when an inmate has made great strides in prison, and even though statistics show that people resentenced under Propositions 36 and 47 pose little danger of recidivism, granting that second chance is a delicate decision that requires courage on the part of judges: they have to bear the risk, however remote, that the petitioner will abuse that mercy in ways that provoke public backlash against their decision.

We believe it would send a powerful message to these judges and others making similar decisions around the country if, while continuing to critique Judge Persky's sentencing decisions and calling for a different approach in future cases, you abstained from your effort to recall him from the bench and instead focused on other avenues of response and reform. These might include educating future judges and jurors about the realities of sexual assault, or pressing for systemic changes in how these cases are handled. We simply ask that you withhold your support for a recall campaign that would set a dangerous precedent against the exercise of merciful discretion in our criminal justice system.

Sincerely,

Akiva Freidlin, Emi Young, Ginny Halden, Jeannie Lieder, Madeleine McKenna, Michael Skocpol, Nick Rosellini, and Vina Seelam *(Drafters) (This letter was also signed by 48 other members of the graduating class.)*

Appendix 3

Respectfully Submitted

Hon. Andrea Y. Bryan (Ret.)

Hon. James H. Chang (Ret.)

Hon. LaDoris H. Cordell (Ret.)

Hon. Ray E. Cunningham (Ret.)

Hon. Raymond J. Davilla, Jr. (Ret.)

Hon. Ron M. Del Pozzo (Ret.)

Hon. William J. Fernandez (Ret.)

Hon. Leonard P. Edwards (Ret.)

Hon. Nazario A. Gonzales (Ret.)

Hon. Charles W. Hayden (Ret.)

Hon. Eugene M. Hyman (Ret.)

Hon. Jerald A. Infantino (Ret.)

Hon. Constance E. Jimenez (Ret.)

Hon. Mary Jo Levinger (Ret.)

Hon. Sandra Faithfull McKeith (Ret.)

Hon. Anna Ollinger (Ret.)

Hon. Diane Ritchie (Ret.)

Hon. Douglas K. Southard (Ret.)

OPEN LETTER ON THE NEED FOR JUDICIAL INDEPENDENCE

The California Judicial Code of Ethics prohibits sitting judges and commissioners from commenting on pending and impending matters. Accordingly, no currently active judicial officer is permitted to comment on the case of People of the State of California v. Brock Turner, which was presided over by Santa Clara Superior Court Judge Aaron Persky. However, this prohibition does not apply to retired judicial officers who no longer handle matters for the court. Because we are permitted to do so and believe that it is important that we express our views, we are writing to respond to the flurry of public and social media criticism of Judge Persky, which has led to the current effort to remove him from the bench.

Judicial independence is one of the core values of our democracy. It is based on the principle that each case should be decided on its particular facts and the applicable law rather than in response to political considerations or public opinion. It exists and thrives only when judges know that doing their job will not put their job at risk.

Judges cannot and should not be immune from criticism. To the contrary, robust public debate about cases that raise important issues is a good thing. Removal of a judge for illegal or unethical conduct may be appropriate. However, calls to remove a judge because of a decision, even a very unpopular one, when that judge exercised discretion permitted under the law, is an entirely different matter. The essence of judicial independence is that judges must be able to make decisions without fear of political repercussions.

We acknowledge and respect the deeply held views of those who disagree with Judge Persky's sentencing decision in the Turner case. The case presents serious questions about our society's treatment of crimes involving sexual assault and of criminal defendants from different socioeconomic backgrounds.

At the same time, the full record in the case shows that Judge Persky made his decision after considering all the evidence presented at trial, the statements of the victim and the defendant, and a detailed report from an experienced probation officer. The probation officer recommended essentially the sentence that was imposed, including the grant of probation.

It is clear to us that Judge Persky took the matter seriously. He read several lengthy excerpts from the victim's statement into the record at the sentencing hearing. He followed the proper procedure, and he explained the reasons for his decision in accordance with the applicable law. Judges acting in good faith routinely reach different decisions. No doubt there are many judges who disagree with Judge Persky's decision. The purpose of this letter is not to take sides as to whether the sentence was adequate or appropriate. Rather, we firmly believe that removing Judge Persky from office under these circumstances would set a dangerous precedent and be a serious threat to judicial independence.

Appendix 4

Law Professors' Statement for the Independence of the Judiciary and Against the Recall of Santa Clara County Superior Court Judge Aaron Persky

(91 law professors as of August 17, 2017)

We the undersigned are part of a broad diversity of law professors from California universities; among our relevant fields of specialization are criminal law, gender and law, and constitutional law. We write in strong opposition to the campaign to recall Judge Aaron Persky of the Santa Clara County Superior Court. We do so because this recall campaign, which just now is beginning the formal process of gathering signatures, threatens the fundamental principles of judicial independence and fairness that we all embed in the education of our students.

The mechanism of recall was designed for and must be limited to cases where judges are corrupt or incompetent or exhibit bias that leads to systematic injustice in their courtrooms. None of these criteria applies to Judge Persky. The recall campaign was instigated in response to a sentencing decision in the case of Brock Turner, where the judge followed a probation report recommendation and exercised discretion towards a lenient sentence, in accordance with the California Penal Code. We appreciate that some people (indeed including some of the signers of this letter) might have chosen a different result, but the core values of judicial independence and integrity require the judge to make a decision based on the record (including, in this case, the recommendation of a skilled professional, a probation officer) – *not* on public outcry about a

controversial case. Judge Persky's decision was controversial, but it was a lawful decision. Other sentencing decisions by Judge Persky that have been challenged by the recall movement have followed the equally common and legitimate practice of accepting a recommendation agreed on by the prosecution and defense.

We believe it is critical to distinguish disagreement with a particular sentence or allegations about a handful of decisions from an attack on a judge's overall record. Thus, it is vital to recognize the following: the Santa Clara County Bar Association issued a 2016 statement opposing attempts to remove Judge Persky

from the bench; this can be found at
http://www.sccba.com/blogpost/1133925/249782/SCCBA-Statement-on-Judicial-Independence. The State Commission on Judicial Performance, an independent state agency, conducted a review and concluded that the claims of bias were unfounded. (https://cjp.ca.gov/wp-content/uploads/sites/40/2016/08/Persky_Explanatory_Statement_12-19-16.pdf). We encourage you to read both documents for details of their reasoning.

The last three elected District Attorneys of Santa Clara County, with 27 years of leadership in that office, are against the recall; surely, they would speak up if they found the judge's record to be improper. Similarly, the defense bar's outpouring of opposition to the recall underscores Judge Persky's reputation for being unbiased against those most harshly disadvantaged by our criminal justice system. A broad range of lawyers who have appeared before Judge Persky have publicly attested to the respect they have for him as a fair and impartial jurist.

In particular, lawyers who represent indigent defendants in our system rightly view the recall as a danger to, not promotion of, progressive values. This is because, historically and empirically, recall actions push judges towards sharply ratcheting up sentences, especially against the poor and people of color, out of fear of media campaigns run by well-funded interest groups. No wonder that former U.S. Supreme Court Justice Sandra Day O'Connor, observing the effects of judicial elections, lamented "political prizefights where partisans and special interests seek to install judges who will answer to them instead of the law and the Constitution."

A fair and equitable justice system requires judges who dispassionately assess the culpability and background of offenders, without fear of public opinion, balancing the goals of retribution, deterrence, and rehabilitation. The recall campaign risks allowing public clamor to distort these crucial acts of judgment. We urge you not to sign the petition, and to oppose the recall. Thank you.

University affiliations are listed solely for the purpose of identifying the individual signers. The statement expresses the views of the individual professors. (89 as of August 15, 2017)

Richard L. Abel, UCLA School of Law
Hadar Aviram, UC Hastings College of Law
Barbara Babcock, Stanford Law School
W. David Ball, Santa Clara University School of Law

Joseph Bankman, Stanford Law School
R. Richard Banks, Stanford Law School
Lara Bazelon, University of San Francisco School of Law
Samuel Bray, UCLA School of Law
Paul Brest, Stanford Law School
Cary Bricker, McGeorge School of Law
Patricia Cain, Santa Clara University School of Law
Robert Calhoun, Golden Gate University School of Law
Linda E. Carter, McGeorge School of Law
Erwin Chemerinsky, UC Berkeley School of Law
Colleen Chien, Santa Clara University School of Law
Gabriel Chin, UC Davis School of Law
Stephen Cody, McGeorge School of Law
Sharon Dolovich, UCLA School of Law
Donald A. Dripps, University of San Diego School of Law
Daniel Farber, UC Berkeley School of Law
Barbara Fried, Stanford Law School
Catherine Fisk, UC Berkeley School of Law
Jeffrey Fisher, Stanford Law School
Richard T. Ford, Stanford Law School
Bryant Garth, UC Irvine School of Law
Paul Goldstein, Stanford Law School
Christine Chambers Goodman, Pepperdine University School of Law
Robert Gordon, Stanford Law School
William Gould, Stanford Law School
Henry T. Greely, Stanford Law School
Thomas Grey, Stanford Law School
Pratheepan Gulasekaram, Santa Clara University School of Law
Angela P. Harris, UC Davis School of Law
Deborah Hensler, Stanford Law School
Robert Hillman, UC Davis School of Law
Daniel E. Ho, Stanford Law School
Scott Howe, Chapman University / Fowler School of Law
Philip Jimenez, Santa Clara University School of Law
Paige Kaneb, Santa Clara University School of Law
Pamela Karlan, Stanford Law School
Gregory Keating, USC Gould School of Law
Amalia D. Kessler, Stanford Law School
Michael Klausner, Stanford Law School

Russell Korobkin, UCLA School of Law
Ellen Kreitzberg, Santa Clara University School of Law
Christopher Kutz, UC Berkeley School of Law
Brian K. Landsberg, McGeorge School of Law
Richard Leo, University of San Francisco School of Law
Laurie Levenson, Loyola Law School
David Levine, UC Hastings College of the Law
Rory Little, UC Hastings College of the Law
Kerry Macintosh, Santa Clara University School of Law
Lawrence C. Marshall, Stanford Law School
Michael McConnell, Stanford Law School
Bernadette Meyler, Stanford Law School
Alison Morantz, Stanford Law School
Mary-Beth Moylan, McGeorge School of Law
Gary Neustadter, Santa Clara University School of Law
Michelle Oberman, Santa Clara University School of Law
Joan Petersilia, Stanford Law School
Donald Polden, Santa Clara University School of Law
Robert Rabin, Stanford Law School
Radhika Rao, UC Hastings College of the Law
Kathleen Ridolfi, Santa Clara University School of Law
Margaret M. Russell, Santa Clara University School of Law
Susan Rutberg, Golden Gate University School of Law
Elisabeth Semel, UC Berkeley School of Law
Steven Shatz, University of San Francisco School of Law
Marci Seville, Golden Gate University School of Law
Jonathan Simon, UC Berkeley School of Law
David Sklansky, Stanford Law School
David Sloss, Santa Clara University School of Law
Robert Solomon, UC Irvine School of Law
Ann Southworth, UC Irvine School of Law
E. Gary Spitko, Santa Clara University School of Law
John Sprankling, McGeorge School of Law
Jayashri Srikantiah, Stanford Law School
Linda Starr, Santa Clara University School of Law
Edward Steinman, Santa Clara University School of Law
David Studdert, Stanford School of Law
Shauhin Talesh, UC Irvine School of Law
Edward Telfeyan, McGeorge School of Law

Ronald Tyler, Stanford Law School
Michael Vitiello, McGeorge School of Law
Gerald Uelmen, Santa Clara University School of Law
Emily Garcia Uhrig, McGeorge School of Law
Michael Wald, Stanford Law School
Robert Weisberg, Stanford Law School
Charles Weisselberg, UC Berkeley School of Law
Stephanie M. Wildman, Santa Clara University School of Law

Appendix 5

Chanel Miller's Letter to the Court

Your Honor, if it is all right, for the majority of this statement I would like to address the defendant directly.

You don't know me, but you've been inside me, and that's why we're here today.

On January 17th, 2015, it was a quiet Saturday night at home. My dad made some dinner and I sat at the table with my younger sister who was visiting for the weekend. I was working full time and it was approaching my bed time. I planned to stay at home by myself, watch some TV and read, while she went to a party with her friends. Then, I decided it was my only night with her, I had nothing better to do, so why not, there's a dumb party ten minutes from my house, I would go, dance like a fool, and embarrass my younger sister. On the way there, I joked that undergrad guys would have braces. My sister teased me for wearing a beige cardigan to a frat party like a librarian. I called myself "big mama", because I knew I'd be the oldest one there. I made silly faces, let my guard down, and drank liquor too fast not factoring in that my tolerance had significantly lowered since college.

The next thing I remember I was in a gurney in a hallway. I had dried blood and bandages on the backs of my hands and elbow. I thought maybe I had fallen and was in an admin office on campus. I was very calm and wondering where my sister was. A deputy explained I had been assaulted. I still remained calm, assured he was speaking to the wrong person. I knew no one at this party. When I was finally allowed to use the restroom, I pulled down the hospital pants they had given me, went to pull down my underwear, and felt nothing. I still remember the feeling of my hands touching my skin and grabbing nothing. I looked down and there was nothing. The thin piece of fabric, the only thing between my vagina and anything else, was missing and everything inside me was silenced. I still don't have words for that feeling. In order to keep breathing, I thought maybe the policemen used scissors to cut them off for evidence.

Then, I felt pine needles scratching the back of my neck and started pulling them out my hair. I thought maybe, the pine needles had fallen from a tree onto my head. My brain was talking my gut into not collapsing. Because my gut was saying, help me, help me.

I shuffled from room to room with a blanket wrapped around me, pine needles trailing behind me, I left a little pile in every room I sat in. I was asked to sign papers that said "Rape Victim" and I thought something has really happened. My clothes were confiscated and I stood naked while the nurses held a ruler to various abrasions on my body and photographed them. The three of us worked to comb the pine needles out of my hair, six hands to fill one paper bag. To calm me down, they said it's just the flora and fauna, flora and fauna. I had multiple swabs inserted into my vagina and anus, needles for shots, pills, had a Nikon pointed right into my spread legs. I had long, pointed beaks inside me and had my vagina smeared with cold, blue paint to check for abrasions.

After a few hours of this, they let me shower. I stood there examining my body beneath the stream of water and decided, I don't want my body anymore. I was terrified of it, I didn't know what had been in it, if it had been contaminated, who had touched it. I wanted to take off my body like a jacket and leave it at the hospital with everything else.

On that morning, all that I was told was that I had been found behind a dumpster, potentially penetrated by a stranger, and that I should get retested for HIV because results don't always show up immediately. But for now, I should go home and get back to my normal life. Imagine stepping back into the world with only that information. They gave me huge hugs and I walked out of the hospital into the parking lot wearing the new sweatshirt and sweatpants they provided me, as they had only allowed me to keep my necklace and shoes.

My sister picked me up, face wet from tears and contorted in anguish. Instinctively and immediately, I wanted to take away her pain. I smiled at her, I told her to look at me, I'm right here, I'm okay, everything's okay, I'm right here. My hair is washed and clean, they gave me the strangest shampoo, calm down, and look at me. Look at these funny new sweatpants and sweatshirt, I look like a P.E. teacher, let's go home, let's eat something. She did not know that beneath my sweatsuit, I had scratches and bandages on my skin, my vagina was sore and had become a strange, dark color from all the prodding, my underwear was missing, and I felt too empty to continue to speak. That I was also afraid, that I was also devastated. That day we drove home and for hours in silence my younger sister held me.

My boyfriend did not know what happened, but called that day and said, "I was really worried about you last night, you scared me, did you make it home okay?" I was horrified. That's when I learned I had called him that night in my blackout, left an incomprehensible voicemail, that we had also spoken on the phone, but I was slurring so heavily he was scared for me, that he repeatedly told me to go find [my sister]. Again, he asked me, "What happened last night? Did you make it home okay?" I said yes, and hung up to cry.

I was not ready to tell my boyfriend or parents that actually, I may have been raped behind a dumpster, but I don't know by who or when or how. If I told them, I would see the fear on their faces, and mine would multiply by tenfold, so instead I pretended the whole thing wasn't real.

I tried to push it out of my mind, but it was so heavy I didn't talk, I didn't eat, I didn't sleep, I didn't interact with anyone. After work, I would drive to a secluded place to scream. I didn't talk, I didn't eat, I didn't sleep, I didn't interact with anyone, and I became isolated from the ones I loved most. For over a week after the incident, I didn't get any calls or updates about that night or what happened to me. The only symbol that proved that it hadn't just been a bad dream, was the sweatshirt from the hospital in my drawer.

One day, I was at work, scrolling through the news on my phone, and came across an article. In it, I read and learned for the first time about how I was found unconscious, with my hair disheveled, long necklace wrapped around my neck, bra pulled out of my dress, dress pulled off over my shoulders and pulled up above my waist, that I was butt naked all the way down to my boots, legs spread apart, and had been penetrated by a foreign object by someone I did not recognize. This was how I learned what happened to me, sitting at my desk reading the news at work. I learned what happened to me the same time everyone else in the world learned what happened to me. That's when the pine needles in my hair made sense, they didn't fall from a tree. He had taken off my underwear, his fingers had been inside of me. I don't even know this person. I still don't know this person. When I read about me like this, I said, this can't be me, this can't be me. I could not digest or accept any of this information. I could not imagine my family having to read about this online. I kept reading. In the next paragraph, I read something that I will never forgive; I read that according to him, I liked it. I liked it. Again, I do not have words for these feelings.

It's like if you were to read an article where a car was hit, and found dented, in a ditch. But maybe the car enjoyed being hit. Maybe the other car didn't mean to hit it, just bump it up a little bit. Cars get in accidents all the time, people aren't always paying attention, can we really say who's at fault.

And then, at the bottom of the article, after I learned about the graphic details of my own sexual assault, the article listed his swimming times. She was found breathing, unresponsive with her underwear six inches away from her bare stomach curled in fetal position. By the way, he's really good at swimming. Throw in my mile time if that's what we're doing. I'm good at cooking, put that in there, I think the end is where you list your extracurriculars to cancel out all the sickening things that've happened.

The night the news came out I sat my parents down and told them that I had been assaulted, to not look at the news because it's upsetting, just know that I'm okay, I'm right here, and I'm okay. But halfway through telling them, my mom had to hold me because I could no longer stand up.

The night after it happened, he said he didn't know my name, said he wouldn't be able to identify my face in a lineup, didn't mention any dialogue between us, no words, only dancing and kissing. Dancing is a cute term; was it snapping fingers and twirling dancing, or just bodies grinding up against each other in a crowded room? I wonder if kissing was just faces sloppily pressed up against each other? When the detective asked if he had planned on taking me back to his dorm, he said no. When the detective asked how we ended up behind the dumpster, he said he didn't know. He admitted to kissing other girls at that party, one of whom was my own sister who pushed him away. He admitted to wanting to hook up with someone. I was the wounded antelope of the herd, completely alone and vulnerable, physically unable to fend for myself, and he chose me. Sometimes I think, if I hadn't gone, then this never would've happened. But then I realized, it would have happened, just to somebody else. You were about to enter four years of access to drunk girls and parties, and if this is the foot you started off on, then it is right you did not continue. The night after it happened, he said he thought I liked it because I rubbed his back. A back rub.

Never mentioned me voicing consent, never mentioned us even speaking, a back rub. One more time, in public news, I learned that my ass and vagina were completely exposed outside, my breasts had been groped, fingers had been jabbed inside me along with pine needles and debris, my bare skin and head had been rubbing against the ground behind a dumpster, while an erect freshman was humping my half naked, unconscious body. But I don't remember, so how do I prove I didn't like it.

I thought there's no way this is going to trial; there were witnesses, there was dirt in my body, he ran but was caught. He's going to settle, formally apologize, and we will both move on. Instead, I was told he hired a powerful attorney, expert witnesses, private investigators who were going to try and find details about my personal life to use against me, find loopholes in my story to invalidate me and my sister, in order to show that this sexual assault was in fact a misunderstanding. That he was going to go to any length to convince the world he had simply been confused.

277

I was not only told that I was assaulted, I was told that because I couldn't remember, I technically could not prove it was unwanted. And that distorted me, damaged me, almost broke me. It is the saddest type of confusion to be told I was assaulted and nearly raped, blatantly out in the open, but we don't know if it counts as assault yet. I had to fight for an entire year to make it clear that there was something wrong with this situation.

When I was told to be prepared in case we didn't win, I said, I can't prepare for that. He was guilty the minute I woke up. No one can talk me out of the hurt he caused me. Worst of all, I was warned, because he now knows you don't remember, he is going to get to write the script. He can say whatever he wants and no one can contest it. I had no power, I had no voice, I was defenseless. My memory loss would be used against me. My testimony was weak, was incomplete, and I was made to believe that perhaps, I am not enough to win this. His attorney constantly reminded the jury, the only one we can believe is Brock, because she doesn't remember. That helplessness was traumatizing.

Instead of taking time to heal, I was taking time to recall the night in excruciating detail, in order to prepare for the attorney's questions that would be invasive, aggressive, and designed to steer me off course, to contradict myself, my sister, phrased in ways to manipulate my answers. Instead of his attorney saying, Did you notice any abrasions? He said, You didn't notice any abrasions, right? This was a game of strategy, as if I could be tricked out of my own worth. The sexual assault had been so clear, but instead, here I was at the trial, answering questions like:

How old are you? How much do you weigh? What did you eat that day? Well what did you have for dinner? Who made dinner? Did you drink with dinner? No, not even water? When did you drink? How much did you drink? What container did you drink out of? Who gave you the drink? How much do you usually drink? Who dropped you off at this party? At what time? But where exactly? What were you wearing? Why were you going to this party? What'd you do when you got there? Are you sure you did that? But what time did you do that? What does this text mean? Who were you texting? When did you urinate? Where did you urinate? With whom did you urinate outside? Was your phone on silent when your sister called? Do you remember silencing it? Really because on page 53 I'd like to point out that you said it was set to ring. Did you drink in college? You said you were a party animal? How many times did you black out? Did you party at frats? Are you serious with your boyfriend? Are you sexually active with him? When did you start dating? Would you ever cheat? Do you have a history of cheating? What do you mean when you said you wanted to reward him? Do you remember what time you woke up? Were you wearing your cardigan? What color was your cardigan? Do you remember any more from that night? No? Okay, well, we'll let Brock fill it in.

I was pummeled with narrowed, pointed questions that dissected my personal life, love life, past life, family life, inane questions, accumulating trivial details to try and find an excuse for this guy who had me half naked before even bothering to ask for my name. After a physical assault, I was assaulted with questions designed to attack me, to say see, her facts don't line up, she's out of her mind, she's practically an alcoholic, she probably wanted to hook up, he's like an athlete right, they were both drunk, whatever, the hospital stuff she remembers is after the fact, why take it into account, Brock has a lot at stake so he's having a really hard time right now.

And then it came time for him to testify and I learned what it meant to be revictimized. I want to remind you, the night after it happened he said he never planned to take me back to his dorm. He said he didn't know why we were behind a dumpster. He got up to leave because he wasn't feeling well when he was suddenly chased and attacked. Then he learned I could not remember.

So one year later, as predicted, a new dialogue emerged. Brock had a strange new story, almost sounded like a poorly written young adult novel with kissing and dancing and hand holding and lovingly tumbling onto the ground, and most importantly in this new story, there was suddenly consent. One year after the incident, he remembered, oh yeah, by the way she actually said yes, to everything, so.

He said he had asked if I wanted to dance. Apparently I said yes. He'd asked if I wanted to go to his dorm, I said yes. Then he asked if he could finger me and I said yes. Most guys don't ask, can I finger you? Usually there's a natural progression of things, unfolding consensually, not a Q and A. But apparently I granted full permission. He's in the clear. Even in his story, I only said a total of three words, yes yes yes, before he had me half naked on the ground. Future reference, if you are confused about whether a girl can consent, see if she can speak an entire sentence. You couldn't even do that. Just one coherent string of words. Where was the confusion? This is common sense, human decency.

According to him, the only reason we were on the ground was because I fell down. Note; if a girl falls down help her get back up. If she is too drunk to even walk and falls down, do not mount her, hump her, take off her underwear, and insert your hand inside her vagina. If a girl falls down help her up. If she is wearing a cardigan over her dress don't take it off so that you can touch her breasts. Maybe she is cold, maybe that's why she wore the cardigan.

Next in the story, two Swedes on bicycles approached you and you ran. When they tackled you why didn't say, "Stop! Everything's okay, go ask her, she's right over there, she'll tell you." I mean you had just asked for my consent, right? I was awake, right? When the policeman arrived and interviewed the evil Swede who tackled you, he was crying so hard he couldn't speak because of what he'd seen.

Your attorney has repeatedly pointed out, well we don't know exactly when she became unconscious. And you're right, maybe I was still fluttering my eyes and wasn't completely limp yet. That was never the point. I was too drunk to speak English, too drunk to consent way before I was on the ground. I should have never been touched in the first place. Brock stated, "At no time did I see that she was not responding. If at any time I thought she was not responding, I would have stopped immediately." Here's the thing; if your plan was to stop only when I became unresponsive, then you still do not understand. You didn't even stop when I was unconscious anyway! Someone else stopped you. Two guys on bikes noticed I wasn't moving in the dark and had to tackle you. How did you not notice while on top of me?

You said, you would have stopped and gotten help. You say that, but I want you to explain how you would've helped me, step by step, walk me through this. I want to know, if those evil Swedes had not found me, how the night would have played out. I am asking you; Would you have pulled my underwear back on over my boots? Untangled the necklace wrapped around my neck? Closed my legs, covered me? Pick the pine needles from my hair? Asked if the abrasions on my neck and bottom hurt? Would you then go find a friend and say, Will you help me get her somewhere warm and soft? I don't sleep when I think about the way it could have gone if the two guys had never come. What would have happened to me? That's what you'll never have a good answer for, that's what you can't explain even after a year.

On top of all this, he claimed that I orgasmed after one minute of digital penetration. The nurse said there had been abrasions, lacerations, and dirt in my genitalia. Was that before or after I came?

To sit under oath and inform all of us, that yes I wanted it, yes I permitted it, and that you are the true victim attacked by Swedes for reasons unknown to you is appalling, is demented, is selfish, is damaging. It is enough to be suffering. It is another thing to have someone ruthlessly working to diminish the gravity of validity of this suffering.

My family had to see pictures of my head strapped to a gurney full of pine needles, of my body in the dirt with my eyes closed, hair messed up, limbs bent, and dress hiked up. And even after that, my family had to listen to your attorney say the pictures were after the fact, we can dismiss them. To say, yes her nurse confirmed there was redness and abrasions inside her, significant trauma to her genitalia, but that's what happens

280

when you finger someone, and he's already admitted to that. To listen to your attorney attempt to paint a picture of me, the face of girls gone wild, as if somehow that would make it so that I had this coming for me. To listen to him say I sounded drunk on the phone because I'm silly and that's my goofy way of speaking. To point out that in the voicemail, I said I would reward my boyfriend and we all know what I was thinking. I assure you my rewards program is non transferable, especially to any nameless man that approaches me.

He has done irreversible damage to me and my family during the trial and we have sat silently, listening to him shape the evening. But in the end, his unsupported statements and his attorney's twisted logic fooled no one. The truth won, the truth spoke for itself.

You are guilty. Twelve jurors convicted you guilty of three felony counts beyond reasonable doubt, that's twelve votes per count, thirty six yeses confirming guilt, that's one hundred percent, unanimous guilt. And I thought finally it is over, finally he will own up to what he did, truly apologize, we will both move on and get better. Then I read your statement.

If you are hoping that one of my organs will implode from anger and I will die, I'm almost there. You are very close. This is not a story of another drunk college hookup with poor decision making. Assault is not an accident. Somehow, you still don't get it. Somehow, you still sound confused. I will now read portions of the defendant's statement and respond to them.

You said, Being drunk I just couldn't make the best decisions and neither could she.

Alcohol is not an excuse. Is it a factor? Yes. But alcohol was not the one who stripped me, fingered me, had my head dragging against the ground, with me almost fully naked. Having too much to drink was an amateur mistake that I admit to, but it is not criminal. Everyone in this room has had a night where they have regretted drinking too much, or knows someone close to them who has had a night where they have regretted drinking too much. Regretting drinking is not the same as regretting sexual assault. We were both drunk, the difference is I did not take off your pants and underwear, touch you inappropriately, and run away. That's the difference.

You said, If I wanted to get to know her, I should have asked for her number, rather than asking her to go back to my room.

I'm not mad because you didn't ask for my number. Even if you did know me, I would not want to be in this situation. My own boyfriend knows me, but if he asked to finger me behind a dumpster, I would slap him. No girl wants to be in this situation. Nobody. I don't care if you know their phone number or not.

You said, I stupidly thought it was okay for me to do what everyone around me was doing, which was drinking. I was wrong.

Again, you were not wrong for drinking. Everyone around you was not sexually assaulting me. You were wrong for doing what nobody else was doing, which was pushing your erect dick in your pants against my naked, defenseless body concealed in a dark area, where partygoers could no longer see or protect me, and my own sister could not find me. Sipping fireball is not your crime. Peeling off and discarding my underwear like a candy wrapper to insert your finger into my body, is where you went wrong. Why am I still explaining this.

You said, During the trial I didn't want to victimize her at all. That was just my attorney and his way of approaching the case.

Your attorney is not your scapegoat, he represents you. Did your attorney say some incredulously infuriating, degrading things? Absolutely. He said you had an erection, because it was cold.

You said, you are in the process of establishing a program for high school and college students in which you speak about your experience to "speak out against the college campus drinking culture and the sexual promiscuity that goes along with that."

Campus drinking culture. That's what we're speaking out against? You think that's what I've spent the past year fighting for? Not awareness about campus sexual assault, or rape, or learning to recognize consent. Campus drinking culture. Down with Jack Daniels. Down with Skyy Vodka. If you want talk to people about drinking go to an AA meeting. You realize, having a drinking problem is different than drinking and then forcefully trying to have sex with someone? Show men how to respect women, not how to drink less.

Drinking culture and the sexual promiscuity that goes along with that. Goes along with that, like a side effect, like fries on the side of your order. Where does promiscuity even come into play? I don't see headlines that read, *Brock Turner, Guilty of drinking too much and the sexual promiscuity that goes along with that.* Campus Sexual Assault.

There's your first powerpoint slide. Rest assured, if you fail to fix the topic of your talk, I will follow you to every school you go to and give a follow up presentation.

Lastly you said, I want to show people that one night of drinking can ruin a life.

A life, one life, yours, you forgot about mine. Let me rephrase for you, I want to show people that one night of drinking can ruin two lives. You and me. You are the cause, I am the effect. You have dragged me through this hell with you, dipped me back into that night again and again. You knocked down both our towers, I collapsed at the same time you did. If you think I was spared, came out unscathed, that today I ride off into sunset, while you suffer the greatest blow, you are mistaken. Nobody wins. We have all been devastated, we have all been trying to find some meaning in all of this suffering. Your damage was concrete; stripped of titles, degrees, enrollment. My damage was internal, unseen, I carry it with me. You took away my worth, my privacy, my energy, my time, my safety, my intimacy, my confidence, my own voice, until today.

See one thing we have in common is that we were both unable to get up in the morning. I am no stranger to suffering. You made me a victim. In newspapers my name was "unconscious intoxicated woman", ten syllables, and nothing more than that. For a while, I believed that that was all I was. I had to force myself to relearn my real name, my identity. To relearn that this is not all that I am. That I am not just a drunk victim at a frat party found behind a dumpster, while you are the All American swimmer at a top university, innocent until proven guilty, with so much at stake. I am a human being who has been irreversibly hurt, my life was put on hold for over a year, waiting to figure out if I was worth something.

My independence, natural joy, gentleness, and steady lifestyle I had been enjoying became distorted beyond recognition. I became closed off, angry, self deprecating, tired, irritable, empty. The isolation at times was unbearable. You cannot give me back the life I had before that night either. While you worry about your shattered reputation, I refrigerated spoons every night so when I woke up, and my eyes were puffy from crying, I would hold the spoons to my eyes to lessen the swelling so that I could see. I showed up an hour late to work every morning, excused myself to cry in the stairwells, I can tell you all the best places in that building to cry where no one can hear you. The pain became so bad that I had to explain the private details to my boss to let her know why I was leaving. I needed time because continuing day to day was not possible. I used my savings to go as far away as I could possibly be. I did not return to work full time as I knew I'd have to take weeks off in the future for the hearing and trial, that were constantly being rescheduled. My life was put on hold for over a year, my structure had collapsed.

283

I can't sleep alone at night without having a light on, like a five year old, because I have nightmares of being touched where I cannot wake up, I did this thing where I waited until the sun came up and I felt safe enough to sleep. For three months, I went to bed at six o'clock in the morning.

I used to pride myself on my independence, now I am afraid to go on walks in the evening, to attend social events with drinking among friends where I should be comfortable being. I have become a little barnacle always needing to be at someone's side, to have my boyfriend standing next to me, sleeping beside me, protecting me. It is embarrassing how feeble I feel, how timidly I move through life, always guarded, ready to defend myself, ready to be angry.

You have no idea how hard I have worked to rebuild parts of me that are still weak. It took me eight months to even talk about what happened. I could no longer connect with friends, with everyone around me. I would scream at my boyfriend, my own family whenever they brought this up. You never let me forget what happened to me. At the of end of the hearing, the trial, I was too tired to speak. I would leave drained, silent. I would go home turn off my phone and for days I would not speak. You bought me a ticket to a planet where I lived by myself. Every time a new article come out, I lived with the paranoia that my entire hometown would find out and know me as the girl who got assaulted. I didn't want anyone's pity and am still learning to accept victim as part of my identity. You made my own hometown an uncomfortable place to be.

You cannot give me back my sleepless nights. The way I have broken down sobbing uncontrollably if I'm watching a movie and a woman is harmed, to say it lightly, this experience has expanded my empathy for other victims. I have lost weight from stress, when people would comment I told them I've been running a lot lately. There are times I did not want to be touched. I have to relearn that I am not fragile, I am capable, I am wholesome, not just livid and weak.

When I see my younger sister hurting, when she is unable to keep up in school, when she is deprived of joy, when she is not sleeping, when she is crying so hard on the phone she is barely breathing, telling me over and over again she is sorry for leaving me alone that night, sorry sorry sorry, when she feels more guilt than you, then I do not forgive you. That night I had called her to try and find her, but you found me first. Your attorney's closing statement began, "[Her sister] said she was fine and who knows her better than her sister." You tried to use my own sister against me? Your points of attack were so weak, so low, it was almost embarrassing. You do not touch her.

You should have never done this to me. Secondly, you should have never made me fight so long to tell you, you should have never done this to me. But here we are. The damage is done, no one can undo it. And now we both have a choice. We can let this destroy us, I can remain angry and hurt and you can be in denial, or we can face it head on, I accept the pain, you accept the punishment, and we move on.

Your life is not over, you have decades of years ahead to rewrite your story. The world is huge, it is so much bigger than Palo Alto and Stanford, and you will make a space for yourself in it where you can be useful and happy. But right now, you do not get to shrug your shoulders and be confused anymore. You do not get to pretend that there were no red flags. You have been convicted of violating me, intentionally, forcibly, sexually, with malicious intent, and all you can admit to is consuming alcohol. Do not talk about the sad way your life was upturned because alcohol made you do bad things. Figure out how to take responsibility for your own conduct.

Now to address the sentencing. When I read the probation officer's report, I was in disbelief, consumed by anger which eventually quieted down to profound sadness. My statements have been slimmed down to distortion and taken out of context. I fought hard during this trial and will not have the outcome minimized by a probation officer who attempted to evaluate my current state and my wishes in a fifteen minute conversation, the majority of which was spent answering questions I had about the legal system. The context is also important. Brock had yet to issue a statement, and I had not read his remarks.

My life has been on hold for over a year, a year of anger, anguish and uncertainty, until a jury of my peers rendered a judgment that validated the injustices I had endured. Had Brock admitted guilt and remorse and offered to settle early on, I would have considered a lighter sentence, respecting his honesty, grateful to be able to move our lives forward. Instead he took the risk of going to trial, added insult to injury and forced me to relive the hurt as details about my personal life and sexual assault were brutally dissected before the public. He pushed me and my family through a year of inexplicable, unnecessary suffering, and should face the consequences of challenging his crime, of putting my pain into question, of making us wait so long for justice.

I told the probation officer I do not want Brock to rot away in prison. I did not say he does not deserve to be behind bars. The probation officer's recommendation of a year or less in county jail is a soft timeout, a mockery of the seriousness of his assaults, an insult to me and all women. It gives the message that a stranger can be inside you without proper consent and he will receive less than what has been defined as the minimum sentence. Probation should be denied. I also told the probation officer that what I truly wanted was for Brock to get it, to understand and admit to his wrongdoing.

Unfortunately, after reading the defendant's report, I am severely disappointed and feel that he has failed to exhibit sincere remorse or responsibility for his conduct. I fully respected his right to a trial, but even after twelve jurors unanimously convicted him guilty of three felonies, all he has admitted to doing is ingesting alcohol. Someone who cannot take full accountability for his actions does not deserve a mitigating sentence. It is deeply offensive that he would try and dilute rape with a suggestion of "promiscuity." By definition rape is the absence of promiscuity, rape is the absence of consent, and it perturbs me deeply that he can't even see that distinction.

The probation officer factored in that the defendant is youthful and has no prior convictions. In my opinion, he is old enough to know what he did was wrong. When you are eighteen in this country you can go to war. When you are nineteen, you are old enough to pay the consequences for attempting to rape someone. He is young, but he is old enough to know better.

As this is a first offence I can see where leniency would beckon. On the other hand, as a society, we cannot forgive everyone's first sexual assault or digital rape. It doesn't make sense. The seriousness of rape has to be communicated clearly, we should not create a culture that suggests we learn that rape is wrong through trial and error. The consequences of sexual assault needs to be severe enough that people feel enough fear to exercise good judgment even if they are drunk, severe enough to be preventative.

The probation officer weighed the fact that he has surrendered a hard earned swimming scholarship. How fast Brock swims does not lessen the severity of what happened to me, and should not lessen the severity of his punishment. If a first time offender from an underprivileged background was accused of three felonies and displayed no accountability for his actions other than drinking, what would his sentence be? The fact that Brock was an athlete at a private university should not be seen as an entitlement to leniency, but as an opportunity to send a message that sexual assault is against the law regardless of social class.

The Probation Officer has stated that this case, when compared to other crimes of similar nature, may be considered less serious due to the defendant's level of intoxication. It felt serious. That's all I'm going to say.

What has he done to demonstrate that he deserves a break? He has only apologized for drinking and has yet to define what he did to me as sexual assault, he has revictimized me continually, relentlessly. He has been found guilty of three serious felonies and it is time for him to accept the consequences of his actions. He will not be quietly excused.

He is a lifetime sex registrant. That doesn't expire. Just like what he did to me doesn't expire, doesn't just go away after a set number of years. It stays with me, it's part of my identity, it has forever changed the way I carry myself, the way I live the rest of my life.

To conclude, I want to say thank you. To everyone from the intern who made me oatmeal when I woke up at the hospital that morning, to the deputy who waited beside me, to the nurses who calmed me, to the detective who listened to me and never judged me, to my advocates who stood unwaveringly beside me, to my therapist who taught me to find courage in vulnerability, to my boss for being kind and understanding, to my incredible parents who teach me how to turn pain into strength, to my grandma who snuck chocolate into the courtroom throughout this to give to me, my friends who remind me how to be happy, to my boyfriend who is patient and loving, to my unconquerable sister who is the other half of my heart, to Alaleh, my idol, who fought tirelessly and never doubted me. Thank you to everyone involved in the trial for their time and attention. Thank you to girls across the nation that wrote cards to my DA to give to me, so many strangers who cared for me.

Most importantly, thank you to the two men who saved me, who I have yet to meet. I sleep with two bicycles that I drew taped above my bed to remind myself there are heroes in this story. That we are looking out for one another. To have known all of these people, to have felt their protection and love, is something I will never forget.

And finally, to girls everywhere, I am with you. On nights when you feel alone, I am with you. When people doubt you or dismiss you, I am with you. I fought everyday for you. So never stop fighting, I believe you. As the author Anne Lamott once wrote, "Lighthouses don't go running all over an island looking for boats to save; they just stand there shining." Although I can't save every boat, I hope that by speaking today, you absorbed a small amount of light, a small knowing that you can't be silenced, a small satisfaction that justice was served, a small assurance that we are getting somewhere, and a big, big knowing that you are important, unquestionably, you are untouchable, you are beautiful, you are to be valued, respected, undeniably, every minute of every day, you are powerful and nobody can take that away from you. To girls everywhere, I am with you. Thank you.

Appendix 6

Brock Turner's Letter to the Court

The night of January 17th changed my life and the lives of everyone involved forever. I can never go back to being the person I was before that day. I am no longer a swimmer, a student, a resident of California, or the product of the work that I put in to accomplish the goals that I set out in the first nineteen years of my life. Not only have I altered my life, but I've also changed [redacted] and her family's life. I am the sole proprietor of what happened on the night that these people's lives were changed forever. I would give anything to change what happened that night. I can never forgive myself for imposing trauma and pain on [redacted].

It debilitates me to think that my actions have caused her emotional and physical stress that is completely unwarranted and unfair. The thought of this is in my head every second of every day since this event has occurred. These ideas never leave my mind. During the day, I shake uncontrollably from the amount I torment myself by thinking about what has happened. I wish I had the ability to go back in time and never pick up a drink that night, let alone interact with [redacted]. I can barely hold a conversation with someone without having my mind drift into thinking these thoughts. They torture me. I go to sleep every night having been crippled by these thoughts to the point of exhaustion. I wake up having dreamt of these horrific events that I have caused. I am completely consumed by my poor judgment and ill thought actions. There isn't a second that has gone by where I haven't regretted the course of events I took on January 17th/18th.

My shell and core of who I am as a person is forever broken from this. I am a changed person. At this point in my life, I never want to have a drop of alcohol again. I never want to attend a social gathering that involves alcohol or any situation where people make decisions based on the substances they have consumed. I never want to experience being in a position where it will have a negative impact on my life or someone else's ever again. I've lost two jobs solely based on the reporting of my case. I wish I never was good at swimming or had the opportunity to attend Stanford, so maybe the newspapers wouldn't want to write stories about me.

All I can do from these events moving forward is by proving to everyone who I really am as a person. I know that if I were to be placed on probation, I would be able to be a benefit to society for the rest of my life. I want to earn a college degree in any capacity that I am capable to do so. And in accomplishing this task, I can make the people around me and society better through the example I will set.

I've been a goal oriented person since my start as a swimmer. I want to take what I can from who I was before this situation happened and use it to the best of my abilities moving forward. I know I can show people who were like me the dangers of assuming what college life can be like without thinking about the consequences one would potentially have to make if one were to make the same decisions that I made. I want to show that people's lives can be destroyed by drinking and making poor decisions while doing so. One needs to recognize the influence that peer pressure and the attitude of having to fit in can have on someone. One decision has the potential to change your entire life.

I know I can impact and change people's attitudes towards the culture surrounded by binge drinking and sexual promiscuity that protrudes through what people think is at the core of being a college student. I want to demolish the assumption that drinking and partying are what make up a college lifestyle I made a mistake, I drank too much, and my decisions hurt someone. But I never ever meant to intentionally hurt [redacted]. My poor decision making and excessive drinking hurt someone that night and I wish I could just take it all back.

If I were to be placed on probation, I can positively say, without a single shred of doubt in my mind, that I would never have any problem with law enforcement. Before this happened, I never had any trouble with law enforcement and I plan on maintaining that. I've been shattered by the party culture and risk taking behavior that I briefly experienced in my four months at school. I've lost my chance to swim in the Olympics. I've lost my ability to obtain a Stanford degree. I've lost employment opportunity, my reputation and most of all, my life. These things force me to never want to put myself in a position where I have to sacrifice everything.

I would make it my life's mission to show everyone that I can contribute and be a positive influence on society from these events that have transpired. I will never put myself through an event where it will give someone the ability to question whether I really can be a betterment to society. I want no one, male or female, to have to experience the destructive consequences of making decisions while under the influence of alcohol. I want to be a voice of reason in a time where people's attitudes and preconceived notions about partying and drinking have already been established. I want to let young people now, as I did not, that things can go from fun to ruined in just one night.

Endnotes

[1] Stanford University Dept. of Public Safety, 1/20/15, PR 019.

[2] https://www.huffpost.com/entry/how-social-media-can-ruin_b_501906

[3] People v. Brock Allen Turner, Police Report, p. 042.

[4] People v. Brock Allen Turner, Vol. 6, p. 328.

[5] People v. Brock Allen Turner, Vol. 6, p. 331

[6] People v. Brock Allen Turner. Vol. 6, p. 268.

[7] People v. Brock Allen Turner, Vol. 8, p. 666, Line 21.

[8] People v. Brock Allen Turner. Vol. 8, p. 679, Line 12.

[9] People v. Brock Allen Turner, Police Report, p. 044.

[10] People v. Brock Allen Turner, Police Report (PR 013).

[11] People v. Brock Allen Turner, Vol. 10, p. 971.

[12] People v. Brock Allen Turner, Vol. 10, p. 971

[13] People v. Brock Allen Turner. Vol. 6, p. 453

[14] People v. Brock Allen Turner, Vol. 7, p 493

[15] People v. Brock Allen Turner, Police Report, (PR 024).

[16] https://padailypost.com/2019/01/08/0-for-16-no-sex-cases-stanford-police-submitted-to-the-da-were-prosecuted/

[17] People v. Brock Allen Turner. Vol. 6, p. 386.

[18] People v. Brock Allen Turner, Vol. 14, pp. 1180-1181.

[19] People v. Brock Allen Turner, Preliminary Examination, Vol. 1, p. 83

[20] People v. Brock Allen Turner, Police Report, p. 019.

[21] People v. Brock Allen Turner, Preliminary Hearing, p. 74.

[22] People v. Brock Allen Turner, Preliminary Hearing, p. 83

[23] People v. Brock Allen Turner, Preliminary Hearing, p. 88

[24] People v. Brock Allen Turner, Preliminary Hearing, p. 88.

[25] People v. Brock Allen Turner, p. 1097.

[26] People v. Brock Allen Turner. Preliminary Hearing.

[27] People v. Brock Allen Turner, Vol. 6, p. 363.

[28] People v. Brock Allen Turner, Vol. 6, p. 378.

[29] https://teachmeanatomy.info/abdomen/areas/peritoneum/

[30] https://dictionary.cambridge.org/dictionary/english/trauma

[31] People v. Brock Allen Turner, Vol. 11, p. 1107.

[32] People v. Brock Allen Turner, Police Report, PR 036.

33 People v. Brock Allen Turner, Vol. 11, p. 1134
34 https://www.lexico.com/en/definition/lifeless
35 People v. Brock Allen Turner. Vol 6, p. 297
36 People v. Brock Allen Turner, Vol. 5, p. 162.
37 https://www.motherjones.com/politics/2016/06/michele-landis-dauber-stanford-rape-recall/
38 People v. Brock Allen Turner, Police Report, PR 004.
39 People v. Brock Allen Turner, Vol. 4, p. 68
40 People v. Brock Allen Turner, Vol 6, p. 264.
41 People v. Brock Allen Turner, Vol. 11, p. 1072
42 https://www.merriam-webster.com/dictionary/trauma
43 People v. Brock Allen Turner, Vol. 11, p. 1089
44 https://www.du.edu/health-and-counseling-center/healthpromotion/bac-calculator.html
45 https://scholarlycommons.pacific.edu/cgi/viewcontent.cgi?article=1181&context=uoplawreview
46 People v. Brock Allen Turner, Vol. 11, p. 1134.
47 People v. Brock Allen Turner. Vol. 6, p. 315.
48 People v. Brock Allen Turner. Vol 4, p. 191.
49 https://www.documentcloud.org/documents/2858997-Probation-officer-s-report-in-Brock-Turner-case.html
50 https://www.documentcloud.org/documents/2858997-Probation-officer-s-report-in-Brock-Turner-case.html
51 https://thecrimereport.org/2018/07/16/why-cant-we-redeem-the-sex-offender/
52 People v. Brock Allen Turner, Police Report, PR 015
53 https://cjp.ca.gov/wp-content/uploads/sites/40/2016/08/Persky_Explanatory_Statement_12-19-16.pdf
54 People vs. Brock Allen Turner. Vol. 14, p. 1179-1180.
55 https://www.cnn.com/2016/06/10/us/stanford-rape-case-court-documents/index.html
56 Prosecutor Alaleh Kianerci's Sentencing Memorandum.
57 https://www.dailymail.co.uk/news/article-3635654/Stanford-rapist-took-photograph-victim-s-breasts-attack-shared-swim-team-friends-deleted-arrest-police-believe.html
58 https://www.dailymail.co.uk/news/article-3635654/Stanford-rapist-took-photograph-victim-s-breasts-attack-shared-swim-team-friends-deleted-arrest-police-believe.html

59 https://www.dailymail.co.uk/news/article-3635654/Stanford-rapist-took-photograph-victim-s-breasts-attack-shared-swim-team-friends-deleted-arrest-police-believe.html

60 https://www.dailymail.co.uk/news/article-7112587/Pictured-Stanford-rapist-Brock-Turner-working-factory-12-hour.html

61 People v. Brock Allen Turner, Defendant's Sentencing Memorandum, Michael Armstrong, p. 4, June 2, 2016.

62 People v. Brock Allen Turner, Vol. 14, p.1189.

63 https://mattmuller.info/the-people-v-judge-persky-72e0c6d75c74

64 People v. Brock Allen Turner, Vol. 11, p. 997

65 https://en.wikipedia.org/wiki/Brady_disclosure#:~:text=The%20Brady%20doctrine%20is%20a,that%20might%20exonerate%20the%20defendant

66 https://law.stanford.edu/stanford-lawyer/articles/debra-zumwalt-jd-79-the-chief-legal-officer-at-the-farm/

67 People v. Brock Allen Turner, Vol. 11, p. 1063, Line 2

68 People v. Brock Allen Turner, Vol. 11, p. 1068, Line 18

69 People v. Brock Allen Turner, Vol. 11, p. 1068, Line 18

70 People v. Brock Allen Turner, Vol. 11, p. 1068.

71 People v. Brock Allen Turner, Vol. 11, pp. 1069, 1070.

72 People v. Brock Allen Turner, Vol. 11, pp. 1069, 1071.

73 People v. Brock Allen Turner, Vol. 11, p. 1071.

74 People v. Brock Allen Turner, Vol. 6, p. 384

75 https://www.theatlantic.com/politics/archive/2016/06/what-makes-the-stanford-rape-case-so-unusual/486374/

76 https://www.chicagotribune.com/opinion/commentary/ct-brock-turner-stanford-rape-20160607-story.html

77 https://www.buzzfeednews.com/article/emaoconnor/meet-the-two-swedish-men-who-caught-brock-turner

78 https://www.opednews.com/articles/Good-Behavior-by-Kathy-Malloy-Brock-Turner_Parents_Rape_Vagina-160830-789.html78

79 https://www.usatoday.com/story/news/nation/2019/06/05/emily-doe-survivor-brock-turner-case-writing-memoir/1361247001/

80 https://www.aclu.org/issues/smart-justice/prosecutorial-reform

81 People v. Brock Allen Turner, Juror Question, Juror No. 3

82 People v. Brock Allen Turner, Vol. 11, p. 1053

83 People v. Brock Allen Turner, Vol. 13, page 6.

84 People v. Brock Allen Turner, Vol. 3 page 41.

85 People v. Brock Allen Turner, Vol. 3, pp 42-43.

[86] People v. Brock Allen Turner, Vol. 3, p. 43.

[87] https://mattmuller.info/the-people-v-judge-persky-72e0c6d75c74

[88] People v. Brock Allen Turner, "Report of Probation Officer," June 2, 2016, p. 11.

[89] https://cjp.ca.gov/wp-content/uploads/sites/40/2016/08/Persky_Explanatory_Statement_12-19-16.pdf

[90] https://www.democracynow.org/2016/6/9/just_before_giving_stanford_rapist_6

[91] lhttps://www.buzzfeednews.com/article/tomnamako/joe-biden-writes-an-open-letter-to-stanford-survivor

[92] lhttps://www.buzzfeednews.com/article/tomnamako/joe-biden-writes-an-open-letter-to-stanford-survivor

[93] People v. Brock Allen Turner, Vol. 1, p. 9.

[94] People v. Brock Allen Turner, Police Report (PR 044).

[95] https://www.dailymail.co.uk/news/article-3635654/Stanford-rapist-took-photograph-victim-s-breasts-attack-shared-swim-team-friends-deleted-arrest-police-believe.html

[96] https://codes.findlaw.com/ca/penal-code/pen-sect-647.html

[97] https://www.ncbi.nlm.nih.gov/pmc/articles/PMC5957776/

[98] http://bostonreview.net/us/judith-levine-rape-and-restorative-justice

[99] https://www.stanforddaily.com/2019/12/04/gsc-approves-partial-funds-to-bring-chanel-miller-to-campus-in-spring-quarter/

[100] Miller, Chanel. *Know My Name.* Viking Press, NY, 2019. P. 242.

[101] https://www.latimes.com/california/story/2020-01-28/california-considers-charging-all-teens-as-juveniles

[102] https://www.latimes.com/california/story/2020-01-28/california-considers-charging-all-teens-as-juveniles

[103] https://www.niaaa.nih.gov/publications/brochures-and-fact-sheets/time-for-parents-discuss-risks-college-drinking Accessed 8-1-2019.

[104] https://www.alcohol.org/effects/sexual-assault-college-campus/

[105] A. Abbey, "Alcohol-Related Sexual Assault: A Common Problem Among College Students." Department of Community Medicine, Wayne State University.

[106] https://www.ncbi.nlm.nih.gov/pmc/articles/PMC4844761/

[107] https://www.alcohol.org/effects/dangers-of-blackouts/

[108] Wilhite, E.R., Mallard, T, Fromme, K, "A Longitudinal Event-Level Investigation of Alcohol Intoxication, Alcohol-Related Blackouts,

293

Childhood Sexual Abuse, and Sexual Victimization among College Students." https://www.ncbi.nlm.nih.gov/pmc/articles/PMC5957776/

[109] Ibid

[110] https://www.wbur.org/commonhealth/2018/10/03/kavanaugh-ford-drinking-blackout

[111] https://www.ncbi.nlm.nih.gov/pmc/articles/PMC1860900/

[112] https://pubs.niaaa.nih.gov/publications/aa72/aa72.htm

[113] https://www.aicr.org/cancer-research-update/2018/2-7/new-study-clarifies-how-alcohol-causes-cancer.html

[114] https://www.ncbi.nlm.nih.gov/pmc/articles/PMC3832299/

[115] https://clinicaltrials.gov/ct2/show/NCT03497442

[116] https://source.wustl.edu/2011/07/the-biology-behind-alcoholinduced-blackouts/

[117] https://www.jneurosci.org/content/31/27/9905

[118] https://www.alcohol.org/effects/dangers-of-blackouts/

[119] https://www.stanforddaily.com/2016/03/21/brock-turner-trial-continues-in-second-week-of-testimony/

[120] https://www.niaaa.nih.gov/alcohol-health/overview-alcohol-consumption/what-standard-drink

[121] https://www.ncbi.nlm.nih.gov/pmc/articles/PMC4329777/

[122] Ibid

[123] People v. Brock Allen Turner, Police report (PR 030).

[124] "People of the State of California, Plaintiff, vs. Brock Allen Turner, Defendant, People's Motions in Limine." March 9, 2016.

[125] Rose, Mark & Grant, Jon., "Alcohol-Induced Blackout Phenomenology, Biological Basis, and Gender Differences." *Journal of Addiction Medicine*. 4 (2):61-73, 6/2010.

[126] Hermens, D, and Lagopoulos, J. "Binge Drinking and the Young Brain: A Mini Review of the Neurological Underpinnings of Alcohol-Induced Blackout*." Frontiers in Psychology*. 2018; 9:12.

[127] Wilhite, E., Fromme, K. (2015). Alcohol-Induced Blackouts and Other Negative Outcomes During the Transition Out of College. *Journal of Studies on Alcohol and Drugs,* 2015 Jul; 76(4): 516–524.

[128] People v. Brock Allen Turner; Motions in Limine.

[129] People v. Brock Allen Turner, Motions in Limine

[130] https://addictionpsychology.org/awards/list-recipients

[131] https://www.stanforddaily.com/2016/03/21/brock-turner-trial-continues-in-second-week-of-testimony/

[132] People v. Brock Allen Turner, Police report (PR 045).

[133] People v. Brock Allen Turner.

[134] Gladwell, Malcolm. *Talking to Strangers*. P. 227. Little, Brown and Company, New York, NY. 2019.

[135] https://www.psychologytoday.com/us/blog/shame-nation/201807/the-impact-public-shaming-in-digital-world

[136] https://www.stopbullying.gov/resources/laws/federal

[137] https://www.localsolicitors.com/criminal-guides/the-law-on-cyberbullying

[138] https://www.irishtimes.com/culture/before-you-join-the-online-mob-think-you-could-be-next-1.3309605

[139] Dauber, Michele (@mldauber). "Elite criminal defense lawyer (Harvard, Duke) compares sentencing white privileged Stanford athlete unrepentant…" https://twitter.com/mldauber/status/1007285026252132352. June 14, 2018.

[140] Dauber, Michele (@mldauber). "Brock Turner is a lying unrepentant sex predator who never showed real remorse for sexual assault…" https://twitter.com/mldauber/status/1027361327457521664. Aug. 8, 2018

[141] https://www.latimes.com/local/lanow/la-me-ln-recall-judge-20180601-story.html

[142] https://padailypost.com/2017/12/07/blowup-over-brock-turner-song/

[143] People v. Brock Allen Turner

[144] https://en.wikipedia.org/wiki/Michele_Dauber

[145] https://www.democracynow.org/2016/6/9/just_before_giving_stanford_rapist_6

[146] https://www.motherjones.com/politics/2016/06/michele-landis-dauber-stanford-rape-recall/

[147] Dauber, Michele (@mldauber). "#brockturner court probation report is fetid pond of victim-blaming rapeyness…" https://twitter.com/mldauber/status/739733922611789825, June 6, 2018, 1:21 AM.

[148] Dauber, Michele (@mldauber). Replying to @GMPaiella. "it is from the probation report which is public doc avail from SC ct for 60 days post-sentencing. If journo Email me pls." https://twitter.com/mldauber/status/739816714943111168. June 6, 2016, 6:50 AM.

[149] Gabriella Paiella (GMPaiella). Replying to @mldauber. "Just emailed, thanks." https://twitter.com/GMPaiella/status/739818339321679873. June 6, 2018, 6:56 AM.

[150] https://www.thecut.com/2016/06/brock-turners-friend-pens-letter-of-support.html

[151] https://www.nytimes.com/2016/06/09/nyregion/drummer-defends-stanford-student-convicted-in-rape-case-her-band-pays-a-price.html

[152] https://www.theguardian.com/us-news/2016/sep/06/brock-turner-stanford-sexual-assault-case-ohio-armed-protest

[153] https://www.theguardian.com/us-news/2016/sep/06/brock-turner-stanford-sexual-assault-case-ohio-armed-protest

[154] https://sanfrancisco.cbslocal.com/2017/12/07/stanford-professor-under-fire-tweeting-anti-brock-turner-song/

[155] Ibid

[156] https://www.youtube.com/watch?v=fKWjMBt4j5Y

[157] https://www.mercurynews.com/2017/12/07/persky-supporter-denounces-recall-leader-for-tweeting-f-brock-turner-song/

[158] https://padailypost.com/2017/12/07/blowup-over-brock-turner-song/

[159] Cyber vigilantism, persecution, and shaming are not to be confused with ethical and lawful activism.

[160] https://www.thecut.com/2017/09/brock-turner-criminal-justice-rape-textbook.html

[161] https://www.vox.com/first-person/2017/11/17/16666290/brock-turner-rape

[162] Ibid

[163] (Twitter, @mldauber, July 5, 2016, 11:33 AM).

[164] https://www.aaronbalick.com/news/the-psychology-of-stranger-shaming/

[165] https://www.huffpost.com/entry/online-shaming-a-virtual-playground-for-adults_b_11250280

[166] https://www.reuters.com/article/uk-factcheck-turner-idUSKCN25F2IA

[167] https://www.verywellfamily.com/characteristics-of-a-bully-2609264

[168] https://www.aaronbalick.com/news/the-psychology-of-stranger-shaming/

[169] https://observer.com/2017/06/mob-mentality-digital-age-twitter/

[170] https://nymag.com/intelligencer/2018/04/an-apology-for-the-internet-from-the-people-who-built-it.html

[171] https://www.mercurynews.com/2018/06/26/opinion-metoo-and-the-downfall-of-mercy-in-criminal-justice/

[172] https://highline.huffingtonpost.com/articles/en/brock-turner-michele-dauber/

[173] https://www.losaltosonline.com/news/sections/comment/257-other-voices/57630-other-voices-why-judge-persky-should-not-be-recalled

[174] https://www.mercurynews.com/2018/05/25/letter-judge-persky-is-among-our-most-capable-jurists/

[175] https://www.npr.org/sections/thetwo-way/2018/06/05/617071359/voters-are-deciding-whether-to-recall-aaron-persky-judge-who-sentenced-brock-tur

[176] https://www.nytimes.com/2016/06/08/us/judge-in-stanford-rape-case-is-being-threatened-who-is-aaron-persky.html Judge Aaron Persky Under Fire for Sentencing in Stanford Rape Case June 7, 2016

[177] https://highline.huffingtonpost.com/articles/en/brock-turner-michele-dauber/

[178] https://abc7news.com/santa-clara-co-to-hold-special-election-to-recall-judge-persky/3044205/

[179] https://www.huffpost.com/entry/public-defenders-judge-aaron-persky_n_576d4c92e4b0dbb1bbba4f91

[180] https://www.stanforddaily.com/2016/06/25/stanford-law-grads-write-open-letter-question-judge-persky-recall/

[181] Ibid

[182] Ibid

[183] Ibid

[184] https://www.paloaltoonline.com/news/reports/1503112952.pdf

[185] Ibid

[186] https://pdfserver.amlaw.com/ca/SCC-Retired-Judges-Open-Letter.pdf

[187] https://pdfserver.amlaw.com/ca/SCC-Retired-Judges-Open-Letter.pdf

[188] https://pdfserver.amlaw.com/ca/SCC-Retired-Judges-Open-Letter.pdf

[189] https://ballotpedia.org/Aaron_Persky_recall,_Santa_Clara_County,_California_(2018)

[190] Palo Alto Daily Post, "I support Emily Doe and oppose the recall," May 17, 2018.

[191] https://www.history.com/news/george-bush-willie-horton-racist-ad

[192] https://padailypost.com/2018/05/16/persky-recall-signs-compared-to-infamous-willie-horton-ad/

[193] https://www.surfsantamonica.com/ssm_site/the_lookout/news/News-2000/Jul-2000/7_17_2000_major_conservative.htm

[194] https://cjp.ca.gov/wp-content/uploads/sites/40/2016/08/Persky_Explanatory_Statement_12-19-16.pdf

[195] https://www.mercurynews.com/2016/06/13/brock-turner-case-santa-clara-county-bar-association-statement/

[196] https://padailypost.com/2018/05/27/recall-persky-campaign-raises-more-than-1-million/

[197] https://www.sfchronicle.com/opinion/editorials/article/Editorial-The-case-against-the-recall-of-Judge-12587849.php

[198] https://padailypost.com/2018/05/10/editorial-vote-no-on-recall-of-judge-persky/
[199] Ibid
[200] https://www.mercurynews.com/2018/05/08/editorial-persky-recall-demands-voters-make-a-sexual-assault-statement/
[201] https://www.mercurynews.com/2018/05/08/editorial-persky-recall-demands-voters-make-a-sexual-assault-statement/
[202] https://www.mercurynews.com/2018/05/08/editorial-persky-recall-demands-voters-make-a-sexual-assault-statement/
[203] People v. Brock Allen Turner, Vol. 14, pp. 1192 – 1193, June 2, 2016.
[204] People v. Brock Allen Turner, Vol. 14, pp. 1192 – 1193, June 2, 2016.
[205] https://www.mercurynews.com/2018/05/25/letter-judge-persky-is-among-our-most-capable-jurists/
[206] https://www.mercurynews.com/2018/06/26/opinion-metoo-and-the-downfall-of-mercy-in-criminal-justice/   Opinion: #MeToo, Persky and erosion of mercy in criminal justice, May 25, 2018
[207] https://www.mercurynews.com/2016/06/11/brock-turner-case-a-look-at-judge-aaron-perskys-record/
[208] https://sanfrancisco.cbslocal.com/2016/08/30/supportive-email-from-assistant-da-to-persky-surfaces/
[209] Ibid
[210] https://www.latimes.com/local/lanow/la-me-ln-persky-20181212-story.html
[211] Ibid
[212] https://www.change.org/p/lynbrook-high-school-fire-new-lynbrook-hire-a-judge-in-brock-turner-s-case-d181cfa6-1c6d-4cc6-88d1-1694395eaab6
[213] https://www.change.org/p/maria-jackson-principal-refuse-to-hire-michael-persky-as-the-lynbrook-high-girls-tennis-coach
[214] https://www.latimes.com/opinion/story/2019-09-12/judge-brock-turner-sex-assault-case-tennis
[215] Marshall, Rachel. "Judge Aaron Persky vs. Mob Rule." San Francisco Chronicle, Sept. 14, 2019.
[216] https://www.paloaltoonline.com/news/reports/1503112952.pdf
[217] https://highline.huffingtonpost.com/articles/en/brock-turner-michele-dauber/
[218] **https://www.theatlantic.com/technology/archive/2018/03/largest-study-ever-fake-news-mit-twitter/555104/**
[219] https://leiterlawschool.typepad.com/leiter/2018/06/stanfords-michelle-daubers-assault-on-the-rule-of-law.html
[220] https://www.si.com/more-sports/2018/06/06/aaron-persky-brock-turner-california-recall-election

221 https://www.paloaltoonline.com/news/2018/05/11/analysis-of-judge-perskys-pattern-cases

222 https://www.mercurynews.com/2011/04/07/no-defendants-found-liable-in-de-anza-rape-trial-no-damages-awarded/

223 https://www.si.com/more-sports/2018/06/06/aaron-persky-brock-turner-california-recall-election

224 https://www.buzzfeednews.com/article/claudiakoerner/judge-in-stanford-sex-assault-case-will-no-longer-hear-crimi

225 https://www.nimh.nih.gov/health/publications/social-anxiety-disorder-more-than-just-shyness/index.shtml

226 https://www.si.com/more-sports/2018/06/06/aaron-persky-brock-turner-california-recall-election

227 https://www.mercurynews.com/2011/04/07/no-defendants-found-liable-in-de-anza-rape-trial-no-damages-awarded/

228 https://www.mercurynews.com/2016/06/30/brock-turner-case-judge-aaron-persky-tackles-new-sex-case/

229 https://www.paloaltoonline.com/news/2018/05/11/analysis-of-judge-perskys-pattern-cases

230 https://www.kron4.com/news/video-stanford-rape-case-judge-aaron-persky-facing-scrutiny-in-separate-sexual-assault-case/

231 https://cjp.ca.gov/wp-content/uploads/sites/40/2016/08/Persky_Explanatory_Statement_12-19-16.pdf

232 Ibid

233 https://www.theguardian.com/us-news/2016/jun/27/stanford-sexual-assault-trial-judge-persky

234 https://www.businessinsider.com/aaron-persky-harsher-sentence-similar-case-2016-6

235 6/27/judge_in_brock_turner_rape_case_handed_el_salvadoran_immigrant_3_years_for_similar_crimes_report_says/

236 https://www.latimes.com/local/lanow/la-me-sex-assault-judge-20160809-snap-story.html

237 https://www.paloaltoonline.com/news/2018/05/11/analysis-of-judge-perskys-pattern-cases

238 https://www.paloaltoonline.com/news/2018/05/11/analysis-of-judge-perskys-pattern-cases

239 https://www.thedailybeast.com/feminists-put-judge-aaron-persky-on-trial

240 https://www.paloaltoonline.com/news/2016/08/09/brock-turner-judge-criticized-for-child-pornography-sentencing

241 Twitter, @mldauber, March 9, 2018, 12:05 PST.
242 https://www.paloaltoonline.com/news/2016/08/09/brock-turner-judge-criticized-for-child-pornography-sentencing
243 Ibid
244 https://www.latimes.com/local/lanow/la-me-sex-assault-judge-20160809-snap-story.html
245 https://www.paloaltoonline.com/news/2018/05/11/analysis-of-judge-perskys-pattern-cases
246 https://www.paloaltoonline.com/news/2018/05/11/analysis-of-judge-perskys-pattern-cases
247 Ibid
248 Ibid
249 https://padailypost.com/2018/05/16/is-there-a-persky-pattern-a-look-at-cases-recall-proponents-say-are-similar-to-that-of-brock-turner/
250 https://www.paloaltoonline.com/news/2018/05/11/analysis-of-judge-perskys-pattern-cases
251 https://www.paloaltoonline.com/news/reports/1503112952.pdf
252 https://www.mercurynews.com/2016/08/26/stanford-sex-assault-case-judge-accused-of-leniency-toward-another-athlete/
253 https://www.mercurynews.com/2016/08/26/stanford-sex-assault-case-judge-accused-of-leniency-toward-another-athlete/
254 Email obtained via California Public Records Request, email to recipient from Sean Webby, Aug. 25, 2017.
255 Email obtained via California Public Records Request, email to recipient rom Sean Webby, Aug. 25, 2017
256 https://www.paloaltoonline.com/news/reports/1503112952.pdf
257 https://www.paloaltoonline.com/news/reports/1503112952.pdf
258 https://www.cbsnews.com/news/stanford-rape-case-judge-aaron-persky-accused-leniency-athlete-again/
259 https://www.mercurynews.com/2016/10/18/judge-orders-weekend-jail-for-student-athlete-who-didnt-satisfy-plea-deal/
260 https://www.mercurynews.com/2016/10/18/judge-orders-weekend-jail-for-student-athlete-who-didnt-satisfy-plea-deal/
261 https://www.paloaltoonline.com/news/2018/05/11/analysis-of-judge-perskys-pattern-cases
262 https://www.mercurynews.com/2016/10/18/judge-orders-weekend-jail-for-student-athlete-who-didnt-satisfy-plea-deal/
263 https://www.paloaltoonline.com/news/2018/05/11/analysis-of-judge-perskys-pattern-cases

[264] Ibid

[265] https://www.cbsnews.com/news/stanford-rape-case-judge-aaron-persky-accused-leniency-athlete-again/

[266] Ibid

[267] https://abc7news.com/1561644/

[268] https://www.paloaltoonline.com/news/reports/1503112952.pdf

[269] https://www.si.com/more-sports/2018/06/06/aaron-persky-brock-turner-california-recall-election

[270] https://www.cbsnews.com/news/stanford-rape-case-judge-aaron-persky-accused-leniency-athlete-again/

[271] https://www.si.com/more-sports/2018/06/06/aaron-persky-brock-turner-california-recall-election

[272] Ibid

[273] https://www.si.com/more-sports/2018/06/06/aaron-persky-brock-turner-california-recall-election

[274] https://www.vox.com/first-person/2018/6/6/17434694/persky-brock-turner-recall-california-stanford-rape-sentencing

[275] https://www.paloaltoonline.com/news/reports/1503112952.pdf

[276] https://www.mercurynews.com/2016/06/11/brock-turner-case-a-look-at-judge-aaron-perskys-record/

[277] https://www.si.com/more-sports/2018/06/06/aaron-persky-brock-turner-california-recall-election

[278] https://eji.org/news/united-states-still-has-highest-incarceration-rate-world/

[279] https://www.publicsafety.gc.ca/cnt/rsrcs/pblctns/pnshnt-rcdvsm/index-en.aspx?wbdisable=true

[280] Int. J Environ res Public Health. 2016

[281] https://www.ppic.org/publication/alternatives-to-incarceration-in-california/

[282] https://www.allianceforsafetyandjustice.org/wp-content/uploads/documents/Crime%20Survivors%20Speak%20Report.pdf

[283] People v. Brock Allen Turner, Probation Report.

[284] Marshall, Rachel. "Judge Persky vs. Mob Rule." San Francisco Chronicle, Sept. 14, 2019.

[285] https://www.latimes.com/politics/la-pol-sac-california-sex-crimes-stanford-cosby-bills-20160930-snap-htmlstory.html

[286] https://abc7news.com/news/santa-clara-county-da-pushes-for-new-sex-assault-bill/1396234/

[287] https://www.latimes.com/politics/la-pol-sac-california-sex-crimes-stanford-cosby-bills-20160930-snap-htmlstory.html

288 https://highline.huffingtonpost.com/articles/en/brock-turner-michele-dauber/

289 https://www.themarshallproject.org/2018/02/25/how-bad-is-prison-health-care-depends-on-who-s-watching

290 https://www.newsweek.com/former-inmates-say-they-were-fed-meat-labelled-not-fit-human-consumption-1461686

291 https://sfbayview.com/2019/01/not-for-human-consumption/

292 https://opencommons.uconn.edu/cgi/viewcontent.cgi?article=1433&context=law_papers

293 https://www.huffpost.com/entry/norway-american-prison-system-reform_n_5d5ab979e4b0eb875f270db1

294 https://www.huffpost.com/entry/norway-american-prison-system-reform_n_5d5ab979e4b0eb875f270db1

295 https://www.mercurynews.com/2016/09/02/brock-turner-a-sex-offender-for-life-he-faces-stringent-rules/

296 https://www.mercurynews.com/2016/09/02/brock-turner-a-sex-offender-for-life-he-faces-stringent-rules/

297 https://oag.ca.gov/sex-offender-reg

298 https://www.prisonlegalnews.org/news/2017/may/5/registration-tracking-sex-offenders-drives-mass-incarceration-numbers-and-costs/

299 https://www.prisonlegalnews.org/news/2017/may/5/registration-tracking-sex-offenders-drives-mass-incarceration-numbers-and-costs/

300 https://www.criminallegalnews.org/news/2018/may/15/ex-offender-registries-common-sense-or-nonsense/

301 https://www.criminallegalnews.org/news/2018/may/15/ex-offender-registries-common-sense-or-nonsense/

302 https://www.criminallegalnews.org/news/2018/may/15/ex-offender-registries-common-sense-or-nonsense/

303 https://thecrimereport.org/2014/02/18/2014-02-farm-bill-sex-offenders/

304 https://www.prisonlegalnews.org/news/2017/may/5/registration-tracking-sex-offenders-drives-mass-incarceration-numbers-and-costs/

305 https://www.criminallegalnews.org/news/2018/may/15/ex-offender-registries-common-sense-or-nonsense/

306 https://www.criminallegalnews.org/news/2018/may/15/ex-offender-registries-common-sense-or-nonsense/

307 https://www.prisonlegalnews.org/news/2017/may/5/registration-tracking-sex-offenders-drives-mass-incarceration-numbers-and-costs/

308 https://www.prisonlegalnews.org/news/2017/may/5/registration-tracking-sex-offenders-drives-mass-incarceration-numbers-and-costs/

[309] https://www.prisonlegalnews.org/news/2017/may/5/registration-tracking-sex-offenders-drives-mass-incarceration-numbers-and-costs/

[310] https://slate.com/news-and-politics/2015/04/internet-shaming-the-legal-history-of-shame-and-its-costs-and-benefits.html

Made in the USA
Monee, IL
17 March 2021

63108261R00174